SELECTED REPORTS
IN
ETHNOMUSICOLOGY
VOLUME IX

TEXT, CONTEXT, AND PERFORMANCE
IN
CAMBODIA, LAOS, AND VIETNAM

UNIVERSITY OF CALIFORNIA
LOS ANGELES

SELECTED REPORTS

IN

ETHNOMUSICOLOGY

VOLUME IX

TEXT, CONTEXT, AND PERFORMANCE

IN CAMBODIA, LAOS, AND VIETNAM

Guest Editor:
Amy Catlin

Managing Editor:
Eran Fraenkel

Assistant Editor:
Therese Mahoney

Music Notation:
Wanda Bryant
Edith A. Johnson

DEPARTMENT OF ETHNOMUSICOLOGY
UNIVERSITY OF CALIFORNIA, LOS ANGELES
1992

Cover: An ancient bronze drumhead, signifying the importance attached to music from earliest times to the present day in mainland southeast Asia. Its surface depicts ten flying herons encircling a procession of twenty feathered men riding feathered deer, all centered around a ten-pointed sunburst.

Selected Reports in Ethnomusicology is a refereed journal published by the Department of Ethnomusicology and Systematic Musicology, University of California, Los Angeles. All communications regarding *Selected Reports in Ethnomusicology* should be addressed to:

Managing Editor
Ethnomusicology Publications
Department of Ethnomusicology and Systematic Musicology
UCLA
405 Hilgard Avenue
Los Angeles, California 90024-1657

ISBN: 0-88287-050-5

CONTENTS

LAOS

VIETNAM

PREFACE

The impetus for this volume stems from the efforts of the Indochina Studies Program of the Committee for Southeast Asian Studies (jointly sponsored by the Social Science Research Council and the American Council of Learned Societies, funded by the Ford Foundation, the Henry Luce Foundation, and the National Endowment for the Humanities) whose purpose has been to foster research on Cambodia, Laos, and Vietnam in the aftermath of the recent disruptive war years. Many of the articles are by scholars who belong to the traditions they study. Their research is now archived in a special collection in the Library of Congress, along with the other projects supported by funds from the Program. Three of the papers, Compton's, Hartmann's, and mine, were contributed by charter members of the Indochina Studies Program Committee. Two were invited from an indigenous Lao scholar, the first voice the Western academic world has heard from Laos in many years. The colloquium also benefited from the participation of Dr. Tran Van Khe, senior ethnomusicologist living in France, but still actively involved in the cultural life of his native Vietnam, as are the other emigré scholars presented here. His paper could not be included in the volume due to technical problems, but like most of the others, it was delivered at the colloquium held at UCLA in July 1988, hosted by UCLA's Department of Ethnomusicology and Pacific Rim Studies Program. Funding for the colloquium was provided by the SSRC Indochina Studies Program, under the capable direction of Drs. Mary-Byrne McDonnell and Toby Alice Volkman. The papers are offered here in the spirit of the ISP, which recognized the import of that unique moment in history when the largely isolated and war-plagued peoples and cultures of Cambodia, Laos, and Vietnam first became accessible again to the international community of humanistic scholars.

This volume could not have been completed without the generous support of UCLA's Department of Ethnomusicology, and the guidance of Professors Charlotte Heth, James Porter, Timothy Rice, and Sue Carole De Vale. Managing Editor of Publications, Dr. Eran Fraenkel, shouldered the major responsibility for seeing this complex work through to its completion. Visiting Assistant Professor Phong Nguyen kindly standardized the fonts and spellings in the Vietnamese section. I also wish to thank Therese Mahoney for lending her Lao expertise to the project, as well as Wanda Bryant, Edith A. Johnson, and Johanna Hofmann, graduate students in the Department, for assistance with notations and proofreading, Jan Steward for artistic direction concerning the cover, and UCLA Professors Robert L. Brown, Nazir Jairazbhoy, and Roger Savage for their contributions made during many collegial discussions.

Amy Catlin
Guest Editor

NOTE ON TRANSLITERATION

The editor has retained the transliteration system preferred by each individual author, rather than attempting to standardize the volume. Terms such as Ramayana and Mahabharata are written without diacriticals throughout to avoid multiple spellings; they remain unitalicized when referring to flexible traditions, whereas printed texts are italicized.

INTRODUCTION [*]

On Interpreting Text, Context, and Performance in Cambodia, Laos, and Vietnam: A Hermeneutical Approach

Amy Catlin

> Hermeneutics has its origin in breaches in intersubjectivity. Its field of application is comprised of all those situations in which we encounter meanings that are not immediately understandable but require interpretive effort. The earliest situations in which principles of interpretation were worked out were encounters with religious texts whose meanings were obscure or whose import was no longer acceptable unless they could be harmonized with the tenets of the faith. But this alienation from meaning can just as well occur while engaging in direct conversation, experiencing a work of art, or considering historical actions. In all these cases, the hermeneutical has to do with bridging the gap between the familiar world in which we stand and the strange meaning that resists assimilation into the horizons of our world. (Linge 1976:xii)

A hermeneutical approach has been chosen for this introduction in order to draw attention to the interpretive achievements of the following articles as they encounter a wide range of music-related performance genres from mainland Southeast Asia. Hermeneutics owes its name to the Greek god Hermes, whom the Romans called Mercury; the son of Zeus and Maia, he carried the gods' messages to mankind, translating and interpreting the divine oral texts using human language. Following Hermes' example, most hermeneutical endeavors to date have been largely textually based, involving both translation and interpretation of verbal texts, whether written or oral. At times the purpose has been to come to an understanding between groups as disparate as gods and men; at other times the goal has been to contemporise texts from the past through re-presentation.

Whatever the intent or consequence, each of us participates in the hermeneutical process on a quotidian basis, as the act of interpretation, whether verbalised or not, is endemic to every human experience and action; indeed, experience itself is essentially hermeneutical. Linge emphasizes the importance of this perspective on interpretation as he continues:

> It is vitally important to recognize that the hermeneutical phenomenon encompasses both the alien that we strive to understand and the familiar world that we already understand. The familiar horizons of the interpreter's world. . . constitute the interpreter's own immediate participation in traditions that are not themselves the object of understanding but the conditions of its occurence. (ibid.)

The writers in this volume, many of whom are both performers and scholars, employ a variety of interpretive approaches from the fields of ethnomusicology, folklore, linguistics, dance ethnology, theater, anthropology, and psychology. By including such a wide variety of approaches, we hope to encourage cross-disciplinary interpretations of the art of performance.

The interpretation of art, however, involves far more than an ordinary event. An uncanny ability to decontextualise and recontextualise itself seems to be the essence of all art, inexhaustibly engaging us in the interpretive process. Hans-Georg Gadamer eloquently states this case while also noting the affective and private quality of the artistic experience in his article, "Aesthetics and Hermeneutics":

> If we define the task of hermeneutics as the bridging of personal or historical distance between minds, then the experience of art would seem to fall entirely outside its province. For of all the things that confront us. . . it is the work of art that speaks to us most directly. It possesses a mysterious intimacy that grips our entire being, as if there were no distance at all and every encounter with it were an encounter with ourselves. (Gadamer 1964, translated in Linge 1976:95)

Our interpretive task is further compounded by the nature of the lively arts, such as the music, dance, and sung poetry included here, for the live performance of art is essentially ephemeral, existing in fleeting shapes and textures experienced in a multiplicity of ways. However, there is always something we refer to in performance as the text, or that element which is to some extent fixed and repeatable. Here we have tried to retain as many complete texts as possible, within the limits of the printed word, and to include musical examples in the form of staff transcriptions whenever the original recordings were available. Our hope of publishing an accompanying videotape of the items discussed here is for the moment impracticable; nevertheless, we offer these translations (themselves inevitably interpretive), representations, and interpretations, for they contain much valuable and original material not otherwise available. Published audio-visual documentation corresponding to the items discussed in many of the papers are referenced in footnotes (Proschan, Catlin, Cravath, Chan Moly Sam, Sam-Ang Sam, and Addiss); others may be obtained by contacting the authors.

The volume cover exemplifies the hermeneutical task at hand. An ancient bronze drumhead, a symbol of the creativity of some of the oldest known inhabitants of the region for whom we have extant artifacts, can be interpreted as signifying the importance attached to music from the earliest times to the present day. Its surface depicts ten right-(east?)flying herons encircling a left-(west?)ward procession of twenty feathered men riding feathered deer (?), all centered around a ten-pointed sunburst. Although the doyen of bronze drum scholarship, A. J. Bernet Kempers, does not include this drum in his inventory of Southeast Asian examples, the images on its tympan can be transcribed from the center outward according to his system of symbols, with some modifications, as follows (1988:87 ff.):

10V1))=))øR))ørev))Z+R))m£d£20))her10R))=))øR))ørev))=))

key to symbols:

10	number of rays of central star
V1	interradial design: chevron
)	concentric circles
=	ladders
ø	tiny dotted circles linked by tangents
R	facing right
rev	reversed direction
Z	Z-shaped meandroid designs
m£	feathered men
d£	feathered deer
her	heron

Fig. 1. Tympan of Bronze Drum (also see cover)
Chaiya National Museum, Thailand, Photo: Robert L. Brown

Fig. 2. Bronze Drum
Chaiya National Museum, Thailand, Photo: Robert L. Brown

This "transcription of the text" prepares us to interpret the aggregate of symbols and images chosen by the makers of this tympan, much as the musical notations and verbal transcriptions in the articles which follow enable us to understand the performances being studied. The rays emanating from the central star may have acoustical as well as cosmological significance, as both enhancer of natural patterns of vibration (Kuttner 1990) and as a symbol of cosmic unity with the "solar star", the life-giving sun (Bernet Kempers 1988:115), or the Pole Star, center of the sky for Turco-Tatars and Mongols who may have influenced Dongsonian thought (ibid.:140). The feathered men may be shamans decorated in the plumes of birds, believed to be enlivened with the spirits of the dead, or to carry the souls of the deceased to the afterworld. The men are unusual in that they ride feathered deer, or perhaps hobbydeer constructed to represent the animal sacred to many ancient peoples (ibid.:173). The flying herons surrounding the clockwise procession move counter-clock(sun)-wise, typical of many Heger Type I drums, and resemble concentric bird patterns found in many parts of the ancient world from Europe to China and Southeast Asia, where the heron continues as a symbol for the souls of the dead (ibid.:170–71).

This seventy-centimeter bronze "drum" (organologically speaking, a gong) is classified due to its tripartite, waisted silhouette and other features as Heger Type I, the oldest of all the types; excavated on Samui Island, off the east coast of peninsular southern Thailand, directly along the ancient sea route from East to West, it now resides in the Chaiya National Museum where UCLA professor of art history Robert L. Brown photographed it in 1983 (see figs. 1, 2). Its mantle depicts the ship of the dead. Like all bronze drums, it once signified the power and wealth of kingship, the military importance of bronze as a ritually sanctioned substance for weapons and armor, and the royal authority to make thunder and summon the rains.[1]

On the volume cover, the image is awash in a field of yellow which carries a dual significance: Yellow as saffron, signifying the influence of Indian religious beliefs on the region's indigenous peoples; or yellow as gold, the precious metal for which the region was named by explorers from India. Yellow, whether obtained from saffron pigment (*kunkuma*) or other natural dyes, has long been the color associated with Lord Shiva, whose origins can be found in descriptions of mystics in the *Vedas* dating from the second millennium B.C.:

> the long-haired . . . wind-clad sages wear yellow and soiled clothes.
> (*Rig Veda* X:136. 1–7. Translated in O'Flaherty 1981:40)

One of the earliest known Buddhist texts, the *Dhammapada* (3rd century B.C.), also refers to mystics wearing the color *kāsāya* (Pali: yellow, reddish-yellow, orange, ochre, saffron, etc.):

> having the yellow robes about their necks.
> (XXII:307. Translated in Carter and Talihawadana 1987:333)

Buddhist monks in the region still wear yellow and its variants today, as do those in India who continue to follow the ancient symbolism for the renunciation of worldliness.

In contrast, gold is the standard measure of wealth, power, and kingship, the worldly counterpart of the monk's saffron robes. The Pali name *Suvaṇṇabhūmī*, "the good-color- (i.e., gold) land" was used as early as the 3rd century B.C. by Buddhist missionaries sent to mainland Southeast Asia by the Emperor Ashoka (Coedes 1968:17), and later in the Rāmāyaṇa for the lands of gold found beyond the sunrise (Higham 1989:244). The yellow/gold cover thus signifies both the secular and the sacred. In a similar way, the present set of articles will explore both secular and sacred realms of performance in Southeast Asia, which frequently interact as do yellow and gold.

TEXT, CONTEXT, AND PERFORMANCE

The volume's conceptual theme owes much to the work of Milton Singer, anthropologist of South Asia. He used the paired terms *text* and *context* (1972b:39–52) to distinguish what philologists and other humanists who work with Indian texts do, from what Indologists do, whom he called "contextualists"—social science-oriented investigators who study the same materials, but focus on social and cultural functions of the texts and text-users. He made

> a plea for collaboration between humanistic scholars who make literary, historical studies of religious texts, and social and cultural anthropologists who make direct observational studies of religious beliefs, attitudes, and practices. (1972c:4)

Singer (1972b:50) later predicted that

> this cleavage between the contextual and the textual approaches will be progressively closed as the texts of different kinds—written, seen, and heard—come to be regarded as the media of cultural transmission cultivated by intellectuals, modern as well as traditional, to link different groups of people into a single and differentiated network of communication.

This cross-disciplinary approach to tradition has indeed come into vogue in recent South and Southeast Asian studies, especially regarding Mahābhārata and Rāmāyaṇa texts (Blackburn et al. 1989; Fleuckiger and Sears 1991; Frasca 1990; Richman 1991; Zerbuchen 1987). Here we are attempting a similar approach toward traditions found within Cambodia, Laos, and Vietnam through interpretions from a variety of disciplines. In this volume, text will be understood as a medium for communication which is to some extent fixed and capable of repetition, whether it be verbal, aural, or visual in substance, including music and dance. Like Singer, we admit of "texts of various kinds: oral, written, inscribed, carved and painted, sung and acted" (Singer 1972c:4). Context is here considered as that which surrounds the text when it is performed, the social milieu, accompanying actions and activities, preparations, and denouements. We can even see performance itself as text, if we consider performance to be a form of meaningful action which can be read, or understood, as text; when recorded aurally or visually, both text and context become conflated into "text as performance." Here once again Milton Singer's writings can be invoked, for in the same volume he first introduced the term 'cultural performance,' and offered it as a viable unit of field study (Singer 1972a:67-80).

It should be mentioned in concluding this section that within the performances under consideration, the musical aspect is an important unifying feature. For at least as long as bronze drums have been produced, music, its sounds, and its instruments have symbolized power and prestige for lowland empires in mainland Southeast Asia as well as serving as markers of ethnic identity and authority among minority groups. The musical elements of each tradition included here are distinct for these reasons, identifiable immediately as belonging to a specific ethnic group, subregion, and center of political power.

CULTURAL SEDIMENTATION IN MAINLAND SOUTHEAST ASIA

Myriad layers of cultural influence are found overlaid upon the autochthonous pan-Southeast Asian cultural stratum long posited by French scholars (Porée-Maspero 1962–1969). Due to its strategic location on the sea trade routes between East and West, the region has experienced confluences of many cultures, among the most pervasive influence being that of South Asia, especially in the domain of writing and verbal texts. The controversy over the extent and depth of Indian cultural influence on Southeast Asia continues today. Some have called it a 'thin and flaking glaze' over the culture and belief systems of the native inhabitants (van Leur 1955:95), but in many cases it appears to be so deeply embedded or transformed through the processes of adaptation and indigenization as to defy separation from local forms. The papers in this volume will add further insights into this and other questions by exploring the role of texts in certain performance traditions of the more- and less-Indianized cultures located within the political boundaries of present-day Cambodia, Laos, and Vietnam.

The volume is organized into four sections, to be viewed in terms of linguistic groupings and diachronicity of migrations to the region as presently understood, from the so-called indigenous inhabitants or earliest arrivals to the most recent immigrants to the region.

Section 1, Tribal Minorities. The Kmhmu are members of the Mon-Khmer linguistic sub-family within the Austroasiatic family, who are believed to be among the earliest inhabitants of mainland Southeast Asia, and users of bronze drums to this day (see fig. 3). More recent tribal immigrants include three non-Chinese groups from Southwest China: Tai Lue, a Tai group who have been migrating into the region for many centuries; and Mien and Hmong, two Miao-Yao peoples who have come to the area during the past two centuries.

Section 2, Cambodia. The Khmer, also members of the Mon-Khmer linguistic group, developed a major civilization in the region which fostered cultural exchange with India. The three papers in this section attest to this influence, as they discuss the representation of Indian mythological themes indigenized by the Khmer through the linked classical arts of dance, music, poetry, and shadow puppetry.

Section 3, Laos. The lowland Lao are descendents of relatively recent non-Chinese speaking Tai immigrants who began arriving in the 13th century from Southern China. They founded a kingdom which maintained cultural relations with such powers as India, Cambodia, and Thailand. Their court- and temple-centered musical ensembles demonstrate these affinities and use music to symbolize power and statehood (see fig. 4), while village and minority traditions of the many Tai, Mon-Khmer, and Miao-Yao speakers are quite distinct.

Section 4, Vietnam. The Viet, like the Khmer, are members of of the Austroasiatic language family who have populated the region for millennia. Here, sacred and secular musical materials of the Vietnamese exhibit appropriations from both Indian and Chinese civilizations, but refashioned in uniquely Vietnamese style.

Fig. 3. Kmhmu Festival, with hanging bronze drum.
(Lefèvre-Pontalis 1896)

Fig. 4. Lao currency ca. 1970
(Note that the image on the bill is printed backwards)

These groupings reflect the lettered and unlettered traditions, as found in performance texts as well as other forms. Prior to Indianization, the peoples of Cambodia and Laos were preliterate, while Chinese characters were used in parts of Vietnam. Today, some of the ethnic groups within the region remain preliterate, whether they are ancient inhabitants or recent immigrants from China.

In its most conventional sense, "text" refers to literature as fixed representations of language. However, as seen in the articles included here in Section 1, "Tribal Minorities, " the tribal use of 'texts' in a broader sense includes the creative manipulation of memorized oral literature, learned poetic procedures, and rules for musical composition, demonstrating the high degree of cultural and artistic sophistication found within these ethnic pockets, despite the absence of writing. Dialogue songs are featured in these articles, which are coupled with courtship ballthrowing as one of the traits of Porée-Maspero's proposed autochthonous pan-mainland Southeast Asian and Southern Chinese "Man" ("barbarian") culture, along with the sacred bronze drum and iron sword as symbols of fecundity, rain, power, and prestige, and the dualism of dryness and wetness, bird and serpent, and highland and lowland (Porée-Maspero 1962-69:704).

As a group, these articles attest to the studied distinctness of tribal minorities in the region, exemplified in sung poetry form, style, and content; at the same time, they show a shared oral tradition functioning as text-based, courtship-centered dialogue songs. Frank Proschan's essay introduces the concept of parallelism, "the ordered interplay of repetition and variation", a creative mechanism found widely in the performance of verbal art. Proschan finds the use of parallelism particularly pervasive in the sung poetic texts of the Kmhmu, and details the playful way in which Kmhmu oral poets manipulate their materials in the context of performance. John Hartmann delineates the performance practice of Tai Lue antiphonally sung narrative poetry, in which singers employ pragmatic procedures he classifies into three types: "comment, border, and connect." He notes that these musical narratives function to transmit Buddhist Jataka tales and Hindu-Buddhist cosmological stories, appropriated into the indigenous courtship dialogue song form. Thus, materials, ultimately from Indian sources, become indigenized through presentation in Lue musical garb, whose characteristic interval structure remains an unmistakable trademark, as well as the style of using a musical instrument characteristic of the region, the $p\bar{\imath}$ (free-reed pipe). His description of Lue poetry as end-rhymed with non-specific line lengths also fits the Hmong dialogue songs which follow. I have interpreted the dynamics of performer-performer and performer-audience interaction in Hmong courtship songs as facilitating the process of mate selection, in which the singing voice is seen as a major tool for sexual seduction and eliciting emotional empathy.

Exemplifying cultural appropriation at the linguistic level, one exception to these unlettered traditions are the Iu Mien Yao, a non-Chinese minority who adopted Chinese characters to preserve their ceremonial texts. Herbert Purnell explores this unique feature in Iu Mien wedding songs, and explains the ways in which lexical tone and musical tune interact, occasionally taking liberties he dubs "musical license", a concept inspired by the notion of poetic license. Tonogenesis being another example of linguistic borrowing exemplified in both Mien and Hmong languages, it is possible that in such cases where melodic considerations prevail, a memory of a pre-tonal melodic aesthetic may be at work. Perhaps ethnomusicologists will one day have a historical perspective on these melodies to compare with linguistic models for language change, and melodogenesis can be considered alongside tonogenesis.

As a consequence of cultural contact with India, other groups—the Khmer, the Lao—fashioned alphabets based upon Indic scripts, and adopted and adapted Indian ceremonial and narrative texts for performance. From these, they created their own secular and sacred performance texts, whether oral or written, sung, played, or danced. Among them are the traditions represented in Sections 2 and 3, Cambodia and Laos. Paul Cravath understands a female mythological character in Cambodia from the perspective of Jungian archetypes and the revival of the Goddess in today's earth movement. The same figure is then examined by Chan Moly Sam from the dancer's perspective concerning magico-religious elements in choreography and music. Similarly writing from a performer's vantage point, Sam-Ang Sam helps us to understand a prominent scene from Khmer shadow puppetry, a performance tradition which may have come from India, in a uniquely Khmer branch story, later borrowed by the Thai, from the indigenized Khmer Rāmāyaṇa.

In Section 3, Laos, the instrumental music of the palace at Luang Prabang is shown to have depended heavily on a nearby Lue tribal village for musicians, a fact not widely known until Patthamavong and Bond conducted their investigation of Lao refugees' memories in the United States. Carol Compton details the transformation of texts and performance style due to the exigencies of contemporary history in Lao dialogue songs of love, which may be infused with Hinayana Buddhist or political themes, depending upon the demands of context. Terry Miller investigates the speech-song continuum in a variety of Thai-Lao genres of sacred chant, many based on written texts which preserve indications of linguistic tone, and finds a close relationship between speech contours and their stylized renderings in song.

These materials contrast with the Vietnamese performance texts which employ Chinese characters for verbal texts as well as for musical notations discussed in Section 4: instrumental musical compositions, sung poetry, and Mahayana Buddhist chant, in which Indian influence via the Northern route through Tibet and China is less direct. Nevertheless, musical performance style in Vietnamese Buddhist chant again reflects its Indian origins, and the use of musical instruments is related to Mahayana and East Asian practices today.

It is evident from these articles that unlike many other dominant traits adopted from India, musical influence does not appear to have been significant in the form and structure of the Southeast Asian music, at least in those genres discussed here, with the exception of certain melodic aspects of Buddhist chant. Instead, the musical styles, instruments, and forms which characterize each ethnic group retain indigenous qualities, attesting to the strength of musical tradition throughout the region.

TEXTUAL TRANSFORMATIONS: FROM SOUTH TO SOUTHEAST ASIA

In contrast to music's conservatism, like that of some other cultural forms linked perhaps by their closeness to biological functions such as kinship organization and cuisine, cultural borrowing in the form of textual appropriation from Indian sources permeates Southeast Asian civilization. The theme of the transformation of Indic myths and legends as they encounter Southeast Asian thought unites many of the papers and merits close scrutiny from a variety of perspectives. Perhaps a description of the way in which one text has undergone this process will be helpful here. (Please note that different spellings are used here to distinguish the Tamil deity, Maṇi Mekhalā Teyvam, the epic heroine and Tamil Buddhist nun, Maṇi Mekhalā, the Tamil epic poem, *Maṇi Mekhalai,* and the Khmerized nymph, Muni Mekhalā.[2]

The origin in a Tamil text of the Muni Mekhalā story, so popular in Khmer dance and art, is not generally known. The papers by Paul Cravath and Chan Moly Sam suggest that the Khmerization of this myth follows the typical acculturation process in which similar traits are the most likely to be adopted, while surrounding traits become adapted to conform with local practices. Evidently the story of Maṇi Mekhalā travelled from India to Southeast Asia as a text, whether oral or written, because of the importance which travellers attached to the sea goddess, Maṇi Mekhalā Teyvam.

It is probable that the Muni Mekhalā of the Khmer dance is based on the tutelary sea goddess (Tamil *teyvam,* deity) of the *Mahājanaka Jātaka* as well as the Tamil poem of the Sangam Period, *Maṇi Mekhalai.* Worshipped by the seafaring Tamil traders as the goddess of the sea (Danielou 1989: ix), she was also the patron goddess of the courtesan community (Richman 1988:20). However, stories of her goddaughter, the Buddhist adept Maṇi Mekhalā, also seem to have inspired the Khmer, as Muni Mekhalā's training in magic from the forest-dwelling sage along with Ream Eysau is often cited (see Chan Moly Sam in this volume).

The name of the goddess, Maṇi Mekhalā, has in Sanskrit a wide variety of interpretations. Mekhalā is usually translated as referring to a belt or girdle worn by members of the three upper *varnas* of Hinduism. Maṇi means "jewel" and jewelled belts on terracotta figures of fertility goddesses were considered as charms for long life. The compound *maṇimekhalā* means "girdled with gems" (Monier-Williams 1899:775). Sacrificial posts described in the *Vedas* were decked with these girdles, wound in a particular manner according to the boon desired, including the bringing of rain (Stutley and Stutley 1977:190).

The name Mekhalā may, however, actually have a geographical relationship to Mekalā (or Mekhalā) Mountain of the Vindhya Range in present-day Madhya Pradesh, the main source of the River Narmada which empties into the Bay of Cambray at Broach, an important trading center during the Buddhist period. A community was given the name Mekalā, as were their kings, and there is evidence in the Mahābhārata to suggest that there was also a city Mekalā (Monier-Williams 1899:831; Dowson 1957:208). Indigenous pre-Hindu religious practice in India commonly venerated the female deities who personified particular springs and rivers, and who later became the ancestors of many Hindu goddesses such as Sarasvati, personification of the river Sarasvat.

The Narmada River itself was called "Mekalā-kanyā," daughter of Mekalā. It is very possible that Mekalā was a tribal goddess of the river Narmada, just as the male deity Mekalā was its god, and quite possible that she could have been adopted by seafaring merchants in Broach as a local patron deity, who carried her southwards. It is equally possible that her fame could have been carried by merchant sailors down the East Coast to Tamil country, as Mekalā Mountain is even closer by land to the Orissan coast than to the West coast.

มณีเมขลา
นางฟ้าเท้าแม่มหาสมุทร
ลี่เมขมอ

Thai depiction.
"Manimekhala. Woman of the sky, equivalent to Simekama" [Ocean + Love Goddess].
From *Manual of Thai Drawings* 1970.

The Goddess Maṇi Mekhalā Teyvam appears in two Buddhist Jātakas in which she rescues the Boddhisattva Mahājanaka himself: the *Sankha Jataka* and the *Mahājanaka Jātaka* (one of ten in the *Mahānipāta* collection), the central hero of each being a seafaring merchant. Episodes from the latter are represented in stone at Bharhut (2nd century B.C.) and in frescoes at Ajanta (5th century A.D.), but there are no known depictions of the rescuing goddess among them. The Khmer version is known widely in Cambodia as *Moha-Chinok* (Pascalis 1931:84). In other stories she saves shipwrecked sailors throughout South and Southeast Asia where Tamil maritime traders traveled—Sumatra, Malaysia, Thailand, and Sri Lanka (Richman 1988:12-13; Sarkar 1980:186-7). In Malaya her story has been retold in modern times, brought in an incomplete form from Sumatra where it may have entered quite early (Sarkar 1980:186–87). She seems to be forgotten as a deity today except in Sri Lanka, where she is still mentioned in Tamil ritual texts to the goddess Pattini

(Obeyesekere 1984), and in landlocked Laos where she is invoked as the goddess of lightning in introductory prayers (see Compton's article in this volume) and integrated into the system of local *phi* spirits as Goddess of the Skies, in conjunction with the Earth Goddess, Nang Thorani (Pascalis 1931:82, 91-92). Seafaring Hokkien Chinese merchants from Kuangdung also worshiped a similar goddess of the seas, called Ma Chor Po, rescuer of shipwrecked sailors. Her temples still exist in Hong Kong, Taiwan, and elsewhere; in Penang, she has been subsumed within the Kuan Im Teng (Kuan Yin Temple) to the Goddess of Mercy (Ong Seng Huat 1989).

Perhaps Maṇi Mekhalā's most vivid representation today is in the realm of Khmer classical dance, although she also occurs in Khmer folktales (Pascalis 1931:82) and as Sakomaṇimekhalā, surveyor of the oceans and heavens and daughter of Preah Bot Otumbor, father of mankind (Udumbara, *ficus glomerata*) (Porée-Maspero 1969:781). The episode discussed in the papers by Cravath and Chan Moly Sam is evidently derived from a branch story incorporated into the Cambodian version of the Rāmāyaṇa (*Reamker*), although the goddess does not occur in any known · Indian version of the Rāmāyaṇa. A similar episode occurs in a Thai Rāmāyaṇa (*Ramakien*) composed by King Rama I in 1807 (Jumsai 1968:17-18), borrowed from the Khmer. At the end of one Khmer Rāmāyaṇa there is also a reference to Mekhalā's great beauty when she taunts Ramesur (*Reamker* 80:31, in Jacob 1986:287). According to Khmer legend, her gem is said to grant all wishes (ibid.:297), just as the Tamil Buddhist adept Maṇi Mekhalā's bountiful bowl could never be emptied.

The dance episode in question can be interpreted as representing the conflict between an indigenous, possibly Dravidian goddess and an Aryan god (Paraśurāmā, "Rāmā of the Axe," from *paraśu*, axe; called by the Khmer Ream Eysor, from Rāmāsura, "opponent of Rāmā," Rāmā + āsura) over her right to the powerful magic jewel. Arjuna (called Voracchun or Varjuna by the Khmers), Indra's son, principal character in the Mahābhārata, and Paraśurāmā's former student in the use of arms, defends Muni Mekhalā, true to his image as a high-minded and just warrior, beloved of women. The episode closely follows that of *Moha Chinok*, the Khmer version of the *Mahājanaka Jātaka* (Pascalis 1931:84).

Evidence suggests an Indian origin for these re-combined myths, perhaps brought as oral texts by the seafaring Tamil traders who had worshipped Maṇi Mekhalā for some time outside the religious realm of orthodox Hinduism. She was one of the figures in the heterodox cults of city-dwelling and seafaring Jain, Buddhist, and non-Brahmin Hindu merchants, but unimportant to Brahmin Hindus who were banned from travel and contact with foreigners by Vedic Hinduism (Obeyesekere 1984:515). The chief Indian literary sources for the goddess Maṇi Mekhalā are all Buddhist: the two Pali Jātakas mentioned, *Mahājanaka* and *Sankha Jataka*, and *Maṇi Mekhalai*, the only known Tamil Buddhist text which survives from the Buddhist period, dated variously from the 2nd to 5th century, under the Chola's rule in the South. This work is titled after the heroine's name for which the usual translation is "The Jewelled Belt," although it may originally have meant "The Jewel of Mekhala," as her belt has no special significance. The work consists of a Tamil narrative poem of thirty chapters, 50–500 lines each, which extolls the virtues of Buddhism. It is attributed to Cattanar, the Grain Merchant Prince of Madurai, who is also credited with having popularised the history of Mani Mekhalā's father's wife, the faithful princess Kannaki. (In the *Cilappatikāram*, "The Tale of the Anklet," another Tamil classic thought by most scholars to have been composed later, he is acknowledged for persuading the Cera king Cenkuttuvan to erect a temple in Kannaki's honor.) The young Jain prince Ilanko Atikal, who is believed to have authored the *Cilappatikāram* after being inspired by Cattanar's work, also depicts the human Mani Mekhalā, but in an earlier period of her life when she was born to Mādhavi and Kovalan, a courtesan and a Jain prince. Mani Mekhalā Teyvam was Kovalan's tutelary goddess, the divine nymph who saved his ancestors from shipwreck and learned to conquer desire. She appeared to Kovalan in a vision before his daughter's birth, and he hoped that by naming his daughter for her, she might be empowered to resist the entrapments which enslaved him: the wiles of Kāman, the god of love (Pope 1911; Richman 1988).

At the end of the *Cilappatikāram*, Mādhavi and Mani Mekhalā enter a Buddhist nunnery, after both Kovalan and his wife Kannaki are martyred and deified. The story continues in the *Mani Mekhalai* epic, when Mani Mekhalā's guardian goddess spirits her away from the monastery to a remote island, in order to protect her from falling in love with a young prince who is seeking her favors. She then undergoes a series of ordeals, pilgrimages, and apprenticeships to spiritual teachers: Vedins, Shaivites, Brahmavadis, Vaisnavites, Jains, and others, learning of her past incarnations and acquiring magical powers. One gift she acquires is the ability to conquer hunger; another the magical food bowl which never empties, with which she feeds the multitudes and abolishes famine. Her greatest accomplishment is the power to fill rainclouds, bring the rain, and endow the fields with produce. In the end she does all these simultaneously before a triple altar to the Buddha, Tivatilakai (guardian of the Buddha image at Mani Pallavam, Mani Mekhalā Teyvam's island), and Mani Mekhalā Teyvam herself; after these charities she becomes an ascetic and receives the final revelations of esoteric Buddhism. In Southeast Asia, her magical bowl becomes the magic jewel which causes lightning, forerunner of rain, reminiscent of the powerful gem of Indic mythology, and she is physically transformed and indigenised to serve the local psyche.

A second example of textual appropriation and transformation occurs in the episode of the Floating Maiden discussed in Sam-Ang Sam's article. Here we find another branch story as an accretion to a few indigenised mainland Southeast Asian Rāmāyanas, especially Khmer and Thai, where it is a favorite shadow puppetry piece (Chagsuchinda 1973). Curiously, one Mahābhārata branch story from Bali has notable parallels. According to dance ethnologist I Wayan Dibia, an episode called "The Death of Subhadra" is performed occasionally in some parts of Bali, also within the shadow puppet tradition. In the episode, while Arjuna is off meditating, his wife Subhadra is sexually harrassed by an unwanted admirer. To escape, Subhadra feigns death while floating in a river, depicted with horizontal puppet movements similar to the Thai and Khmer examples. The existence of similar traits in both traditions suggests a possible common origin in indigenous Southeast Asian myth.

No doubt similar evidence for appropriations could be documented in the papers which follow, and although it would be difficult to demonstrate empirically Murdoch's claim (1960:253-4) that 90 percent of all culture is borrowed, his assertion that borrowing is a sign of all major civilizations cannot be disputed. What is not borrowed, however, the distinctiveness belonging to each tradition which excludes all others, often contains the subtler aesthetic and affective elements of a culture such as musical sound. Indeed, music and similar aesthetic features function as ethnic or cultural markers, identifying a group and ensuring the perpetuity of the cultural "species" by infusing its heightened moments with the unmistakable experience of belonging for its members. And for those members who care to reflect upon that experience, as well as for those excluded from membership who wish to understand the unfamiliar, hermeneutics provides the key.

NOTES

*   I would like to acknowledge with gratitude the participation of my colleagues at the University of California who have contributed to the ideas explored in this introduction: Roger Savage for hermeneutical guidance, Robert L. Brown for suggestions from the field of South and Southeast Asian art, Fredric Lieberman for literary polishing, and Nazir Ali Jairazbhoy for his scholarly and editorial counsel.

1.   For a fictionalized account of the arrival of the first bronze drum in Java ca. 300 B.C., see Hood 1980:57–123.

2.   Although still often spelled and pronounced *mani* in Khmer, the spelling and pronunciation are sometimes given as *muni* in consideration of her great powers and acquired knowledge. In Cambodia today *muni* is an honorific for hermits and sages of the past as well as for scholars, whether male or female [from the Sanskrit for an inspired or ecstatic person, saint, seer or ascetic (Monier-Williams 1899:823)].

REFERENCES

Bernet Kempers, A. J.
    1988   *The Kettledrums of Southeast Asia: A Bronze Age World and its Aftermath.* Rotterdam: A. A. Balkema.

Carter, John Ross, and Mahinda Talihawadana
    1987   *The Dhammapada.* New York: Oxford University Press.

Chagsuchinda, Pensak, trans.
    1973   *Nang Loi: the Floating Maiden. A Recitation from an Episode of the Ramakien* (A Thai Version of the Indian Epic Rāmāyana) by Rama II, King of Thailand 1809-1824. Monograph Series 18. Lund: Scandinavian Institute of Asian Studies.

Coedes, G.
    1968   *The Indianized States of Southeast Asia.* Kuala Lumpur: University of Malaya Press.

Danielou, Alain
    1989   "Preface" to *Manimekhalai.* Merchant-Prince Shattan. Tr. Alain Danielou with T. V. Gopala Iyer. New York: New Directions Books.

Davids, T. W. Rhys
    1921   *Pali-English Dictionary.* London: The Pali Text Society.

Dowson, John
    1957   *A Classical Dictionary of Hindu Mythology and Religion, Geography, History and Literature.* London: Routledge & Kegan Paul.

Flueckiger, Joyce Burkhalter, and Laurie J. Sears, eds.
    1991   *Boundaries of Text: Epic Performance in South and Southeast Asia.* Michigan Papers on South and Southeast Asia 35. Ann Arbor: University of Michigan Press.

Frasca, Richard Armando
    1990   *The Theater of the Mahabharata: Terukkuttu Performances in South India.* Honolulu: University of Hawaii Press.

Higham, Charles
    1989   *The Archaeology of Mainland Southeast Asia: From 10,000 B.C. to the Fall of Angkor.* Cambridge: Cambridge University Press.

Hood, Mantle
    1980   *The Evolution of Javanese Gamelan Book I: Music of the Roaring Sea.* International Institute for Comparative Music Studies, Berlin. Pocketbooks of Musicology 62. New York: C. F. Peters Corporation.

Jacob, Judith M., trans.
    1986   *Reamker: The Cambodian Version of the Rāmāyaṇa.* London: Royal Asiatic Society.

Jumsai, M. L. Manich, trans.
    1968   *Thai Rāmāyaṇa.* Bangkok: Chalermnit.

Lefèvre-Pontalis, Pierre
    1896   *Chanson et fêtes du Laos.* Paris: Ernest Leroux.

Linge, David E.
    1976   *Philosophical Hermeneutics: Hans-Georg Gadamer.* Berkeley: University of California Press.

Manual of Thai Drawings [Original title in Thai]
    c. 1970   Bangkok: Borisat Khonachang Chankat.

Monier-Williams, Sir Monier.
    1899   *A Sanskrit-English Dictionary.* Oxford: Clarendon Press.

Murdoch, George P.
    1960   "How Culture Changes." In *Man, Culture, and Society,* ed. H. L. Shapiro. New York: Oxford University Press.

O'Flaherty, Wendy Doniger
    1981   *Siva: The Erotic Ascetic.* Oxford: Oxford University Press.

Obeyesekere, Gananath
1984   *The Cult of the Goddess Pattini.* Chicago: University of Chicago Press.

Ong Seng Huat
1989   "The Temple on the Knoll." *Pulau Pinang* (Jan-Feb):24–27.

Parkin, Robert
1991   *A Guide to Austroasiatic Speakers and Their Languages.* Honolulu: University of Hawaii Press.

Pascalis, Claude
1931   "Manimekhala en Indochine." *Revue des Arts Asiatiques* 2/7 (June):81–92.

Porée-Maspero, Eveline
1962–69   *Etude sur les Rites Agraires des Cambodgiens.* 3 vols. The Hague: Mouton.

Pope, G. U.
1987   *Manimekhalai.* Reprint of 1911 ed. Madras: Pioneer Book Service.

Proschan, Frank
1989   *Kmhmu Verbal Art in America: The Poetics of Kmhmu Verse.* Phd diss., University of Texas.

Richman, Paula
1988   *Women, Branch Stories, and Religious Rhetoric in a Tamil Buddhist Text.* Syracuse, N.Y.: Maxwell School of Citizenship and Public Affairs.

Richman, Paula, ed.
1991   *Many Rāmāyaṇas: The Diversity of a Narrative Tradition in South Asia.* Berkeley: University of California Press.

Ricoeur, Paul
1981   *Hermeneutics and the Human Sciences.* Edited and translated by John B. Thompson. Cambridge: Cambridge University Press.

Sarkar, Himansu Bhusan
1980   *Literary Heritage of South-East Asia.* Calcutta: Firma K.L.M.

Shattan, Merchant-Prince
1989   *Manimekhalai.* Tr. Alain Danielou with T.V. Gopala Iyer. New York: New Directions Books.

Singer, Milton
1972a   *When A Great Tradition Modernizes: An Anthropological Approach to Indian Civilization.* New York: Praeger.

1972b   "Search for a Great Tradition in Cultural Performances." In *When A Great Tradition Modernizes: An Anthropological Approach to Indian Civilization.* Ed. Milton Singer, 67–80. New York: Praeger.

1972c   "Text and Context in the Study of Contemporary Hinduism." In *When A Great Tradition Modernizes: An Anthropological Approach to Indian Civilization.* Ed. Milton Singer, 39–52. New York: Praeger.

Stutley, Margaret and James Stutley
    1977   *Harper's Dictionary of Hinduism.* New York: Harper and Row.

Swaminatha Iyer, U. V.
    1965   *Manimekalai.* Madras: Kapir Accukkutam.

van Leur, J. C.
    1955   *Indonesian Trade and Society: Essays in Asian Social and Economic History,* Tr. James S. Holmes and A. van Marle. The Hague: W. van Hoeve.

Zerbuchen, Mary Sabina
    1987   *The Language of Balinese Shadow Theater.* Princeton, N.J.: Princeton University Press.

POETIC PARALLELISM IN KMHMU VERBAL ARTS:
FROM TEXTS TO PERFORMANCES[1]

Frank Proschan

Parallelism—the ordered interplay of repetition and variation—has been identified by Roman Jakobson as the constitutive essence of poetry. Parallelism may employ any of the resources and components of language and speech: it may be lexical, semantic, grammatical, prosodic, or rhythmic, for example, or simultaneously several of those. At its deepest level, all of language can be seen as the realization, with variation, of a certain basic stock of repeated grammatical figures. In English, for example, the sequence of subject-verb-object constitutes a grammatical model that is repeated infinitely, with infinite variability. In English style guides and writing courses, we are taught that good form requires that corresponding phrases of a sentence or paragraph employ parallel syntactic structures.

Far more interesting are those language phenomena that employ other forms of parallelism based on sound or meaning in addition to grammatical parallelism. One readily recognizable type of parallelism includes those forms that combine a high degree of lexical and phonological repetition with a low degree of variation. Every language has its examples: The Russian folklorist Jakobson (1987) cites the American political slogan, "I like Ike," while former president Reagan was inclined to cite the Russian folk proverb, *"doverie no proverie"* (Trust, but verify). The appeal of both examples to English-speaking listeners derives in large part from the fact that this kind of phonological parallelism is *not* a prominent device of most English-language verse, being limited for the most part to small genres such as riddles and sayings. Within certain language communities, however, or within certain genres of those communities, lexical and phonological parallelism is not merely an artistic device employed occasionally for striking effect. In many language traditions, parallelism becomes canonical, even compulsory, within certain genres or more broadly across several genres. Scholars of the verbal arts of Eastern Indonesia, for instance, have examined the parallelism that is obligatory in ritual language of various sorts (Fox 1988). The verbal art traditions of mainland Southeast Asia offer another rich and relatively unexplored terrain.

Jakobson defines canonical parallelism as existing when "certain similarities between successive verbal sequences are compulsory or enjoy a high preference," especially when these sequences occur "in metrically or strophically corresponding positions" (1987:146, 145). Such parallelism is a pervasive feature of the verse and narrative forms of Kmhmu and other Austroasiatic language groups, as for instance Vietnamese (Nguyen Van Huyen 1934), Mon (Guillon 1971), Khmer (Jacob 1979), Mnong Gar (Condominas 1977), Maa' (Boulbet 1972, 1975), and Lac (LeGay and Da Got 1971); it also figures into the poetics of other Southeast Asian language groups such as Hmong (Catlin

1982), Mien (Saepharn 1988), Tho [i.e., Tay-Nung] (Nguyen Van Huyen 1941), Rhade (Sabatier 1933), and others. Except for Nguyen Van Huyen's masterful explication of parallelism in the antiphonal verse of the Vietnamese (1934), the phenomenon has essentially gone unstudied. It is unmistakable from cited texts (even those presented only in translation), but unremarked by the authors and unnoticed by scholars of comparative poetics.

Folklorists and linguists working with the oral traditions of other regions have recently shown great interest in the forms and functions of poetic parallelism (e.g., see Sherzer and Urban 1986 and Sherzer and Woodbury 1987 for Native American traditions; Fox 1971, 1977, 1988 and Metcalf 1989 for Austronesian traditions). These scholars have investigated parallelism as a feature differentiating genres within the verbal arts of one language, as a feature characteristic of all or most genres of verbal art in a given language, or as an areal feature common to numerous contiguous or related languages. Parallelism in verbal art has also been compared with parallel structures in other forms of expressive behavior (e.g., ritual practice or material culture). The use of form-content parallelism as an organizing principle for extended verbal art forms has recently been demonstrated to be a productive analytical tool that unlocks subtleties of meaning embodied in texts (see Woodbury 1987 and Urban 1986, among others).

What follows is offered as a contribution to that larger enterprise, of particular importance from two standpoints: First, it establishes that there remain unstudied traditions of parallelism that equal or exceed in their complexity and artistry those already known to scholars. Second, it demonstrates the necessity of considering not just "texts," but far more importantly "performances" of parallelistic genres. The nature of performance is such that text models with given, pre-existing structures are creatively realized in specific contexts—temporal, social, historical—in unique and varied manners, as we shall see. I will consider how parallelism characterizes Kmhmu verbal arts, drawing examples from various verse and non-verse genres. A particularly complex form of crosswise parallelism, described by the Kmhmu as "reverse words," is unlike any that has previously been described and will be given special explication. As a structuring principle of Kmhmu verbal art, strict and regular parallelism provides a skeletal organization bringing coherence and continuity to "texts." But during specific performances situated in given spatio-temporal and sociocultural contexts, that skeleton is fleshed out, distorted, and played with for artistic effect. The bare bones of the parallel structure will be compared here with the fully realized, and far more complex, performance.

PARALLELISM IN KMHMU VERBAL ART GENRES

Parallelism pervades Kmhmu verbal art: in verse forms including songs and prayers; in shorter rhymed genres such as proverbs and riddles; in non-metrical, non-rhymed narrative forms such as tales and myths; and in non-narrative speech including oratory, prayers, and conversation. And, as in Vietnamese (Nguyen Van Huyen 1934) and Khmer (Jacob 1979), parallelism in the form of reduplication is a characteristic feature of Kmhmu morphology, continuing as a productive morphological process and artistic device of contemporary speakers (Svantesson 1983). In the extra-verbal realm, parallel actions are frequent in ritual practice: offerings are made twice; ritual libations are drunk in pairs; and so on. As part of the humorous banter that takes place when liquor is consumed,

Kmhmu will insist that you drink not one but two glasses of rice whiskey. After all, they joke, you cannot walk with just one leg and neither should you have just one drink.

Examples of pervasive parallelism in verse, narrative, and other genres will be drawn from recordings made among Kmhmu in the United States and from previously printed materials.[2] In the case of those examples drawn from my own sound recordings, the examples will be presented initially in a somewhat schematized form that I call "text models." This format shows their structure most clearly, omitting certain embellishments, elaborations, or emendations that were actually performed. In the case of examples drawn from previous publications, a similar schematization has generally been done already by the collector or transcriber. The complexities even of these "stripped-down" versions are already daunting, as we shall soon see. The more fully and accurately transcribed performances introduce another set of complications, as we shall see later.

Kmhmu *teem* or *trneem* sung verse[3]

To begin, let us consider one relatively simple example of parallelism, a quatrain from a courtship song sung by Chanh Thammala, originally from the Muong Sai region of Luang Prabang province, Laos. Ta' Chanh is now living in Stockton, California, where this song was recorded in 1982. The song, which would be known by Kmhmu from Luang Prabang as a *teem* "song" (and in the northern Kmhmu areas as a *trneem*), is one that a young man would sing to his beloved and her parents and kin, praising them for their wisdom, virtue, and prosperity while belittling himself (the entire song with its translation and a partial musical transcription are presented as Appendix 1). It is one of a number of *teem trklé'* "courtship song" sung at different stages of the process of courtship and marriage. Here the singer describes the travails he endured while traveling to his beloved's village:

ô' mèèn koon hnooq ñè' kndruum
    bu' ma' déé.
	I remained still a small child under my
	    mother's breast.

ô' mèèn koon hnooq ñè' kndruum
    kiaq ma'.
	I remained still a small child under my
	    mother's arm.

ô' yat daa blooq rôôm gook, hlian cqkvaa
    pryaak kôh plwam.
	I was in the rattan thicket, I separated
	    the medicine plant, cut the leeches.

yat daa blooq rôôm gook, yoh cqkvaa
    pryaak hrwam glaaq.*
	I was in the rattan thicket, I parted the medicine
	    plant, cleared off the stones.

* These verses are marked with a single asterisk in the full text provided as Appendix 1.

This pair of couplets features a very high proportion of repetition and relatively little new information in the second and fourth lines, and thus a high degree of parallelism. In the first couplet, *bu'* "breast" is replaced by *kiaq* "upper arm"; the reflexive pronoun *déé* is omitted. A close equivalence is preserved semantically, syntactically, metrically, and phonetically between the paired lines.

At the semantic level, a sort of synecdoche is employed in the second line: The general expression "under my mother's breast" is used in Kmhmu just as we would in English to refer to a nursing baby; the more restricted expression "under my mother's upper arm" substitutes one part of that process for the more general whole. In certain language traditions where parallelism is pervasive, the semantic relation of the first term to the second term is always that of general-to-specific (or unmarked-to-marked, using Jakobson's terminology).[4] In other traditions the order is reversed; the first term is always specific and the second general. And in others, the terms are considered to be semantically equivalent. Fox, for instance, has proposed as a general characteristic of parallel pairs that "dyadic sets are essentially neutral pairs; one element in a set is not 'superior' to another element and either element may precede the other in expression" (1971:247), although he goes on to note somewhat contradictorily that one may be semantically "dominant" as compared to the other.

Mannheim (1987) notes the contrasting situation of clearly established "semantic hierarchy" of parallel terms in Southern Peruvian Quechua.[5] In Kmhmu verse, we can distinguish two possibilities: In the first, the parallel partners are related hierarchically, with one marked and the other unmarked. There is, though, no compulsory sequence. Either term may precede the other, so that we can consider the relation hierarchical but reversible. While the example above moved from unmarked to marked, in the second couplet the marked term *hlian* (go out) is followed by the unmarked term *yoh* (go). We will see below a general semantic pattern of obscurity resolving to clarity, but within this pattern a specific, marked "part" may precede a general unmarked "whole," for example. The marked term may be too specific to be clearly understood initially, its obscurity resolved only when its more general partner follows.

The second possibility in Kmhmu verse is that the parallel pair may be two words drawn from the same semantic domain that are neither synonymous nor hierarchical—they are equivalent without being the same. Thus, in English, "magenta" might be a marked partner for "red," while "red" and "green" are equivalent partners. The pair *kôh*, (cut [in a given manner]), and *hrwam* (clear, cut down) and the pair *plwam* (leech) and *glaaq* (stone) are not related as marked or unmarked, specific or general. Instead, they are comparable or equivalent terms from the same semantic domains (in the first pair, ways of cutting,[6] and in the second, items from the realm of nature that present obstacles to one's progress).

At the syntactic level, the noun *bu'* is replaced by the noun *kiaq*, and the reflexive pronoun *déé* is omitted. The reflexive pronoun is both semantically and syntactically optional in expressions such as this. Similarly, the personal subject pronoun *ô'* (I) is omitted from the fourth line (as it is omitted before the verbs *hlian* and *yoh*, *kôh* and *hrwam*), consistent with a tendency in Kmhmu to omit subject pronouns (and more generally, subject nouns) in most cases. Throughout, words are replaced by parallel words of the same grammatical class (verb-for-verb, noun-for-noun) and filling the same syntactic role (subject-for-subject, object-for-object). Syntactic parallelism joins the four lines, which all begin with stative or existential verbs *mèèn* ([Lao] remain, continue) and *yat* (be, reside). The first implies a continued existence, roughly corresponding to an imperfect tense (its Kmhmu gloss would be *meh*), while the second is more definite and finite, like a perfect tense. In the lines of the second couplet, a similar verbal progression is established with the stative verbs (*mèèn* and *yat*) followed by active verbs (*hlian, cqkvah, kôh, yoh, cqkvah, hrwam*). There is thus a syntactic parallelism established among the verbs, in which we move from imperfect-to-perfect and from stative-to-active. This sequence of gradation operates between the two paired couplets and within each line of the second couplet.

Another possible domain for parallelism is at the metrical level, where we can distinguish two different possibilities. In the first, patterns of stresses are repeated in corresponding positions of parallel lines. Generally, such parallelism is especially frequent in languages such as English, where syllable stress is used to distinguish meaning between words. Where stress is predictable from the morphological constraints of the word, it does not provide as rich a resource for this kind of parallelism. This is the case for Kmhmu, where stress serves no sense-discriminatory function in normal conversational prosody and is not used as a basis for parallelism. Instead, the basis for metrical parallelism in Kmhmu verse is count—a line is typically constituted from paired stichs of five or seven syllables. In counting syllables, diphthongs are treated like simple vowels as the nucleus of a single syllable, and minor presyllables are given full count as a single syllable, even if they are often reduced in normal speech (and even if they may be prolonged or artifically emphasized in sung verse).

In the verse presented above, the syllabic structure of lines is as follows:

5 + 5
5 + 4
6 + 7
5 + 7

Elsewhere within the same song, lines are composed of paired distichs: 5 + 5 syllables long, 5 + 7 syllables long, 7 + 5 syllables long, or 5 + 4 syllables long, or of single stichs seven syllables or six syllables long. Based on a larger collection of songs we can generalize that lines composed of paired, five- syllable distichs are typical or canonical, but there is wide latitude for various combinations of five-syllable and seven-syllable phrases, and less frequently for combinations of four-syllable or six-syllable phrases (cf. Proschan 1989:376–78).

Phonologically, the quatrain shows much the same kind of gradation as it did syntactically. The first couplet is heavily salted with nasals: the only non-nasal consonants are five instances of /k/, one each of /d/ and /b/, and a pair of the cluster /dr/. The vowel structure is one where back vowels are sandwiched between the less frequent front vowels (the vowel /e/ in parentheses marks the schwa vowel of the minor presyllable; the optional subject pronoun ô' is also enclosed in parentheses):

(ô) èè oo oo è - (e) uu u a éé
(ô) èè oo oo è - (e) uu ia a

In the second couplet, by contrast, the consonant inventory is far richer: two instances of /d/ and two /t/, two /g/ and five /k/, and two /p/ and two /c/ among the stop series; two /h/, four /r/, five /y/, one /hr/, and one /hl/ among the continuants; and two /bl/, two /kv/, one /pl/ and one /gl/ among the clusters. The nasals are also well represented, but not to the exclusion of the non-nasals as in the first couplet. And where the first couplet was heavy in back vowels, the second couplet is emphatically front vowels, especially in the second stich of each line:

(ô) a aa oo ôô oo - ia (e) aa (e) aa ô wa
a aa oo ôô oo - o (e) aa (e) aa wa aa

As we saw with the verb structure, so in terms of phonology there is a pattern moving from upper left to lower right; that is, the back vowels of the first couplet are echoed in the vowels of the first stichs of the second couplets, and in each line of the second couplet we see the same gradation from back-to-front that marks the structure of the couplet as a whole.

Another form of parallelism at the phonological level is more familiarly known as rhyme, exhibited only minimally in this first example. Exact rhyme unites *hnooq* and *blooq*, *plwam* and *hrwam*. It could be claimed that a close rhyme unites *koon, hnooq, blooq, rôôm,* and *gook,* or *kôh* and *yoh,* or *ñè'* and *déé,* but there are no examples elsewhere in Kmhmu verse of such sounds being assimilated to one another. In choosing a simple example that could let us see the complex workings of parallelism on the semantic, syntactic, lexical, and phonological levels, we have wound up with only the most minimal use of rhyme. But, it would be wrong to assume from this example that rhyme is not a prominent device of Kmhmu parallelism. The second instance of rhyme in this quatrain, *plwam* and *hrwam,* introduces a characteristic of Kmhmu parallel verse that makes all we have seen until now seem simple. This is what the Kmhmu call *hrlo' prgap* or "reverse words" (also known in some areas as *kham prgaay* or *hrlo' prgap prgaay*). As found here, this involves a rhyme that is displaced, cross-wise, between two parallel lines. Before moving on to a consideration of reverse words, let us offer examples of other genres of Kmhmu verbal art that use parallelism.

Kmhmu *hrlo' boor* prayers and blessings

The prayers and blessings of the Kmhmu are known as *hrlo' boor* and are generally used in the context of religious rituals and ceremonies. These are somewhat difficult to elicit outside of their ritual context. Some Kmhmu claim that they cannot remember them except when needed. Generally spoken in a heavily rhythmic semi-chant, prayers and blessings make frequent use of parallelism. An example, drawn from Lundstrom and Tayanin's study of music in the annual agricultural cycle of the Kmhmu (1982:78, 140–141), is used ritually to drive away spirits and call on the rice to grow:

gaay eem hqo'!	Recover, oh rice!
kto' eem blaaq!	Set buds, oh elephant grass!
hqo' Stpuut gaay guut daa gii!	Rice of Stpuut village come here!
hqo' Môq Loot root daa gii!	Rice of Môq Loot village come here!
druuñ lee gaa tqkwl!	Termites, do climb on the tree stumps!
mwl lee looq tmpo'!	Larvae, do crawl in the valley!
gaay jem mat!	Recover every seed!
sat jem jwaq!	Grow every plant!

In this instance, parallelism is used in each of the four couplets, combined with a variation of *hrlo' prgap* (reverse words). The reverse words here are used in a form of chiasmus, in which the last word of one line is rhymed with the first word of the next (or, using an alternative analysis, the last word before a caesura is rhymed with the first word after it). This same kind of parallelism is used in many proverbial expressions.

Kmhmu *kham tqkap tqkaay* sayings and proverbs

Kmhmu have many succinct sayings or proverbs that employ parallelism of various sorts. Most are very short, as for instance this example drawn from a publication of Damrong Tayanin (1984:9):

vaar smruat klam hla'	Hot early, carry rice basket
kma' smruat klam tôq	Rain early, carry bamboo water container

The saying explains that when it is hot early in the morning, one can expect rain by mid-day. As in the previous example, a form of chiasmus is employed in which the last word of the first line is rhymed with the first word of the second, again combined with parallelism joining the two lines together. A similar structure is employed in an extended proverbial expression, used by young people seeking knowledge from their elders:

ôô i' meh koon hmmé', plé' kñoom,	Oh, we are the new child, the young fruit,
siim praa méc, séc praa neeq.	The still unhearing bird, the still unknowing bird.
beq boo meh mat bri' jôq, mat môq kaal.	We lean on you, the high sun, the new moon.
kak gooy klvis, klis gooy smgar.	If we bend, straighten us; if we make a mistake, correct us.
boo meh thav, meh kèè,	You are the elder, the old one,
meh thaav, meh khun.	The village headman, the priest.
jwa' snaat, jaat kmhmu',	The pistol bullet, the Kmhmu tradition,
kmhmu' kuq, spuq ram.	The village people, the treasure basket.

Here again, lines are linked together by lexical parallelism (lines 5 and 6) or syntactic parallelism (lines 1 and 2, 5 and 6, 7 and 8). Within a line, two clauses separated by a caesura may also be linked together by lexical parallelism (line 2, 3, 4, 5, 6). Within each and every line, the paired clauses are linked together by syntactic parallelism. Finally, we again have instances of the use of phonological chiasmus with rhymed words on either side of a caesura (line 2, 4, 7, 8) or linking two successive lines (lines 2 and 3, 7 and 8).

Kmhmu *hrlo' trdoh* tales and stories

Parallelism is frequent in Kmhmu narratives, although it is not compulsory in the same degree as it is in verse forms. At the largest level, narratives frequently employ what Woodbury (1987) calls form/content parallelism, in which actions are repeated with variation. For instance, a synoptic outline of the actions initiating a Cwaq myth, where the Kmhmu culture hero Cwaq is in his avatar of Ta' Ñii Graan (Lazy Grandfather Ñii), clearly shows the nature of such repetition:

1. Ta' Ñii Graan's (Cwaq's) parents go to work in the field, he babysits his brother, makes a magical drum of wax, and hides it under the bed. Cwaq takes the magical drum from the bed and beats on it. Others come to hear, and Cwaq crushes his wax drum and hides it under the bed.[7]

2. Cwaq's parents go to work in the field, he babysits his brother, makes a magical drum of wax, and beats on it. Others come to hear, Cwaq crushes the wax drum and hides it under the bed. People tell his parents about it.

3. Cwaq's parents pretend to go to the field, but instead prepare a net and a jar of water. Cwaq babysits his brother, makes a drum of wax, and beats on it. His father catches him in the net and his mother throws water on him. He loses his magic power to beat the drum and they hang it in the corner.[8]

An examination of the text (Appendix 2) will show that this form/content parallelism is reflected in lexical parallelism (on a somewhat larger scale than that of a line, as in the cases above). Thus, in each episode Cwaq beats out virtually the same message on the drum and certain phrases are repeated exactly several times. However, variation enters in frequently.[9] Thus, different words are used to describe how Cwaq babysits his brother and how he crushes the magical drum into a ball of wax and hides it under the bed. Nevertheless, it is clear that lexical parallelism is not nearly as frequent or elaborate in Kmhmu oral narrative as it is in the verse genres and epigrams considered above.

KMHMU REVERSE WORDS: *HRLO' PRGAP*

We have been introduced to the special form of parallelism that the Kmhmu call *hrlo' prgap* or *hrlo' prgap prgaay*.[10] This cross-wise parallelism has been presented thus far only in its most simple forms. To gain a better idea of the complex possibilities, let us consider another quatrain drawn from the concluding verses of the same song sung by Ta' Chanh Thammala. Here the singer begins his leavetaking, imploring his beloved not to forget him:

an boo sdu' rééq, smoot srlwaq ha' yo' ha'.	If you observe the new forest, watch the thatch burn and burn.
an boo sdu' rééq, smoot srlwaq plôq yo' plôq.	If you observe the new forest, watch the thatch sprout and sprout.
an boo sr'ééq juu, smoot crna' mwaq yo' mwaq.	If you miss your lover, watch the area around the villages.
an boo sr'ééq juu, smoot pha'ôq mwaq yo' mwaq.**	If you miss your lover, watch the whole region around the villages.

*   ** These verses are marked with two asterisks in the full text provided as Appendix 1.*

We can schematically represent this quatrain as follows, using zero to represent the repeated words that provide a frame for the parallel words, and using letters to represent rhyming parallel words (note that for the present purpose we are indicating words and not syllables). In the hierarchical arrangement of the quatrain, the two final lines are more important than the two beginning lines. Hence the schema below represents this semantic hierarchy by indicating the reverse words with lower case letters and their consequential counterparts with upper case letters and by inverting the alphabetical sequence of the first lines in order to maintain a proper alphabetical sequence for the more important final lines.

0	0	b	a	0	d	c	0	c
0	0	b	a	0	d	e	0	e
0	0	A	B	0	C	D	0	D
0	0	A	B	0	E	D	0	D

The basic structure of Kmhmu reverse word parallelism is apparent from an even more truncated schematic representation, as follows. Here we indicate another aspect of hierarchical organization: each stich is a unit related both to its conjoined stich in the same line and its corresponding stich in sequential lines and each couplet is linked to the other. These relations are marked with brackets:

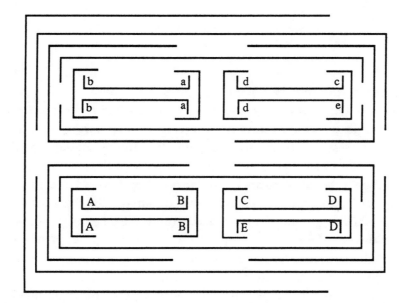

Thus we have the pairs of *sdu' rééq* and *sr'ééq ju'*, *srlwaq ha'* and *crna' mwaq*, *srlwaq plôq* and *pha'ôq mwaq*, incorporated into a framework of words repeated exactly from line to line. In the present case, all of the words in the verses are meaningful in context, but this is not always the case. Further, there is a hierarchy of meaning. In this example, as in the one previously discussed, the lines of substance are the second couplet in the quatrain, the singer's entreaties to his beloved not to forget him. In the earlier example, the substantive content is also in the two final lines, where the singer describes the hardships he endured in traveling to his lover's village. The first couplet of each quatrain is evocative while the second couplet is consequential. Can this semantic organization give us some clues to the nature of reverse word parallelism?

Let us consider one final example, drawn from the beginning of the same song. Here the singer sets the scene, describing the elders gathered to hear him sing. In contrast to the previous example, the first two lines have no discernible sense: the words themselves are all meaningful in isolation, but they have no conceivable connection to one another.

ktaam haac raa-jaa kndruum trwal dwk.	Crab, burrow, rajah, under, pheasant, butt head.
ktaam haac raa-jaa kndruum trwal dèèn.	Crab, burrow, rajah, under, pheasant, sit.
an-ñaa dén aam graam kndruum go' bwk hool.	Everyone sits crosslegged under the sooty beams.
an-ñaa dén aam graam kndruum pèèn hool.***	Everyone sits crosslegged under the sooty planks.

*** *These verses are marked with three asterisks in the full text provided as Appendix 1.*

The parallel words are by now obvious: *ktaam* and *aam graam*, *rajah* and *an-ñaa*, *trwal* and *hool*, *bwk* and *dwk*, *dèèn* and *pèèn*. Interestingly, despite the large number of possible ways that Kmhmu use reverse words in parallel verse, the schematic structure of this quatrain corresponds exactly to the second example above, despite the large difference in their semantic organization (note that again we represent words, not syllables, and that repeated frame words are omitted here):

```
b   a      /    d    c
b   a      /    d    e
A   B      /    C    D
A   B      /    E    D
```

The reverse words of the first two lines are all words whose solitary, decontextualized meanings are transparent. Only *raa-jaa* is a loan word from Lao, and it is probably an ancient loan (from the same semantic domain as *an-ñaa*, referring to dignitaries within the Tai social hierarchy). Interestingly, these two words form the only pair in the quatrain in which the rhyme words are also syntactically and semantically related (excepting *kndruum*, "underneath," which is repeated without change). The noun *ktaam* (crab) is paired with an adverbial construction, *aam graam* (crosslegged); the noun *trwal* (silver pheasant) is paired with the verb *hool* (smear with ashes or soot, as in ritual face-painting); the verb *dwk* (butt one's head) is paired with the noun *bwk* (crossbeam); and the verb *dèèn* (replace) is paired with the noun *pèèn* (plank).

Consistent with the larger semantic pattern we have traced above of natural images answered by cultural images, the first couplet invokes entities from the semantic domain of nature (*ktaam*, "crab"; *haac*, "dirt heaped up around hole by burrowing crab or other animal"; *trwal*, "silver pheasant"). The second couplet refers directly to the immediate social and material context in which the song is sung. In other cases, the reverse words in the first couplet are semantically more obscure. They may be loan words from Lao, incorporated for their sound shape rather than for their meaning.[11] In some cases, as we shall see below, the reverse words may not have any meaning outside of their context. They may follow the constraints of Kmhmu morphology and phonology, but have no existence independent of their use as reverse words.[12]

· This quatrain shows a phonological gradation like that in our first verse example above, from low-front to high-back vowels. The opening stich of each line is almost exclusively long /aa/ (fourteen occurrences), with a pair of short /a/ and a pair of /é/, all low-front vowels; the schwa of the minor presyllable /k-/ is the only non-low, non-front vowel. The closing stich of each line is primarily high and back vowels: four occurrences of /uu/, a pair of /oo/, a pair of /wa/, a pair of /w/, and one /o/; the exceptions are the low front vowel /èè/ which occurs twice and the schwa in the minor presyllable /kn-/:

```
(e) aa aa aa aa / (e) uu wa w
(e) aa aa aa aa / (e) uu wa èè
a aa é aa aa / (e) uu o w oo
a aa é aa aa / (e) uu èè oo
```

In the cases we have just considered, the reverse words have been incorporated into a regular and complete quatrain, with two linked couplets, each comprising two linked distichs, the second couplet answering to the first. We can consider these as examples of an archetypal or canonical shape of Kmhmu reverse word parallelism. Yet this model does not exhaust the possibilities within the canon. Indeed, a talented singer may use the typical or canonical verse structure only occasionally, preferring to display virtuosity by playing with the diverse possibilities.[13] Consider another quatrain from the closing verses of the song, as the singer is preparing to depart (sung just prior to the first example considered above):

tnéc hla' rlaay, sii baay hla' rlaat	The bamboo leaf droops, the long-bean leaf hangs down,
smbraat 'maat cii véc, smbraat 'maat cii gaay	It is time to leave, to go home, it is time to leave, to depart,
hla' lum go' smgaat, hla' lèèq go' smgaat	The *lum* leaf is tasty, the basil leaf is tasty,
koon hnwm go' smbraat, thav kèè go' smbraat.****	Girl friend, I must leave, grandparents, I must leave.

    **** *These verses are marked with four asterisks in the full text provided as Appendix 1.*

Here, it is lines 1 and 3 that include the reverse words, with lines 2 and 4 carrying the semantic load. The first and third lines also involve internal rhyme (in line 1, a mirror rhyme or chiasmus like that we have seen above in some of the shorter sayings and proverbial expressions); these are represented below with numbers. The reverse words are again represented with upper and lower-case letters; a hash mark indicates a close but not exact rhyme. Auxiliary particles *cii* (future marker) and *go'* (apposition) are not shown here.

c	1	d	/	d	1	a
A	B	C	/	A	B	D
1	f'	a	/	1	h'	a
E	F	A	/	G	H	A

This parallelistic structure is not unique in Kmhmu verse and represents just one of many variations possible, in addition to the paired couplet structure of the first examples.

    To understand how and why these reverse words are used by the Kmhmu with such frequency, and to appreciate the special fascination and enjoyment they provoke, we must broaden our consideration beyond the texts themselves and begin to examine how reverse words and parallelism are used in performance. It is useful to move away from the schematized, stripped-down examples we have been using thus far to consider how in fact these mental templates, or models, are elaborated and modified when they are actually sung.

PARALLELISM IN TEXTS, CONTEXTS, AND PERFORMANCES

    Until now, our discussion has concerned only texts of Kmhmu verbal art, abstracted from the performance contexts in which such texts are generated and realized. We have seen a range of parallelistic devices, some very simple and others of a daunting complexity. We have much that we can still learn about parallelism by considering it in performance, as distinct from its existence in the skeletal structures of artistic texts.

    To begin, a consideration of performance practice and context can give us a fuller sense of the attraction that parallelism holds for Kmhmu, especially the *hrlo' prgap* reverse words. Let us recall that parallelism necessarily involves repetition with variation. Canonical repetition contributes to an expectation on the part of hearers that what comes next will be similar to what preceded, that succeeding lines will be predictably similar. Canonical variation, contrariwise, leads hearers to expect that successive utterances will be unlike those that preceded. The combination of repetition and variation in canonical parallelism, then, can be understood to produce both anticipation and surprise.

This highly charged combination of the expected and the unexpected could lead either to a neurotic fearfulness or to a delighted playfulness. The latter, according to Kmhmu, accounts for the special fascination that parallelism holds for them. When I asked Kmhmu friends why they are so fond of *hrlo' prgap*, they tend to explain by pointing out that they are fun to listen to: auditors try to guess from hearing the beginning how things will turn out in the end. There is thus a sort of internal dialogue established, a call and response or question and answer between the first half and the second half. This is not the same as a riddle session where one's guesses are public, but more a matter of testing one's own wit privately against the singer's, without risk of embarrassment.

Performance contexts

What are the performance contexts and situations in which Kmhmu parallel verse is featured? One genre of song in which parallelism and reverse words are ubiquitous is that of *teem trklé'* "courtship songs," including the one used as our primary example above but also including others performed in antiphonal dialogues between two singers. Kmhmu speak of *teem trklé'* (courtship songs), *pat hrôôq trklé'* (courting with the Jew's harp), and *hrlo' trklé'* (courtship speech), all of which are performed in similar circumstances by young lovers.

Instrumental music plays an important part in traditional Kmhmu courtship. Typically, a Kmhmu youth will come in the evening to visit his girlfriend's house, sometimes playing on the *sqkuul* (mouth organ) as he approaches the house, or circling around the house playing the *sqkuul* until he is invited in. The girl can recognize the distinctive style of her lover's *sqkuul* music. Once inside, they sit near one another, yet still under the watchful eye of her parents, and he plays on the *hrôôq* (Jew's harp). The nature of the Jew's harp is such that its performer can enunciate vowel sounds quite clearly, and even some consonants, and the instrument can thus be used as a speech surrogate to convey precise lexical information.[14]

Ta' Cheu Rathasack, who demonstrated the *hrôôq* for me in Stockton, California, explained that, because it is a quiet instrument, the girl will often snuggle closer to the boy. Using the *hrôôq*, he will profess his love, compliment his sweetheart, praise her character and beauty, and propose marriage. The girl may respond musically by playing on the *toot*, a two-holed transverse flute. She does not generally enunciate words with the *toot*, but each song has a meaning or recalls words or phrases.

Also a typical part of the amusements practiced by courting lovers are a number of forms of play languages, in which words of affection are disguised through regular, systematic transformations of the morphology of the Kmhmu word.[15] Like "pig Latin" or Cockney rhyming slang, these play languages are relatively simple to learn, easy to perform, and provoke mirth and pleasure—not least when the performer makes a mistake or fails. A final form of verbal art used in the context of courtship is *hrlo' trklé'* (courtship speech), which takes in both the negotiations between families and the various kinds of speechifying between lovers or between a boy and his prospective parents-in-law. This includes flowery oratory, hard business negotiations, mutual praise, and antiphonal self-abnegation, in which each speaker seeks to situate himself below the other in prestige, virtue, financial position, etc; a sort of dialogue of debasement. In the *teem trklé'* (sung love dialogues), the same sort of diminution of self and glorification of the other is characteristic, both in exchanges between lovers and between suitor and parents-in-law. Kmhmu in the U.S. are shy and out-of-practice in the dialogic boy-girl *teem trklé'*, but it has been possible to record some of the songs for lovers and prospective parents-in-law, including the song we have used above to introduce Kmhmu poetic structures.

Ta' Chanh Thammala's song would customarily have been sung by a courting youth to his prospective bride and future parents-in-law, who would have responded to it with a comparable answering song. At other points during the courtship process, the dialogue is more rapid, with singers exchanging single quatrains with one another. In either case, but especially in the latter, the respondent would seek to answer the previous verse(s) with a verse or song referring to the images used by the other singer. The most desired response is one that is united through parallelism with the verse it answers, especially one that involves a more skillful and artistic use of reverse words. When I have discussed Ta' Chanh's song with other singers, for instance, they have more than once responded to his verses with an answering verse using the same reverse words or others that rhyme.

Kmhmu courtship traditions are part of a much larger cultural complex in East Asia, and especially Southeast Asia, of antiphonal love dialogues, usually between a boy and girl who engage in a friendly competition in verse (Proschan 1989:74–79). As with the Kmhmu, parallelism is frequent in these traditions. In some it is canonical, as Nguyen Van Huyen has shown for Vietnamese (1934). A basic semantic structure is common to many, if not most, of the love dialogue traditions—the pattern we have seen in Kmhmu verse in which the first couplet of a quatrain refers to natural phenomena in an often oblique manner and the second couplet refers to events or attributes of the human domain. This is the case for the Chinese love dialogues in the Book of Songs (cf. Granet 1932), for the Vietnamese songs (Nguyen Van Huyen 1934), and for many other traditions (Proschan 1984).

This semantic structure implicates a complex metaphoric system that reflects the cultural and ideological context in which these traditions are embedded. It is worth noting the explicit connection Jakobson makes between metaphor and parallelism. Both make use of relations of similarity or equivalence: In the first case "similarity connects a metaphorical term with the term for which it is substituted" (1987:113) and in the second "similarity is superimposed on contiguity" and this reveals "what elements are conceived as equivalent and how likeness on certain levels is tempered by conspicuous difference on other ones" (1987:86,83). The poetic parallelism in love dialogues functions both at the micro-level of poetically appropriate "equivalents" and at the macro-level of culturally situated metaphoric conceptions. The canonical form of the ancient Chinese love poems has been explained as revealing a cultural ideology establishing an equivalence between nature and man. Liu explains

> The parallel relationship between man and nature is not one of transparent comparison, where the first term is effaced by or subordinated to the second. Both terms exist at once. . .[and] a third term englobes both images. (1983:652)

In the case of Kmhmu parallel verses, as we have seen, typically (although not always) enigmatic or obscure images drawn from nature are followed by concrete images drawn from the social realm. This is true not only of courtship songs, but indeed of the full range of Kmhmu sung verse. The parallel verse structure thus replicates a larger cultural conception in which the social and natural worlds are linked as parallel pairs.

Structured texts and varied performances

If we can learn much about parallelism from an examination of performance practice and social context, we can learn even more from a close analysis of a recorded performance. Let us return to the song sung by Chanh Thammala, although now not in a schematic, regularized text but in a more detailed transcription. In the regularized texts presented above, we have omitted certain things: melodic vocables sung at the beginning, middle, or end of a line, and phatic communication such as terms of direct address to the listeners (dear, lover, mother, relations).[16] Lines have been distinguished based on poetic structure and not on the timing of pauses or the organization of melodic lines. We have not yet noted that parts of lines may be repeated, or phrases may be omitted as the model text is actually performed. When we begin to consider these as well, the already complicated nature of Kmhmu parallelism becomes even more complex.

The particular verses we have used as examples above include only a small number of address terms and they do not include partial lines. We shall return to them to illustrate some important issues concerning the organization of lines as they are actually performed, but let us first consider a verse that shows the extent to which the text model may be modified and emended in performance. In its regularized form, the verse model is as follows:

ô' pan taay déé thii mwaq moot,
    gaay bwp rqkô' 'yaq.
	I reached close to this village, came
	    and saw rice baskets

ô' gaay taay déé thii mwaq moot,
    gaay bwp rqkô' boom.
	I came close to this village, came and
	    saw rice jars.

ô' pan taay déé root mwaq gii,
    mwaq gii bwp cav raq.
	I arrived in this village, arrived in root
	    this village and saw the important elders.

ô' pan taay déé root mwaq gii,
    gaay bwp déé cav moom.*****
	I arrived in this village, came and saw the
	    powerful elders.

*****These verses are marked with five asterisks in the full text provided as Appendix 1.*

A more detailed transcription offers a much fuller sense of how the text model is realized in an actual performance. In this presentation, lines are established based on marked pauses in which the singer is silent (a line too long to be printed on a single line is indented, but there is no pause dividing it when sung). A prominently pronounced glottal stop marks the end of several lines. Several different vocables are used (*eem, qeey, ôô, rww, eey, heey*) as well as phatic communication (*ma' koon éém* "sweetheart, fiancée") and a quotative (*briaq leey* "others say"); these are marked in boldface below.

em, suu maa **ma' koon éém** suu maa. [glottal]
em, ô' pan taay déé thii mwaq moot, thii mwaq moot, gaay bwp rqkô' 'yaq, **briaq leey.**
em, ô' pan taay déé thii mwaq moot.
qeey, ô' gaay taay déé thii mwaq moot, gaay bwp rqkô' boom **ôô rww.**
em, ô' pan taay déé root mwaq gii, root mwaq gii bwp cav raq. [glottal]
qeey, ô' pan taay déé root mwaq gii, gaay bwp déé cav moom **eey heey.** [glottal]

Em, forgive me, sweetheart, forgive me. [glottal]
Em, I reached close to this city, close to this city, I saw rice baskets, others say.
Em, I reached close to this city.
Qeey, I came close to this city, I saw rice jars, ôô rww.
Em, I arrived in this village, arrived in this village and saw the important elders. [glottal]
Qeey, I came close to this village, saw the powerful elders, eey heey. [glottal]

This example illustrates clearly the extent to which the basic parallel structure and quatrain form can be modified and elaborated by the singer during performance. The modifications in the present instance serve to extend the verse through repetition and emendation. Occasionally, the text model may be amended through the omission of one clause in a line or through the replacement of one parallel clause by words that are not incorporated into the parallel structure. Thus, for instance, the following:

ô' yat thii mwaq moot,	I was near to this village
gaay guuñ knoor knhni'	and saw footprints in the path
(ô' yat thii mwaq moot,)	(I was near to this village)
gaay guuñ rqkô' 'yaq	and saw rice baskets
ô' phat déé root mwaq gii,	I arrived at this village
gaay guuñ h'é' rooy boor	and saw 100 stacks of firewood
ô' gaay taay déé root mwaq gii,	I arrived here in this village
gaay guuñ h'é' ban boor.	and saw 1,000 stacks of firewood.

In performance lines one and two are sung without pause and line four is divided into two phrases separated by a glottal stop and pause:

qeey ô' yat thii mwaq moot, gaay guuñ knoor knhni' éém lèèv
ô' gaay yoh, gaay guuñ rqkô' 'yaq éém rww.
qeey sah ô' phat déé root mwaq gii, gaay guuñ h'é' rooy boor éém lèèv.
em ô' gaay taay déé root mwaq gii. [glottal]
gaay sah, gaay guuñ h'é' ban boor éém lèèv eey.
I was near to this village and saw footprints in the path, I came on and saw rice baskets, my
   relations.
I say, then I arrived at this village and saw one hundred stacks of firewood, my relations.
I arrived in this village.
Came, I say, and saw one thousand stacks of firewood, my relations.

This example also demonstrates the frequent occurrence of various forms of enjambment, in which lines that are distinct semantically and syntactically are run together during performance. In this example, the first and second lines of the text model are combined in singing into a single, unbroken line. At the same time, the last line of the text model is broken apart. The most common occasion for such enjambment comes between the last line of one couplet or quatrain and the first line of the succeeding one. Thus, one verse we have already considered in its regularized model is realized in performance as follows:

em, ktaam haac rajah kndruum trwal dwk, eey. [glottal]
qeey sah, ktaam haac rajah kndruum trwal dèèn, anña dén amgraam kndruum go' bwk hool,
   briaq lav.
em, anña dén amgraam kndruum pèèn hool. [glottal]

Crab hole, rajah, under, pheasant, bump, eey.
Say, crab hole, rajah, under, pheasant, replace, everyone sits crosslegged under the sooty
    beams, others say.
Everyone sits crosslegged under the sooty planks.

This aural enjambment serves several purposes. Recalling that parallelism in general and especially reverse words derive their fascination in large part from the dynamic tension between the expected and the unexpected, between predictability and surprise, enjambment of this sort accentuates the desired effect. Listeners attempting their own personal solution to the enigmatic riddle of the first lines do not have the luxury of time. It is laid out clearly and leisurely in its initial statement, but the second time through it is sung more briskly and immediately followed by the solution. The concluding line then restates and summarizes the entire quatrain, presenting the desired and consequential semantic content in a clear and unhurried fashion. Tension and anticipation are created and then released during the performance, providing for a far richer and more stimulating involvement by the hearers in the song.

Similarly, tension and anticipation are used to heighten the hearers' enjoyment with other forms of enjambment, tying together the two lines of a couplet or tying together two couplets. For instance, a frequently used quatrain asking the indulgence of the listeners is followed immediately by a verse of greater meaning:

em, phaa môôy da' tmnis.
qeey, sah phaa baar da' tmnis, klis môôy da' sannaa, klis baar da' sannaa; ******
    ô' mèèn koon hnooq ñè' kndruum bu' ma' déé rww.
em ô' mèèn koon hnooq ñè' kndruum kiaq ma' eey.
qeey sah ô' yat da' blooq rôôm gôôk hlian cqkvah pryaak kôh plwam.
qeey yat da' blooq rôôm gôôk déé yoh cqkvah pryaak hrwam glaaq.

One cut, a penalty.
I say, two cuts, a penalty, one mistake by agreement, two mistakes by agreement. I was still a
    small child under my mother's breast.
I was still a small child under my mother's arm.
I say, I was in the rattan thicket, I parted the plants, cut the leeches.
I was in the rattan thicket, I parted the plants, cleared off the stones.

In this way, the expressive means available to the singer are used to establish larger structural continuity and to provide seamless transition between verses. Further, the timing of pauses and the use of enjambment contribute suspense and anticipation that increase the hearers' vicarious involvement in the performance and increase their pleasure.

If, as we have seen, a consideration of the performance of sung verses can expand our understanding of the Kmhmu use of parallelism, what can we discover from an examination of the performance of a Kmhmu narrative? In our discussion above, we noted that parallelism at the large scale of form-content parallelism is frequent in Kmhmu narrative, but that we do not encounter the same canonical lexical parallelism in narrative as we do in verse forms. To be sure, there are isolated instances in many tales of parallel lines and phrases, as for example an excerpt from a narration by Khan Suksamphan of the Kmhmu origin myth of the flood.[17] The example is presented first in a format that accentuates the parallelism:

Môôy aathit gii an boo tôm déé dé' mah.   In one week you must cook yourselves rice,

an boo tôm déé dé' mah.	you must cook yourselves rice.
Môôy aathit an noo pôq déé dé' huut,	In one week you should cut out the wax,
dé' seq liit briiq ni'.	to close up the drum.

As we may by now expect, in the performance itself the text model is realized somewhat differently, as shown in a more detailed transcription. (The first column shows the time that each line takes to speak, and the second column shows the length of the pause between each line. Times are shown in decimal fractions of one second. Italics indicate that the lines are spoken by a character; here, the bamboo rat.)

1.73		Môôy aathit gii an boo tôm déé dé' mah,
	1.44	
1.11		an boo tôm déé dé' mah.
	.49	
.71		Môôy aathit
	.73	
.90		an noo pôq déé dé' huut,
	1.27	
.93		dé' seq liit briiq gni'.

Interestingly, we see that the pause between sentences is shorter by far than the pauses within sentences, especially those pauses within sentences that coincide with grammatical pauses (indicated by commas). Based on the length and distribution of pauses in the rest of the story, we can determine that the pause after the third line is an expressive device and not a hesitation. As with enjambment in the sung verses, during performance the parallelism in the text model is realized in a way that subverts its seeming structural regularity while thereby calling greater attention to itself. Another example comes from the same story, again presented first in a regularized form:

Hlian rméét kaal.	Out came the Rmeet first.[18]
Hlian rméét ni' kaal,	Out came the Rmeet first,
hlian buh yiak tnlaq yaq nan.	came out rubbing off the charcoal
	from the hot iron.
Vaay ni' i' gaay dôôy.	After that, we came next.
Gaay hoo mèèv gii gaay dôôy.	The Chinese and Hmong came next.
Ca' mèèv ca' yaav gaay dôôy.	The Hmong and Mien came next.
Améérikaa, phalaqséét gii noo hlian knswt,	Americans and French came out last
noo graa,	so beautiful,
noo klook.	so white.

In the performance itself, we again encounter a purposeful use of timing and pauses for expressive effect:

1.06		Hlian rméét kaal.
1.49		
.70		Hlian rméét ni'
	.50	
2.08		kaal, hlian buh yiak tnlaq yaq nan.
	1.18	

1.14	Vaay ni' i' gaay dôôy.
2.20	
3.11	Gaay hoo mèèv gii gaay dôôy. Ca' mèèv ca' yaav gaay dôôy.
.95	
2.17	Amééríkaa, phalaqséét gii noo hlian knswt,
1.57	
.92	noo graa, noo klook.

Out came the Rmeet first.
Out came the Rmeet
    first, came out rubbing off the charcoal from the hot iron.
After that, we came next.
The Chinese and Hmong came next. The Hmong and Mien came next.
Americans and French came out last,
    so beautiful, so white.

Through variation in the tempo and rhythm of speech, and especially through strategic uses of pauses, even in places where they do not coincide with syntactic boundaries, the narrator achieves great artistic effect through his transformation and modification of the regular parallel structure, just as a singer does with the parallelism of verse genres.

CONCLUSION

In its diverse forms, parallelism pervades Kmhmu verbal art. In verse forms, parallelism is canonical, and in narrative forms it is an optional artistic device. One characteristic Kmhmu form of parallelism, the use of *hrlo' prgap* reverse words, is of a complexity not heretofore documented among the numerous global traditions that employ parallelism. Whether the parallelism is simple or complex, it provides a text model or structure that is differentially realized in performance. Certain characteristic devices used in performance, including emendment, amendment, enjambment, and the manipulation of pauses, have been identified and discussed. The contention is that these devices are used purposefully by the performer to heighten the artistic effect and increase the hearers' enjoyment of the performance.

Comparative studies of poetic parallelism have heretofore considered primarily what we have here called "text models." These regularized, skeletal structures represent parallelism as being rigorously patterned, even to the point sometimes of being rigidly uninteresting. If the practices of the Kmhmu are any indication, the underlying structures of parallelism provide a regular and predictable base on which a performer constructs a varied and less predictable performance. Parallelism in performance, like parallelism as a whole, combines repetition and variation, the expected and the unexpected, to the delight and enjoyment of its hearers and performers. It is our hope that future comparative studies of the realization of parallel structures in performance will enrich the global study of creativity in the realm of verbal art.

APPENDIX 1

Courtship song sung by Chanh Thammala

Musical Transcription and analysis by Amy Catlin
Text transcription and translation by Frank Proschan

The musical expression here artfully supports both semantics and poetic structure in a vocal style that is uniquely Kmhmu. Tonal materials are roughly equivalent in intonation to the gapped pentatonic scale, degrees 123 56, over a span of one octave plus a fourth, or 5̣6 123 56 i̇, with rare instances of the seventh degree in the upper range. Vocal quality is open with stylistic use of clear glottal stops to separate the rapid notes in figurational passages, often hummed to a nasal phoneme. This separation gives an aural impression similar to that of a flute or free-reed pipe with fingerholes. There is no detectable metric pulse.

Melodies alternate between untexted interludes (*qeey* or *em*, also found in Khmer vocalization) and single lines of sung text. The one basic interlude motive, with variants called here a, c, e, and f, consists of a basically descending 5321 structure with oscillations, prolonged notes, and rapid descending figures and infixes. Variants consist of approach from higher points, such as a) 16...53 (5653) 21, e) 65321, and f) 176...5(35653) 21. The most commonly used is the simplest: c) 5321, with repetitions and infixes. All basic forms are introduced within the first four lines of text.

The sung text alternates between two basic melodies, called here b and d. The first, b, consist of 35321 in its simplest form with many repeated notes used syllabically in recitative style and descending/oscillating melismas at the end of the line. The second, d, begins in the lower register on 6, sometimes approached from above with a slide, prolonged and often with increasing amplitude to the nonext *qeey*. This is followed by syllabic text recitation on the lowest tone, 5, in alternation with 6, and ascending, often by sliding, to 1 by the end of the line. Minor variants contain one or two higher notes.

These three basic themes, interlude descending to the 1, recitation descending to the 1, and ascending to the 1 from below, provide the tonal and temporal signposts to listeners, intensifying the poetic materials, whose rhymes and replacements always resolve on reposeful 1. Semantically the b and d melodies function as antecedent/consequence, as thoughts are introduced on the b melody and are resolved or concluded on the d melody. Visually, the slope of each four-part unit can be shown thus: 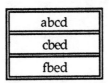 an inverted arch.

This is reinforced by the use of the b melody for such introductory lines as "Forgive me" (1, 14, 43) and "Open the door" (31). This d melody is greatly prolonged in the final two statements, confirming and making use of the stronger cadential effect associated with this lower-register ascent to the 1. Thus the melodic structure provides a satisfying sense of completion in its tripartite form:

abcd
cbed
fbed

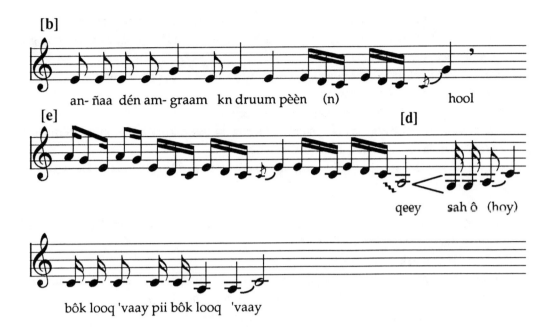

[b]

an- ñaa dén am- graam kn druum pèèn (n)   hool

[e]   **[d]**

qeey   sah ô (hoy)

bôk looq 'vaay pii bôk looq 'vaay

qeey sah, suu maa cav suu maa eey.

qeey, suu maa cav tqhlaay déé rww rak eey heey.

(***)   em, ktaam haac rajah kndruum trwal dwk eey.

    qeey sah, ktaam haac rajah kndruum trwal dèèn, an-ñaa dén amgraam kndruum go' bwk hool, briaq lav. (***)

em, an-ñaa dén amgraam kndruum pèèn hool.

qeey sah, ô' bôk looq 'vaay pii bôk looq 'vaay.

em, chaay looq dôk pii chaay looq tèèq, ô' tèèq boo dé' paan khôôt cav naay.

qeey, ô' tèèq paan 'mèèp cav naay déé rww rak ôô khooq eey.

em, phaa môôy da' tmnis.

qeey sah, phaa baar da' tmnis, klis môôy da' sannaa, klis baar da' sannaa, (*) ô' mèèn
    koon hnooq ñè' kndruum bu' ma' déé rww.

em, ô' mèèn koon hnooq ñè' kndruum kiaq ma' eey.

qeey sah, ô' yat da' blooq rôôm gôôk hlian cqkvah pryaak kôh plwam.

qeey, yat da' blooq rôôm gôôk déé yoh cqkvah pryaak hrwam glaaq. (*)

em, suu maa ma' koon éém suu maa.

(*****)   em, ô' pan taay déé thii mwaq moot, thii mwaq moot, gaay bwp rqkô' 'yaq, briaq leey.

em, ô' pan taay déé thii mwaq moot.

qeey, ô' gaay taay déé thii mwaq moot, gaay bwp rqkô' boom ôô rww.

em, ô' pan taay déé root mwaq gii, root mwaq gii bwp cav raq. (*****)

qeey, ô' pan taay déé root mwaq gii, gaay bwp déé cav moom eey heey.

qeey, ô' yoh da' kcô' blôôq déé eey, gaq gaq du' tmpwr déé rww

em, ô' yoh theq da' dôôq c'ô', iy ma' koon éém ma', trjeer siaq hmbraq déé rww.

em, pak tbaq dôk vôt viat.

qeey sah, r'iat taaq hmbraq bo' nè' twk siiq taal knhni' hmbraq éém rww.

qeey, ô' yat thii mwaq moot, gaay guuñ knoor knhni' éém lèèv, ô' gaay yoh, gaay guuñ
      rqkô' 'yaq éém rww.

qeey sah, ô' phat déé root mwaq gii, gaay guuñ h'é' rooy boor éém lèèv.

em, ô' gaay taay déé root mwaq gii.

gaay sah, gaay guuñ h'é' ban boor éém lèèv eey.

em, plwam go' rñaay, rvaay èèv, sqpôk pôk rña' iy heey, kma' séñ knduur éém lèèv.

em sah, tuu laay, ma' koon éém, tuu laay heey.

qeey, tuu laay kmat so' éém lèèv, tuu laay koon éém tuu laay, tuu laay kmat aay scaaq
      éém rww.

em, khaay tuu, ma' koon éém, khaay tuu.

eey sah, khaay tuu rmpaaq laat éém rww, sqlar liat yaak paaq éém lèèv, sqlar vaaq
      yaak too.

em, cii dé' sqplaak don rndéén.

eh, cii téén hme' go' rak, kmban jak kmuul éém gaa cii téén hme' go' rak, kmban jak
      kmuul éém guut déé eey, kjuh da' prlôq éém lèèv, ñak traak.

qeey, kmban da' prlôq éém eey, ñak yaan déé rww rak ôô khooq eey.

em, kha' éém eey, saay naam éém rww.

em sah, raam éém eey, pqga' éém eey, traak i' pe', kmuul i' pe', déé eey.

(****)   qeey, tnéc hla' rlaay déé rww, sii baay hla' rlaat, smbraat 'maat cii véc, smbraat
      'maat cii gaay déé eey.

qeey em, hla' lum go' sam gaat eey naaq, hla' lèèq go' smgaat, koon hnwm go' smbraat,
thav kèè go' smbraat. **(****)**

(**)   em, an boo sdu' rééq, smoot srlwaq ha' yo' ha'.

em, an boo sdu' rééq, smoot srlwaq plôq yo' plôq éém lèèv, an boo sr'ééq juu,
      smoot crna' mwaq yo' mwaq. **(**)**

qeey, an boo sr'ééq juu, smoot pha'ôq mwaq yo' mwaqle' bréén.

qeey ôô, ma' koon éém, suu maa ma' koon éém.

eey sah, tlul sul hvooy hvot, boo lèèv, tlul sul hvooy hvèèn, tlyèq qèèn da' plah,
      tlyèq qèèn da' plooy, naaq graa ñooy trphooy rmbôh iy ma' koon éém, naaq graa ñen
trphèn rmbôh iy ma' koon éém.

● ● ● ● ● ● ● ● ● ●

I say, forgive me elders, forgive me, eey.

Forgive me elders, everybody, rww dear eey heey.

Crab hole, rajah, under, pheasant, bump, eey.

Say, crab hole, rajah, under, pheasant, replace, everyone sits crosslegged under the
      sooty beams, others say.

Everyone sits crosslegged under the sooty planks.

I say, I'll see if I'm able to cut, I'm not able to cut.

I know how to cut, I don't know how to do it, I'll do as you ask, by the rules, my
      elders.

I'll do just what the elders ask me, my dear, eey.

One cut, a penalty.

I say, two cuts, a penalty, one mistake by agreement, two mistakes by agreement.
    I was still a small child under my mother's breast.

I was still a small child under my mother's arm.

I say, I was in the rattan thicket, I parted the plants, cut the leeches.

I was in the rattan thicket, I parted the plants, cleared off the stones.

Forgive me, sweetheart, forgive me.

I reached close to this city, close to this city, I saw rice baskets, others say.

I reached close to this city.

I came close to this city, I saw rice jars.

I arrived in this village, arrived in this village and saw the important elders.

I came close to this village, saw the powerful elders, eey heey.

I go to the poison tree, eey, the turtledove flies "*gaq gaq,*" I arrive in front of the
    granary, sweetheart, the horse sounds "*trjeer.*"

Break the bamboo shoots, twist and squeeze them.

I say, the horse carries a pack, everywhere are horses' footprints.

I was near to this village and saw footprints in the path, I came on and saw rice
    baskets, my relations.

I say, then I arrived at this village and saw one hundred stacks of firewood, my
    relations.

I arrived in this village.

Came, I say, and saw one thousand stacks of firewood, my relations.

Leeches and worms, tigers growled, many mosquitoes bit me, it rained on my head,
    my relations.

I say, the door lock, sweetheart.

The door lock, pickled meat, dog, relations, the door lock, child, relations, the door
    lock, pickled meat, elephant, relations.

Open the door, sweetheart, open the door.

I say, open the door latch, my relations.

The short bolt is difficult to open, relations, the long bolt is difficult also.

There will be fish spines where I walk, wherever I tread, I grip the silver railing,
    relations, and climb where I walk, I grip the silver railing, relations, and enter, spit at
    the door, relations, and hit the buffalo.

I grip the doorway, relations, hit the bronze drum, my dear.

I am your servant, relations, I am humble, relations.

I say, I am embarassed, relations, I am shy, we have no buffaloes, we have no silver.

The bamboo leaf droops, the long-bean leaf hangs down, it is time to leave, to go
    home, it is time to leave, to depart.

The *lum* leaf is tasty, miss, the basil leaf is tasty, girl friend, I must leave,
    grandparents, I must leave.

If you observe the new forest, watch the thatch burn and burn.

If you observe the new forest, watch the thatch sprout and sprout, if you miss your lover,
watch the area around the villages.

If you miss your lover, watch the whole region around the villages, better yet.
Forgive me, sweetheart, forgive me.
The flute sound flutters, the flute sound sways, carry a water gourd, place it down,
    carry a water gourd, place it down, miss, your face is light and beautiful, sweetheart,
    miss, your face is light and fairskinned, sweetheart.

APPENDIX 2

Ta' Ñii Graan story, reworked from Ferlus 1979 (excerpt)

1.
cwaq gni', gee meh ta' ñii graan, sqmeh gee gni'.
hôôc yôq ma' gee ci' yoh hèèl,
    an ta' ñii graan ni' bo' hèèm.
bo' hèèm lèèv gee laaq yaan dwn dii jrap hni',
    yôq ma' yoh eh hré' lèèv.
gee véc da' gaaq moot huut dii bwwn jrap hni',
    le' lii hèèm:
"ee hèèm ci' laaq i' dé' yaan hèèm."
hôôc gee le' tam:
"dreey yeey kluq,
    tam yaan kluq too suu too taan,
    too 'maan too mwaq kluq."
briaq yoh ci' yoh jèèq.
gee qôôp mñèèq gee pwat da' kndruum jrap hni',
    kndruum jrap hni' ani'
    le' yat.

2.
da' sbaq ni', baq gaay an gee yat da' gaaq.
"méé bo' hèèm ni yoh la' em w',
    pñneeñ hèèm i' ci' yoh da' hré',
    ci' yoh hèèm."
gee gaay véc moot huut laaq yaan gni', gaay tam:
"dreey yeey kluq,
    tam yaan kluq,
    tam yaan ta' ñii graan kluq,
    too suu too taan,
    too 'maan too mwaq kluq."
briaq yoh yèèq, gee nôôm ñop ñaq ro' kndruum jrap gni'.
bat ni' noo pntuun yôq ma' dé' lèèv

3.

sbaq lè', yôq ma' neeq lèèv swq briag lav, putuun yôq ma' dé'.
yôq ma' ni' le' 'mook an gee yoh bo' hèèm yoh la' da' kntiiq,
    briaq ci' yoh da' hré'.
snaa le' uun rya' da' kluaq suam da' hô',
    hôôc snaa le' cap ôm bwr ani' yôq ma' ni',
    cap rep gaa da' pndrèèq.
gee le' véc lèèv oor hèèm déé véc, véc laaq yaan gni'.
laaq hôôc gee tam:
"dreey yeey kluq,
    tam yaan kluq too suu too taan,
    too 'maan too mwaq kluq."
craaq, yôq gni' dwaq rep kdwp kmpôq snaa,
    ma' ni' dé' ôm bwr géét.
gee nôôm dqme' go' bay de',
    le' tmluuy uun hni' lèèv.

1.

Cwaq here, his real name was Ta' Ñii Graan.
Well, his parents had to go clear the field
    if Ta' Ñii Graan would watch his younger brother.
He watched his brother, and he made a bronze drum and hid it under the bed,
    while his parents went to make the field.
He went home and took the wax from under the bed,
    and sang to his brother:
"Oh, brother, we will make a bronze drum."
Then he beat on it:
"*Dreey yeey kluq,*
    beat the drum, *kluq,* all around,
    in every village, *kluq.*"
The others came to see.
He crushed the wax drum and he hid it under the bed,
    under the bed there,
    right there.

2.

The next day, the next day came and he stayed at home.
"You take your younger brother and go out—em, uh—
    take care of your brother while we go to the field,
    you watch your brother.
He returned home, took the wax and made a drum, then beat it:
"*Dreey yeey kluq,*
    beat the drum, *kluq,*

Ta' Ñii Graan beats the drum, *kluq*,
all around,
all around in every village, *kluq*."
The others came to listen, but he crushed the drum and put it under the bed.
This time, they told his parents about it.

3.
The next day, his parents knew about what the others were telling them.
The parents told him to take care of his brother in the village,
    and the others would go to the field.
The parents hid their shoulder bag in the room there,
    then they made rice water then, the parents,
    and grabbed a net and climbed onto the roof.
He went home, took his brother home, and made another drum.
When it was finished he beat it:
"*Dreey yeey kluq*,
    beat the drum, *kluq*, all around,
    every village, *kluq*."
Craaq! His father dropped the net over his head,
    and his mother poured the rice water down.
He lost his magic power to beat the drum,
    and they hung it in the corner.

NOTES

1.   My research with Kmhmu since 1982 has been supported by the University of Texas at Austin, the National Endowment for the Arts, the Indochina Studies Program of the Social Science Research Council and American Council of Learned Societies, the Lao Khmu Association, the Asian Cultural Council, and the Smithsonian Institution.

2.   Copies of the sound recordings of Kmhmu verbal art in America are archived at the Smithsonian Institution, Office of Folklife Programs and at the Library of Congress (as part of the Social Science Research Council, Indochina Studies Program deposit). An audio cassette of the songs and story included in Proschan (1989) may be purchased from the Archivist at the Office of Folklife Programs.

3.   In the Kmhmu orthography used here, "e" is a schwa, "w" is a barred i, "ô" is a closed o, "o" is an open o, and "q" is the consonant engma (-ng-). An "h" before a consonant marks devoicing, and an "h" after a consonant marks aspiration.

4.   Jakobson notes that "The general meaning of the marked [term] is characterized by the conveyance of more precise, specific, and additional information than the unmarked term provides" (1990[1980]:138).

5.   See also Thomas (1985) for a discussion of the semantic links between couplets in the Malaysian *pantun*.

6.   See Suwilai Premsrirat's fascinating study of Kmhmu cutting words and their semantic organization (1987).

7.   Amy Catlin points out the implications of this story for the technique of lost-wax bronze casting, traditionally used in the manufacture of the great bronze drums of Southeast Asia (Bernet Kempers 1988).

8.   Vietnamese scholar Dang Nghiem Van points out the widespread Southeast Asian belief that a ghost or spirit's evil power may be bound up and controlled by a net or plaited lattice thrown over its head. Thus, the ubiquitous plaited bamboo *talèèv* used throughout highland Indochina to mark a ritually taboo house or village, and the practice of Vietnamese in Hai Hung province who hang a piece of old netting on their doors as protection against malignant spirits. See Dang Nghiem Van (n.d.).

9.   Folklorists will note the narrative technique of incremental repetition, a typical method of advancing narrative in European balladry (Gummere 1907). The relations of poetic parallelism and incremental repetition are obvious—in fact, it is not infrequent that folklore scholars use the latter restricted term to describe the much broader category of parallelism.

10.   The term can be glossed as *hrlo'* "word, language, speech," *prgap* "reverse, return," and *prgaay* "return, give back, reciprocate." The Kmhmu prefix *pr-* is a reflexive and intensifier (quite strikingly similar in functions and meanings to the English prefix *re-*).

11.   As Metcalf notes, "One common technique, familiar in parallel speech worldwide, is to borrow words from the languages of neighboring peoples" (1989:39). In many cases, it should be noted, Lao words are incorporated in a semantically motivated context, where they can be considered as the marked partner, as contrasted to an unmarked Kmhmu word. See, for instance, the verse discussing door locks and latches in Appendix 1, where Lao words are used as the initial partner and Kmhmu words later. Metcalf considers such loan words as synonymous with their native language counterparts and chooses in his translations to disregard "subtle . . . nuances" that distinguish a borrowed term from its native language partner, glossing them both with the same English word (1989:40). For Kmhmu, who are highly self-conscious about the intrusion of Lao loan words into their own language and about Kmhmu words "leaking" into their speech when they are speaking Lao, such an approach is indefensible (cf. Lindell et al. 1977:22–23, 98).

12.   In this respect they are like the *"piat*-words" that Metcalf describes in the *piat* or parallelistic prayers of the Berawan, an Austronesian group. These are "concocted elements . . . not recognizable outside narrowly defined environments within *piat*. . . . Their meaning can only be deduced from the word in everyday Berawan that accompanies them" (1989:41). The final quatrain of our primary example (Appendix 1) employs such neologisms.

13.   See, for instance, the extended song analyzed in Proschan (1989:324-380), where the twenty verses make use of nineteen different structures, all recognizably related to the typical pattern but elaborated in diverse ways.

14.   For a fuller discussion of the use of the Jew's harp as a speech surrogate, among the Kmhmu and throughout Southeast Asia and Oceania, see Proschan (1989:382-408).

15.   For more on Kmhmu play languages, see Ferlus (1974) and Proschan (1989:408-420).

16.   According to Jakobson's model of communication, widely embraced by scholars of verbal art and the ethnography of speaking, "phatic" communications check the channel and verify that the communication is proceeding effectively (1987 [1960]:66–71). Jakobson took the term from Malinowski, who speaks of "a type of speech in which ties of union are created by a mere exchange of words . . . serving the direct aim of binding hearer to speaker" (1927:315).

17.   The entire text is included in Proschan (1989:482–521).

18.   *Rmeet* is very likely from Old Man *rmeñ*, the Mon ethnonym for themselves—Ed. (See Robert Parkin, *A Guide to Austroasiatic Speakers and Their Languages*. Honolulu: University of Hawaii Press, 1991, p. 61).

REFERENCES CITED

Bernet Kempers, A. J.
    1988   *The Kettle Drums of Southeast Asia: A Bronze Age World and its Aftermath.*
                Rotterdam: A. A. Balkema.

Boulbet, J.
    1972   *Dialogue lyrique des Cau Maa' (Tam pöt maa').* Publications de l'Ecole Française
                d'Extrême-Orient 85.

    1975   *Paysans de la forêt.* Publications de l'Ecole Française d'Extrême-Orient 105.

Catlin, Amy
  1982   "Speech Surrogate Systems of the Hmong: From Singing Voices to Talking Reeds."
            In *The Hmong in the West*, ed. Bruce T. Downing and Douglas P. Olney, 170–201.
            Minneapolis: University of Minnesota, Center for Urban and Regional Affairs.

Condominas, Georges
  1977   *We Have Eaten the Forest*. New York: Hill and Wang.

Dang Nghiem Van
  n.d.   "Myths on the Origin of Ethnic Groups." Typescript.

Ferlus, Michel
  1974   "Le javanais en Khamou." *Asie du Sud-Est et Monde Insulindien* 5:171–175.

  1979   "Le recit Khamou de Chuang et ses implications historiques pour le Nord-Laos."
            Asie du Sud-Est et Monde Insulindien 10(2-4):327–364.

Fox, James J.
  1971   "Semantic Parallelism in Rotinese Ritual Language." *Bijdragen tot de Taal-, Land-
            en Volkenkunde* 127:215–255.

  1977   "Roman Jakobson and the Comparative Study of Parallelism." In *Roman Jakobson:
            Echoes of his Scholarship*, ed. J. D. Armstrong and C. H. van Schoonweld, 59–90.
            Lisse: Peter de Ridder.

Fox, James J., ed.
  1988   *To Speak in Pairs*. New York: Cambridge University Press.

Granet, Marcel
  1932   *Festivals and Songs of Ancient China*. New York: E. P. Dutton.

Guillon, Emmanuel
  1971   "Sur 21 chansons populaires mones." *Homme* 11(2):58–108.

Gummere, Francis
  1907   *The Popular Ballad*. Boston: Houghton, Mifflin and Company.

Jacob, Judith M.
  1979   "Observations on the Uses of Reduplication as a Poetic Device in Khmer." In
            Studies in Tai and Mon-Khmer Phonetics and Phonology, ed. Theraphan L.
            Thongkum et al., 111–130. Bangkok: Chulalongkorn University Press.

Jakobson, Roman
  1987   *Language in Literature*. Cambridge: Harvard University Press.

  1990   *On Language*. Cambridge: Harvard University Press.

LeGay, Roger, and K'Mloi, Da Got
  1971   "Prieres lac accompagnant les rites agraires." *Bulletin de la Société des Etudes
            Indochinoises*, N.S. 46:111–213.

Liu, David Jason
    1983   "Parallel Structures in the Canon of Chinese Poetry." *Poetics Today* 4:639–653.

Lundstrom, Hakan
    1984   "A Kammu Song and its Structure." *Asian Folklore Studies* 43:29–39.

Lundstrom, Hakan, and Tayanin, Damrong
    1982   "Music in the Fields." In *The Kammu Year: Its Lore and Music,* ed. Kristina Lindell
                et al., 60–130. London: Curzon Press.

Malinowski, Bronislaw
    1927   "The Problem of Meaning in Primitive Languages." In *The Meaning of Meaning,* ed.
                C. K. Ogden and I. A. Richards, 296–336. New York: Harcourt, Brace and Company.

Mannheim, Bruce
    1987   "Couplets and Oblique Contexts: The Social Organization of a Folksong." *Text*
                7(3):265–288.

Metcalf, Peter
    1989   *Where Are You/Spirits.* Washington D.C.: Smithsonian Institution Press.

Nguyen Van Huyen
    1934   *Les chants alternés des garçons et des filles en Annam.* Austro-asiatica 3. Paris: Paul
                Geuthner.

    1941   *Receuil des chants de mariage Tho de Lang-son et Cao-bang.* Hanoi: Ecole Française
                d'Extrême-Orient.

Proschan, Frank
    1984   "Love Dialogues in Southeast Asia: Highland and Lowland, Vocal and
                Instrumental." Paper presented at the annual meeting of the American Folklore
                Society, San Diego, California.

    1989   "Kmhmu Verbal Art in America: The Poetics of Kmhmu Verse." Ph.d. diss.,
                University of Texas.

    1990   *Kmhmu Verbal Arts in America.* 90-minute audio cassette. Available from the
                Archivist, Smithsonian Institution Office of Folklife Programs.

Sabatier, L.
    1933   "La chanson de Damsan." *Bulletin de l'Ecole Française d'Extrême-Orient* 33:143–
                302.

Saepharn, Kaota
    1988   "The Mountain Poets: Verbal Dueling of the Iu Mien of Laos." Unpublished paper.

Sherzer, Joel, and Urban, Greg
    1986   *Native South American Discourse.* Berlin: Mouton de Gruyter.

Sherzer, Joel, and Woodbury, Anthony C.
    1987   *Native American Discourse.* Cambridge: Cambridge University Press.

Suwilai Premsrirat
  1987   *Khmu, A Minority Language of Thailand*. Pacific Linguistic Series A-75. Canberra: The Australian National University.

Svantesson, Jan-Olof
  1983   *Kammu Phonology and Morphology*. Travaux de l'Institut de Linguistique de Lund 18. London: Curzon.

Tayanin, Damrong
  1984   *Kam Booraan: Ancient Sayings*. Lund: self-published.

Thomas, Phillip L.
  1985   "Phonology and Semantic Suppression in Malay. *Puntun*." *Semiotica* 57.87–99.

Urban, Greg
  1986   "Semiotic Functions of Macro-parallelism in the Shokleng Origin Myth." In *Native South American Discourse*, ed. Joel Sherzer and Greg Urban, 15–58. Berlin: Mouton de Gruyer.

Woodbury, Anthony C.
  1987   "Rhetorical Structure in a Central Alaskan Yupik Eskimo Traditional Narrative." In *Native American Discourse*, ed. Joel Sherzer and Anthony Woodbury, 176–239. Cambridge: Cambridge University Press.

MAP OF THAI REGIONS WHERE *KHAP LUE* IS REPORTED[*]

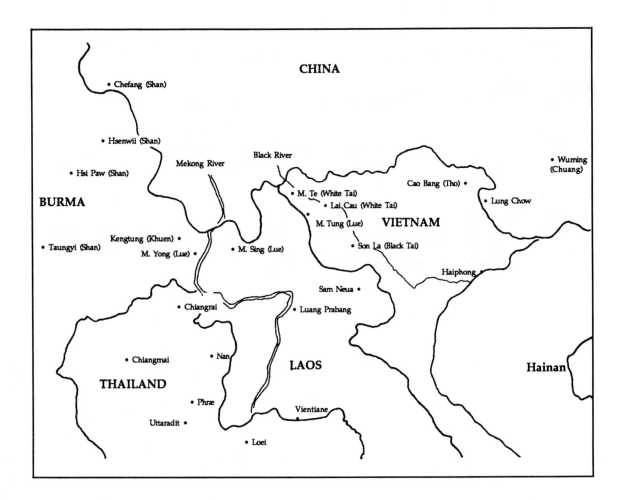

* In comparative-historical terms, the region covers both the Southwestern and Central Tai branches of the Tai family as set forth by Fang-kuei Li (1977).

THE CONTEXT, TEXT, AND PERFORMANCE OF *KHAP LUE*

John F. Hartmann

Definition of the term *khàp*[1]

The term khàp appears in many Tai[2] languages and, in general, means "to sing."[3] In Tai dialects that are in close contact with one another, and thus share many linguistic and cultural traits, the expression *kham khàp* is used. The form kham means "word(s)" and thus, kham khàp is "sung words" as opposed to "spoken words." The genre of khàp is particularly prominent today in contiguous Tai dialects and languages in the northern tier of Southwestern Tai: Lue (centered around the city of Ching Hung)[4] in the Sipsongpanna regions of Yunnan, China; Lao of northern Laos; and Tai Dam (Black Tai) in the area of the Red River in northwestern Vietnam (see map). The word itself appears in all of the dialects of Southwestern Tai and even in the Central Tai dialect of Tho in northeastern Vietnam (F. K. Li 1977:195). In the realm of actual performance, khàp is antiphonal chanting, usually with members of the opposite sex taking turns. Khàp Lue means "to sing in the Lue manner."

Earliest historical references

The tradition of khàp is possibly the oldest form of formal sung performance in the Tai domain, as witnessed by the earliest historical references in both Thai and Western sources. In his seventeenth-century account of *The Kingdom of Siam*, the French diplomat and scholar Simone de la Loubere wrote (1969:68):

> They sometimes accompany the voice with two short sticks, which they call *crab* [*kràp*] and which they strike one against the other; and he that sings thus, is titled *Tchang cap* [*chàaŋ khàp*].

One of the earliest (ca. fifteenth–seventeenth century A.D.) Thai epic poems, *Phra Law*, has several references to khàp in the text of the poem itself (see Hartmann et al. 1989; Bickner 1991). The following excerpts, which are the third and fourth stanzas of the poem, give us a picture of a khàp performance in a fifteenth-century Thai court and, in fact, of what is still found in khàp Lue performances today: two singers taking turns in chanting a poetic narrative with reed pipe accompaniment in the background—in a formal setting, where the idealized audience is an all-wise, meritorious monarch and his retinue.

[Stanza 3]

ruú	malák	sòp	sàat	thûan	yĭŋ	chaay
know	much	all	rule	all	woman	man

Knowing much of the rules of versification, all you ladies and gentlemen,

càk	klàaw	klɔɔn	phráʔ	lɔɔ	lə̂ət	phûu
will	tell	poem	royal	Law	surpass	person

I will tell you in verse the story of Phra Law, The Unsurpassed,

phayrɔ́ʔ	ríap	banyaay	phrɔ́ʔ	yîŋ	phrɔ́ʔ	naa
euphonious	smooth	narrate	euphonious	ints.	euphonious	emph.

in smooth, even more euphonious narration,

sǒm	pĭi-lúu	sĭaŋ	lúu	lɔ́ɔ	láw-loom	cay
united	pipe	sound	pipe	tempt	soothe	heart

accompanied by the seductive and soothing sounds of the pipe.

[Stanza 4]

sǔan	sĭaŋ	**khàp**	ʔàan	ʔàaŋ	day	paan
joyous	sound	sing	read	recite	whatever	comparable

The joyous sounds of sung recitation—compare them to what you will,

faŋ	sanɔ̀ʔ	day	puun	prìap	dây
listen	melodius	whatever	comparable	compare	can

Listen to the melodious sounds and compare them to whatever you can,

klaw	klɔɔn	klàaw	kon	kaan	kon	klɔ̂ɔm	cay	naa
polish	verse	twist	artful	work	artful	lulla by song	heart	emp.

—Verses which have been polished and fashioned into an artful song to soothe the heart!

thawaay	bamrəə	tháw	tháy	thirâat	phûu	mii	bun
offer	serve	foot	big pers.	all-wise king	person	have	merit

—An offering made at the foot of The Great and All-wise King, The Meritorious One.

Collocations of khàp

In the poem, the word khàp appears in the environment of so-called "elaborate constructions," that is, where a single word—in this case khàp—is juxtaposed with other words related to it in meaning so as to create a "thicker" or "packed" semantics. Alliteration and assonance are also employed so as to fill phonological space with an intensified poetic experience. Some of the collocations used with khàp are Thai words that carry the meaning of "to sing," "to read," "to recite," "to praise," and "to be fast," the latter indicating the rapid syllable-timed rhythm of a sung performance. The citations below illustrate these elaborate (poetic) verbal constructions and, at the same time, the actual functioning of khàp in the Thai court of the fifteenth-seventeenth centuries.

line 51   **khàp ʔàan ʔàaŋ**: 'to sing-read-recite'

sŭan	sĭaŋ	**khàp**	ʔàan	ʔàaŋ
joyous	sound	sing	read	recite....

the joyous sounds of sung recitation....

line 254, 394   **khàp sɔɔ yɔɔ**: "to sing-sing-praise"

khàp	sɔɔ	yɔɔ	raacha	thian	thúk	mɯaŋ
sing	sing	praise	king	lesser	every	kingdom

Sing praises to the lesser kings of every kingdom.

khàp	sɔɔ	yɔɔ	yót	ʔàaŋ
sing	sing	praise	rank	recite

Sing praises to those of rank.

line 820 **khàp...sɔ̌ɔŋ**: sing-two (alternate singing)

khàp	khĭaw	maa	tɛ̀ɛ	cháw
sing	fast	come	since	early morning

sɔ̌ɔŋ	hây	chəən	phra-câw
two	let	invite	lord/king

Sing fast from early in the morning in two's as an invitation to the king.

Dialect area differences: khàp vs. *mohlam* vs. *sɔɔ*

What is called khàp in one dialect region of Southwestern Tai may receive a different label elsewhere. In Laos, khàp is found in the north, and it extends across the border into the Lue areas of Yunnan and northern Thailand. In Tai Dam (Black Tai) khàp also means "to sing." In the southern parts of Laos, what appears to be the same phenomenon is called *mohlam*. Wongthes (1991:165) states:

> In present-day Laos, the word *khap* is still used to refer to different types of songs. However, there are some Thai-Lao-speaking groups who use the word *lam* instead of *khap*. This term is common among the Thai-Lao of Isan and southern Laos. . . . In the regions of the Chao Phraya River, the words *khap* and *lam* are commonly used, for example in the expression *khap sepha* and *lam thad*.[5]

In her study of mohlam, Compton (1979:96) notes that lam in Laos begins "from the far south of Laos and works northward. The northern styles generally are referred to as /khắp/ 'to sing'."

The geographical locations of Lao khắp—which Compton calls a "style"—are Sam Neua, the Vientiane Plain, Xieng Khouang, and Luang Prabang. Except for Luang Prabang, the musical accompaniment for Lao khắp is the *khaen*, not the *pii*. In Luang Prabang, however, the khắp observed by Compton was accompanied by a *pii phaat* ensemble:

> consisting of a *pii*, wooden xylophone (*naaŋ nâat*), small cymbals (*síŋ*), two high-pitched, two-stringed violins (*sɔ́ɔ ʔíi*), and a two low-pitched, two-stringed violins (*sɔɔ ʔɔ́ɔ*).

For Luang Prabang, the northern capital of Laos, Compton lists five different styles of khàp: *Khap Thum, Khap Salaam, Khap Sam Saaw, Khap Lohong Khon, Loht Kay, Khap Maa Nyohng.*

In the dialect of northern Thailand, also known as "Kam muang," the word khàp is replaced by *sɔɔ*, which is translated by Purnell (1963:93) as "Northern Thai traditional singing (two people usually with accompaniment)." In the excerpt from *Phra Law* cited earlier, khàp and *sɔɔ* appeared as synonyms in the elaborate expression *khàp sɔɔ yɔɔ* "sing-sing-praise."

Each Tai dialect, different from a neighboring "sister dialect," also has its own particular variant khàp style, both in terms of melodic trademark, instrumental accompaniment, and performers. The Tai Lue of Sipsongpanna and adjoining areas of Burma (chiefly Moeng Long) and Laos (notably Ban Houei Sai) employ the pi, [Siamese *pii*] a bamboo free-reed pipe, for musical accompaniment—the same instrument referred to in the early Siamese text, *Phra Law*. The Lao use the khaen, [Siamese *khɛ̌ɛn*] a bamboo free-reed mouth organ, as the accompanying instrument in a khàp performance. The Tai Lue and the Lao performers are invariably male-female pairs who take turns singing parts of a continuous text. The Tai Dam appear to prefer to engage two or more singers of the same sex in an extended performance, but they also have male-female exchanges identical to the Lao mohlam.[6]

The khàp as practiced today in all three areas is doubtless considerably diminished in importance and form. The author's Tai Lue consultants reported that in former times, when the ruling prince of Chiang Rung was still in power, singers would be called to perform in his presence. At such royal performances, the singers would prostrate themselves before the prince and his entourage and further reduce their presence by occluding their faces with a Chinese-style folding fan held in their right hand. Wongthes (1990) also refers to the *chang khap* [*chàang* means "expert or craftsman"; a chàang khàp would be a "professional singer"]. Wongthes states that the chang khap sings songs that "praise the king, morality, and male-female love."[7] In the Lue texts transcribed, translated, and analyzed by the author (Hartmann 1984), all three elements appear, but the emphasis is on the moral content of the narratives, which are essentially *Jatakas*; praise to the king occurs in the opening lines of the performance, and references to male-female love appear in the initiating repartee of the male-female lines as they take turns singing a portion of the extended narrative.[8]

Because of the revolutionary political and social changes that have taken place in the last generation in all three areas, the past support from the local princes and the elite audiences that maintained the tradition of the khàp in the past are no longer there. What we witness now are performances that are reduced in grandeur and frequency; the older Tai traditions are dying out here as elsewhere.[9] In place of the family of the ruling princes are families with some money and prestige, no doubt, who have singers come to their homes, not palaces, to sing for (non-royal) weddings and house-warmings. Itinerant Lue singers travel considerable distances even today to perform at such special occasions and thus keep the ebbing tradition alive.[10] In Yunnan, itself, the state—as elsewhere—broadcasts khàp performances alongside the music of other ethnic groups in the region as a matter of managing the politics of the minorities in the Han nation.[11] In Laos, the central government produces video tapes showing the variety of musical and dance performances as a display of "unity in diversity," but much of it has an artificial look and feel to to it. The same is true of Vietnam; recent video tapes show interviews with professional singers employed by the central government for purposes that can only be called propagandistic: songs extolling the collective and exhorting the peasants to increase production.

The pragmatics of a khàp lue performance

As was mentioned earlier, a khàp Lue performance consists of a male-female pair taking turns chanting connected episodes of a narrative, with a single free-reed player (seated to the left of the pair) providing accompaniment and introductory and concluding flourishes. Superficially, such an arrangement looks not unlike the setting of a performance of courtship poetry, such as the Lao mohlam. However, in the case of the Lue, the courtship form has been appropriated for the serious transmission of narratives that promote and preserve the Jatakas and Hindu-Buddhist cosmology, the foundation of Lue culture. Schweisguth (1951) notes that equivalent forms of "ces échanges poétiques" are popular in Cambodia, Vietnam, Burma, and Thailand. The social origin of such linguistic behavior, he claims, is the separation of young men and women, especially in terms of division of labor and festivals connected with seasonal activities of the agriculturalist—of which the Lue are perfect examples. This male-female exchange is illustrated by the following opening segment of a female Lue singer, who picks up from where her male counterpart left off:

> Listen first! Our goodly brother has just sung as gently as the drip-drop of water that trickles from the heads of the rice plants and flows down to touch everything, deeply cooling and refreshing the heart. We will sing joyfully the story of *Bua Rah*. Now, I, Saeng, will try to follow faithfully the words already spoken. Our brother has already warned us as to what will come so that I will know the line of

the story. The next part of the story I will tell to the end. I, Saeng, will describe what happened accordingly, little by little.

On a purely textual level, it is interesting to note what can be termed the *pragmatic* structure of such a performance. Analysis of a transcript of the text of the khàp Lue performance dealing with the topic of the "Creation and Destruction of the Universe" reveals a pragmatic structure that can be divided into a *procedural* and a *narrative* function. The former is the straightforward telling of the story; the latter is the manner or format of presenting chunks of narrative. The procedural function has, in turn, three functions: *comment, border,* and *connect.*

The comment function establishes the "I-Thou" relationship between singer and audience and informs the latter of what both parties do: "I will sing, tell a story, narrate; You will listen, hear what I have to say, compare"—and so forth. Comment also serves to constantly bring the audience back into the narrative activity by reinvoking their participation as listeners and revalidators of time-honored truths and beliefs. Openings—or introductions—and closings—or conclusions—are part of the comment apparatus.

The border material serves to frame narrative material—to set off major events of the story line—and, in the case of the Jataka-based Lue tradition, to provide an authoritative stamp: "It is said that once upon a time . . . Note what was just said and remember it. "

The connective utterances are short, two or three syllable utterances that are inserted from time to time as filler or connective tissue: "and so, thus, then, therefore." A less fluent narrator will rely on more connective phrases more frequently to fill what would otherwise be dead vocal space. The pipe player keeps the cadences of the performance alive with his instrumental accompaniment, and the singer is expected to match the musical beat with an uninterrupted flow of chanted syllables. By the same token, when there is a complete breakdown on the singer's part, the piper will go on playing, and thus provide an interlude, during which the singer can recall, recover, and resume—or yield to his or her opposite, who will then carry the story onward.

The poetic form of khàp lue

The khàp Lue performances are in the poetic form known as *ràay,* which is without doubt one of the most ancient of indigenous Southwestern Tai poetic forms. Some writers refer to ràay as "poetic prose" because line length is not important. Bidya (1955) refers to ràay as "quasi-poetry." What distinguishes it from straight prose is the fact that the line is the basic unit, and lines are linked by rhyme, with the last syllable of one line rhyming with one of the early syllables of a succeeding line. Not all lines need be linked in an unbroken chain. Where a thought is concluded or a transition to a new topic is being made, linking lines are, in fact, dropped as a transitional signal. Line length varies from three to eleven syllables, and rhymes interlock at unpredictable points. Alliteration and assonance are richly employed. A form of ràay known as *ràay yaaw* [long ràay] is used by monks in chanting Jataka tales, and the khàp Lue models itself after the the same form.

To conclude this paper on khàp Lue, we quote the opening lines of a male Lue singer narrating the destruction of the universe through fire. The entire text is published in Hartmann (1984:127).[12]

Text II: *The Conflagration*[13]

1. caw^3 həy^4 caw^3
   lord   O!   lord

   Lord O! Lord

2. ʔan^4 vaa^5 bat^1 dew^4 van^4 nii^6
   that   say   time   once   Pt.   Pt.

   It is said that once upon a time

3. faŋ   t ɔʔ   mɛɛ   too^1 tii^5 nɔn^4 dək^1
   listen   Pt.   woman   person   Rel.   sleep   late

   Listen, my woman partner, who went to sleep late

4. kaŋ ^{5} luk^5 caw^6 lɛʔ
   hurry   arise   early   Pt.

   And hurried to get up early

5. yaŋ^4 phum^1 yuŋ^3 sut^1 tii^5 vii^1 nɔɔ^4 van^4
   still   hair   rumple   beyond   Rel.   comb   Pt.   Pt.

   Your hair is still snarled beyond combing

6. lɔn^1 see^1 vaa^5 phum^1 yii^4 vay^6 nii^6
   if   lose   say   hair   mess   put   Pt.

   Your hair stays messed up

7. mən^1 haŋ^4 tii^5 fɔə^1-fɛt^2
   like   nest   Rel.   twin

   Like twin nests

8. phum^1 vet^5 vay^6 nii^6
   hair   put up in a bun   put   Pt.

   Your hair stays messed up

9. sin^3 nɨŋ^5 baw^2 thɔɔ^1 nɔɔ^4 van^4
   Clf.   one   not   move   Pt.   Pt.

   Not one strand moves

10. mən¹   naŋ²   vaa²   thə¹-ləp¹   xam⁴   nii⁶
     like   with   that   sheet   gold   Pt.

It is like a piece of gold leaf

11. xaw³   pay¹   lup⁵   naa³-phak²
     enter   go   stroke   forehead

Stroking the forehead

12. seŋ¹   ciŋ²   vaa⁵   cap¹   vaa⁵   taan³
     voice   so   say   hold   say   speak

Voices hold forth in conversation

13. pii⁵   noŋ⁶   yɛm⁶   cum⁵   xoo¹   ʔɔn¹
     older sibling   younger sibling   smile   moist   laugh   before

Our brothers and sisters enjoy themselves meanwhile

14. ʔan⁴   vaa⁵   bat¹   dew⁴   van⁴   nii⁶
     that   say   time   once   Pt.   Pt.

It is said that once upon a time

15. faŋ⁴   tɔʔ⁵   too¹   caaŋ⁵   kɔn¹
     listen   Pt.   person   artisan poetry

Listen! You who are a poet

16. taa¹   nəə⁶   nin⁴   nok⁵   paw³
     eye   flesh   black   bird   kind of bird

With eyes as black as the Paw Bird

17. pɔɔ⁵   hak²   xaw³   lɔt⁵   lɛw⁶
     father   since   enter   pass through   already

Our father has gone through his part already

18. tok¹   kɔn²   ʔɔn⁴   taaŋ⁴
     fall   first   before way

He has led the way

19. luk⁵   lɛʔ⁵   diʔ¹   vaaŋ⁴   seŋ¹   sɔn⁶
     child   Pt.   will   put   voice   again

I, the son, will sing more....

NOTES

1. The pronunciation of the term khàp will vary from dialect to dialect. In Siamese (Central Thai) it is pronounced with a low tone khàp; in the Lue dialect of Sipsongpanna with a high tone kháp. In the Lao dialect studied by Compton (1979), the tone is mid-rising khǎp. In this paper, we shall use the Siamese pronunciation for the most part for convenience—except when directly quoting other sources.

2. *Tai* is used in this paper in a comparative-historical sense and refers to the proto-language from which modern languages such as Thai (Siamese) and Lao have developed. Some writers prefer to use *Thai-Lao* in place of Tai in order to bring more balance to what some perceive as a Thai (Siamese) bias in much research that deals with Tai groups outside of Thailand. See Hartmann (1980) and Wongthes (1989:62).

3. Khàp appears in several of the oldest pieces of Siamese literature. The form is also mentioned in the Lao Chronicle, *Phongsawadan Lan Chang* (Wongthes 1989).

4. In Siamese: Chiang Rung.

5. Lam tàd is also a Central Thai term which refers to antiphonal (improvised) singing.

6. Evidence is based on cassettes and videotapes; further on-site fieldwork waits to be carried out in order to gain a complete understanding of the complete repertoire of Tai musical forms in the region.

7. No examples of text or any other detail about the verbal content are given by the Wongthes.

8. Traditional Lao mohlam is decidedly replete with talk of male-female love; but then too, mohlam deals with the profane—in contrast to the sacred—while the khàp Lue has content that is more sacred, i.e., about the creation of the world and the lives of the Buddha, interspersed with local folklore.

9. The performing arts of the Tai-Ahom in Assam have disappeared completely according to Wongthes (1989:167), other than "some short religious chants that are used in some rituals."

10. Lue singers from Moeng Yong in Burma, for example, travel to Chiangrai and other points in northern Thailand to perform khàp.

11. In northern Thailand the state-owned radio stations recorded and broadcast khàp Lue performances as early as the 1970s. Evening radio waves are filled with the music of the many ethnic minorities living in the region.

12. Tai Lue has six tones on smooth syllables, labeled here with the numbers 1-6. Checked syllables can carry tones 1, 2 or 5, depending on the syllable-initial consonant. In this segment of khàp Lue, rhymes are indicated in boldface. Tonal rhymes appear in Proto-Tai tone categories A (tones 1 and 4), B tones (2 and 5), and C (tones 3 and 6). The tones of Lue of Chieng

Rung are: 1–high level; 2–mid rising; 3–low, glottalized, slight rise; 4–mid falling; 5–mid level; 6–low level, glottalized, slight rise.

13.   The bolded words in the following text indicate external linking rhymes used in Thai wherein the final syllable of a line will rhyme with a nonfinal syllable, usually of the succeeding line.

REFERENCES CITED

Bickner, R. J.
    1991   *An Introduction to the Thai Poem "Lilit Phra Law"* (The Story of King Law). Monograph Series on Southeast Asia: Special Report no. 25 DeKalb: Center for Southeast Asian Studies, Northern Illinois University.

Bidya, His Highness, Prince
    1955   "Sebha Recitation: The Elements of Siamese Poetry." *Thought and Word* 7:24–32.

Compton, C. J.
    1979   *Courting Poetry in Laos: A Textual and Linguistic Analysis.* Special Report Series no. 18. DeKalb: Center for Southeast Asian Studies, Northern Illinois University.

Hartmann, J. F.
    1980   "A Model for the Alignment of Tai Dialects in Southwestern Tai." *Journal of the Siam Society* 68:72–6.

    1984   *Linguistic and Memory Structures in Tai-Lue Oral Narratives.* Pacific Linguistics Series B No. 90. Canberra: The Australian National University.

Hartmann, J. F., J. Henry, and W. Kongananda
    1989   "Lexical Puzzles and Proto-Tai Remnants in an Old Thai Text." *Crossroads* 4(2):71–85.

Loubere, Simon de la
    1969   *A New Historical Relation of the Kingdom of Siam.* (English translation of the 1669 French original.) New York: Oxford University Press.

Li, Fang-kuei
    1977   *A Handbook of Comparative Tai.* Oceanic Linguistics Special Publication No. 15. Honolulu: University of Hawaii Press.

Purnell, H. C.
    1963   *A Short Northern Thai—English Dictionary.* Chiang Mai: Overseas Missionary Fellowship.
Schweisguth, P.
    1951   *Etude sur la littérature siamoise.* Paris: Imprimerie Nationale.

Wongthes, Pranee and Sujit
    1989   "Art, Culture, and Environment in Thai-Lao-Speaking Groups." In *Culture and Environment in Thailand*, edited by the Siam Society, 161–169. Bangkok: The Siam Society.

HOMO CANTENS: WHY HMONG SING
DURING INTERACTIVE COURTSHIP RITUALS

Amy Catlin

In looking beyond verbal texts, scholars have begun to explore performance in context (Blackburn 1981; Blackburn et al. 1989; Kirschenblatt-Gimblett 1975), the dynamics of performer-audience interaction (Beeman 1981; Milner 1972; Schechner and Schuman 1976; Schechner 1979; Wadley 1989) and interactive performance genres (Dundes and Özkök 1972; Proschan 1985). Following Beeman's example, the pragmatic theories of Charles Peirce will be used here as a basis for investigating these areas within the text-context-performance paradigm as found in secular courtship rituals of the Hmong.

Peirce (Hartshorne and Weiss, 1963; Freeman 1934) proposed three levels of interaction to explain sign phenomena: *firstness,* or expression, *secondness,* or reception, and *thirdness,* or interpretation and response. Although all three levels pertain to performances of texts in specific contexts, they do not encompass those elements that precede or are consequential to the actual performance. Hence, Peirce's three levels will be expanded here to include *pre-firstness,* involving the broader historical and cultural context, the preparation of texts, and artistic training, and *post-thirdness,* involving issues related to diachronic change and outside interpretation, or the hermeneutical response, which this article exemplifies.

Hmong performers and spectators interact in a multitude of ways during the singing of ritualized courtship dialogue songs while simultaneously playing catch. The question I will examine is, why should the Hmong sing courtship songs as they do at their New Year festivals? As a corollary to this question, I examine why, in order to be performed, the verbal texts of Hmong songs need to be sung rather than spoken or recited and why the context of ball-tossing games generally surrounds this singing.

PRE-FIRSTNESS

Cultural context

The Hmong belong to the non-Chinese minorities of south and southwest China, where they number over five million (Bender 1990:28); in the past two centuries some two million have settled in Vietnam, Laos, and Thailand, and since 1975, about 100,000 have migrated from Laos to Thailand, the United States, France, French Guiana, Australia, and Canada. The larger context of the Hmong New Year festival provides the one annual occasion when Hmong from all clans gather and where courtship games and songs are performed throughout the world. Hmong social organization is based upon exogamous clans whose rituals other than the New Year are clan-specific. These inter-clan mating games are similar to the dialogue songs documented in fertility festivals in ancient China; they are also related to the "flower battles" of rural China in which boys and girls from different villages sing courtship songs while tossing ferns, flowers, or scented sachets. (Granet 1951, cited in Mottin 1980:226) Similar courtship rituals continue in China today during harvest, New Year, and spring festivals, among others (Liang 1987:80-93). The date for the Hmong New Year is traditionally the thirtieth day of the last month in the Hmong calendar, although Christmas vacation has been adopted in the West. Today, the largest Hmong New Year festivals in the United States occur in Fresno, California and La Crosse, Wisconsin, where crowds of as many as 15,000 Hmong gather in public parks for a week of festivities.

Preparation of texts

Courtship song texts are of undetermined authorship and age, but archaic references and poetic elements attest to their considerable antiquity. Texts are orally composed and may be manipulated freely in performance, while following the poetic constraints which characterize the form. Musical presentation of these oral texts is determined largely by word tone, sung according to rhythmic conventions and learned without benefit of a verbalized theory. These elements are not considered here as part of the preparation of text, but rather as an aspect of live performance, or firstness.

Artistic training

Songs are transmitted orally, either by observation or by individual example, although written texts are now sometimes used, using the Roman Popular Alphabet (RPA) devised by a team of American and French missionary linguists, or occasionally in the Pahawh Hmong script in which a special punctuation mark indicates singing (Smalley 1990:78). Children do not sing in Hmong society; rather, the act of singing is considered to be an aspect of courtship that ceases upon marriage, especially for women, although some later achieve status as ritual singers or bards, the exemplary singers of noncourtship genres.

The system of setting the verbal texts to music is difficult to follow and only the cleverest manage to intuitively grasp the technique, which has been explained in the literature (Catlin 1982, 1987, summarized in Smalley 1991:61-62; Mareschal 1976). Basically, eight tones of Hmong speech are distributed over a minimum of four pitches of various interval structures, each characteristic of a region, with some individual variation permitted. There is considerable overlap of speech tones in the middle register, as the highest and lowest notes are reserved for only three tones. This feature, plus the fact that the "high-falling" word tone is sung on the lowest pitch, causes many listeners to lose the meaning of text when sung. Blue Hmong singers are especially free with these rules, allowing melodic considerations to affect pitch choices. Vocal inflections subtly depict emotion, following highly stylized conventions for each genre, generally using a smooth, straight tone. The timbre of this tone is very intense and strained for younger courting singers, both male and female. The best singers pushing the chest voice so high that controlled falsetto breaks are possible, creating a sobbing effect that depicts the singer's tension in a heartrending manner. Such a tone is also penetrating and carries a good distance, essential during the din of a typical New Year festival.

The desire to produce this effect may influence the decision to sing in gapped scales, as the Hmong do consistently, rather than in stepwise melodic motion. In Xiengkhouang province these scales conform to Chinese pentatonicism. Other regions have their own distinct melodic characteristics and pulse-based meters as well as metric forms of irregular non-recurring units, without a regular inherent pulse.

There are no terms in Hmong for the tone positions or musical pitch levels used in singing and instrumental music. Hmong was, for the most part, an unwritten language until the 1950s when the RPA system of Romanization was implemented; the original orthography created by a Hmong messianic leader in Laos is considerably less widespread (Smalley 1991:151). Today more Hmong are making use of writing to prepare their songs for performance at the New Year. These texts are frequently published in Hmong sources, and a musical notation system for learning the technique is in preparation (Catlin and Vangyi, unpublished). Meanwhile, cassette tapes of performances serve as examples for imitation as well as for entertainment and bride-hunting.

FIRSTNESS

Expression

The central texts of the courtship ritual are the dialogue songs, performed within the context of the New Year celebration. Two such songs in White Hmong will be discussed and contrasted here in terms of text, context, and performance. The first was sung by an unmarried girl, the second by a recently bereaved widow. Hmong transcriptions in RPA and English translations will be given at this stage, although in a sense they both belong in the stage of post-thirdness, since transcription and translation inevitably involve interpretation. The two most widely used dialects spoken in Laos and the United States are White Hmong (*Hmoob Dawb*) and Blue Hmong (*Hmoob Ntsuab/Mong Njua* or *Hmoob Leej*). In the case of the first text, two bilingual White Hmong men were asked separately to prepare transcriptions and translations. The first was and was found by the second White Hmong translator to be incorrect in some instances. The second Hmong translator then prepared his own, which I found to contain considerable use of euphemism for explicit passages, among other liberties, when checked with Heimbach's *White Hmong-English Dictionary* (1969). I have thus decided to give the White Hmong transcription by Shur Vang Vangyi as prepared, but have translated the text myself more literally, using Heimbach's dictionary. The second text is given as transcribed, although due to its more complex language the transcription simplifies the utterance in many cases; the translation is also primarily prepared by Shur Vang Vangyi. Thus, the determination of exactly what constitutes the text becomes problematic from the beginning.[1]

At the level of firstness, or expression, we can assume a very high level of anxiety and/or excitement on the part of the performers while searching for a potential mate, or merely interacting with a member of the opposite sex under the scrutiny of an audience of parents, friends, and outsiders. Why then is the game of catch combined with the already demanding task of inter-gender socializing with a stranger, forbidden in normal life? The answer may lie in the consoling security found in the long-standing courtship tradition of ball tossing, a simple motor activity involving reciprocal interaction, in which the ball can serve as a welcome distraction for staring eyes. Similarly, singing a time-honored song from the past may help performers to relax by focusing attention away from the serious business at hand—meeting and evaluating potential mates.

What are the elements that constitute the message expressed at the level of firstness? The entire cluster of actions, including the performers' costumes, facial and gestural expressions, qualities of eye contact, ball tossing, words and melody of the poetry sung, conversation, and laughter all merge in the performance event. Where does the "text" lie in this convergence? The verbal text of the song is only one text at work: there are also "scripts" for behavior, or behavioral subtexts that determine the types of interaction acceptable between boy and girl. The cultural script for such occasions demands that the girl reluctantly consent to overcoming her shyness—a desirable trait of Hmong women—before she begins to sing. There are also cultural subtexts for evaluating character and other cognitive subtexts of many kinds brought into play.

The following is the transcription and translation of the verbal text of *Kwv Txhiaj Plees* (from *txhiaj*, riddle; *plees*, brazen, wanton, shameless), a typical courtship song performed in 1984 by an unmarried White Hmong girl during the New Year festivities held outdoors in Fountain Valley, California

Verbal Text #1
Sung by Xia Muas (from Xiengkhouang Province)
Videorecorded in Fountain Valley, California, December 31, 1984
Hmong transcription by Shur Vang Vangyi
English translation by Amy Catlin

(1) Niaj yais...
Oh...

Taj no ntshai luag leej tub ntaus plees nkauj
Now I fear this young man will strike at this shameless young woman,

Nraum twb hais zoo ua luaj no es
Out here in the clear and open,

Koj tsis muaj siab tiag
But if you do not really have the heart (*siab:* liver),

Tsis txhob daj dee me ntxhais nkauj xwb no es
Do not become involved with this unmarried little girl

Yog muaj siab tiag ces
But if you do have the heart,

Wb li tuav tes zuj zawv mus nce tag lub niag toj do/tsoob rua
Let us hold hands and go up the big round *empty* hill/*to open* the sexual act

Plees nkauj nraum hais zoo luaj no es
Like a shameless young woman says,

Cia wb mus tab wb lub teej cuab es
Let us both see and take care of each other,

Saib wb leej niam leej txiv puas nco/tshuas yuas
We will both see if our mother and father *miss/like us*

Txiv leej tub om.
My dear boy.
(2) *Niaj yais...*
Oh...

Txiv leej tub, ntaus plees nkauj
My dear boy, if you strike at this shameless young woman

Nraum zoo luaj no es
Out here in the clear and open,

Cia me noog uab lag txawj ya es
Let the little jungle crow (*corvus macrorhynchos*) and kestrel (*falco tinnunculus*) birds fly

Yuav qe txawj raws
They want to be able to chase after eggs

Yuav raws dua tus ceg khaub/po
They want to chase again and land on the *dry branch/rotten (branch)*

Plees nkauj nraum zoo luaj no ces cia wb mus tab
This shameless young woman is out in the open, let us both begin

Wb lub teej cuab es
Let us both decide to start our family

Tsis tshob pub leej niam leej txiv paub/hnov.
And not allow our mother and father to *know/hear.*

Ces zoo siab ua luaj no os
What great happiness!

A characteristic form of parallelism is central to the structure of this two-part verbal text. In each part (*fab, zaj,* classifiers for the sections or verses) the rhyming words are replaced by a second pair of rhyming words when the entire part is repeated. Thus, *do* and *nco* are replaced by *rua* and *tshuas* when the first verse is repeated; *khaub* and *paub* are replaced by *po* and *hnov*. Final "consonants" are actually tone markers in RPA; thus the vowels rhyme while tones need not be parallel.

Context

An unmarried, adolescent girl stands singly, as in the present case, or in a line, usually wearing an elaborate Hmong costume that identifies her subgroup within the Hmong tribe as well as her family and individual skills at needlework. She waits, holding the courtship ball, typically shading herself with a flowery parasol. A male or a group of males, often dressed in embroidered costumes made by their womenfolk, approaches to propose a game. Once the ball is tossed a male may begin to sing or he could entreat the female to sing, as in the present case, when all five male spectators encouraged her for several minutes by saying, "Sing!" (*Hais zoj!*) She might respond in song, although many do not, professing shyness or a lack of skill; repeated entreaties may elicit her song. Sometimes the game is played for forfeits, so that one who misses a ball must carry a piece of his or her costume to the opposite side; the thrower of the missed catch will guard the ransomed piece until it is retrieved in private. Sometimes a song is the price to pay for its retrieval; in the past, marriage was sometimes the price. Nowadays one seldom sees forfeits being exacted, but once I saw a girl hand a quarter to her partner each time she dropped the ball. A boy or girl may proudly wear the opponent's forfeited sash or belt about the festival grounds for a few hours until some agreement is reached between them. In some Hmong circles even this exchange of love tokens can signify an unconditional contract of marriage that the girl's parents may enforce.

Hmong girl catching courtship ball (right hand).
New Year Festival, San Diego, CA, December, 1985.
Photograph: Amy Catlin

Performance

The musical tools used in Hmong singing support the effort to appear detached from the verbal message, coolly uninvolved. Virtually all musical decisions follow an austere set of rules: words with either high or rising tones are sung on the highest pitch, those with falling tones on the lowest pitch, and all others are distributed between a minimum of two pitches between the two extremeties. As few as four pitches may thus suffice for the entire rendition. The following transcription shows the musical decisions made by this singer in rendering her text.

Musical Example 1:

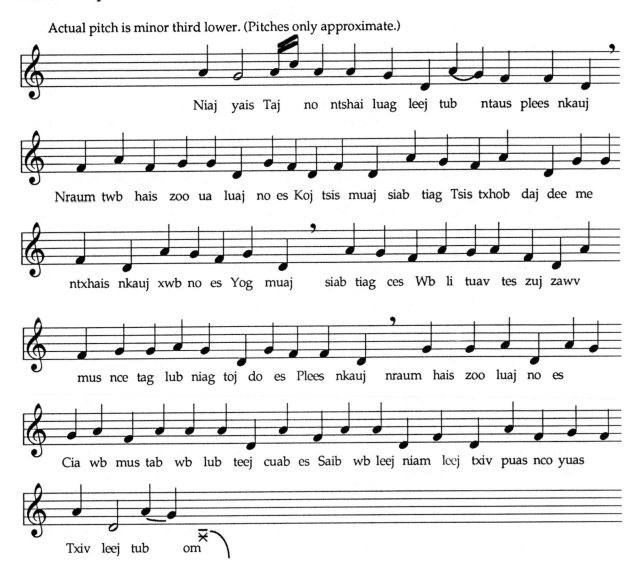

Actual pitch is minor third lower. (Pitches only approximate.)

Niaj yais Taj no ntshai luag leej tub ntaus plees nkauj

Nraum twb hais zoo ua luaj no es Koj tsis muaj siab tiag Tsis txhob daj dee me

ntxhais nkauj xwb no es Yog muaj siab tiag ces Wb li tuav tes zuj zawv

mus nce tag lub niag toj do es Plees nkauj nraum hais zoo luaj no es

Cia wb mus tab wb lub teej cuab es Saib wb leej niam leej txiv puas nco yuas

Txiv leej tub om

SECONDNESS: RECEPTION

At the level of secondness, or message reception, we must include two sublevels: the partner and the observers at the site. Other listeners such as the Hmong who later listen to the tape recordings made of these events and outside interpreters such as ourselves are relegated to post-thirdness.

The ostensible, intended audience for the display may be the partner, but, in fact, many others are present and a show is made of taking away recordings. Thus, singing to a partner may only be symbolic, a chance to achieve some fame for artistic skill and perhaps a desirable mate as a result.

If we assume that courtship between two individuals is indeed the "real" activity, how might singing and ball tossing help accomplish it? Many Hmong have said that beauty, wealth, family, skills, and personality are important in choosing a wife, but by far the most highly prized attribute of a potential wife is her ability to sing. This recalls the adulation of singers in many societies. The New Year ball game is one of the few arenas where such skills may be displayed. Recordings made by potential matchmakers are carried throughout the country after New Year and are listened to avidly by the singles crowd. My own Hmong assistant became entranced with a recording I brought from California to Rhode Island for him to transcribe; when he wrote to her appreciatively, she sent him her photo which he mounted above his desk at home. Carrying this one step further, some young women have made their own tapes for distribution and sale at the New Year festival, complete with a portrait on the cassette box. Many of the younger singers are learning from cassettes now. But since singing is usually forbidden after marriage, this skill is valued as a cultural treasure to be given to one's descendents, a courtship tool designed for sexual selection. As stated earlier, Hmong children do not sing. There are no Hmong children's songs or musical games. In adolescence, singing for courtship begins. After marriage, singing is reserved for funerals, weddings, and in exceptional cases as a means of communicating thoughts or tales too large for ordinary speech, on the stage before the entire community in contests celebrating the Hmong bardic tradition.

Why then is ball throwing involved? Using Erving Goffman's concept of "focused interaction" (1974), tossing a ball while singing affords a unique opportunity to demonstrate through variations in eye contact and facial expression just how interested one is in the partner. The singer's ability to remain calm under stressful social conditions, and even to be entertaining and playful, are fully tested in this activity. Surprisingly, one can learn a good deal about another person by playing a game of catch, even more by listening to and watching that person sing a song, and perhaps still more by observing the friends and relations who encourage and react to the singer.

Unless there is singing involved, these ball games attract only casual attention during the course of the festival days, and only close friends and relatives of the players stand behind them to coax or initiate discussion between potential mates. However, with the introduction of song, the players become the center of a throng of cassette-wielding onlookers who strain to hold their tape recorders as close as possible, especially to the female singer. Her recording will then be circulated freely among boys seeking mates, for the ability to sing is a prime factor in choosing a wife. Other girls may then also learn from her recorded example. One can always find the best singers at a festival by surveying the field for the largest clumps of observers and recordists, tennis balls bobbing above the center of the crowd. Observers often encourage or tease the singers during the performance, but for the best singers rapt attention prevails until the final syllable of the song, when all recorders click shut in near-perfect unison. Kudos may follow, but responses are generally swallowed up by the resumption of normal festival sounds.

THIRDNESS

Interpretation and Response

At this level, the musical performance of verbal texts functions in one way to facilitate multiple interpretations, freeing the singer and the listener from the chains of normal discourse. In another article (Catlin 1985) I have suggested that Hmong song can be seen as a "critique of pure speech" and the boundaries which speech imposes on utterances and their interpretation, in the sense that for the Hmong singing appears to "criticize" pure speech by virtue of its active extension of the boundaries of speech. This fits with a standard Hmong explanation for the use of singing, which states that they are too shy a people to speak the thoughts expressed in their songs. By singing, shyness can be transcended, and verbal and nonverbal statements occur which could never be made in the context of pure speech and its attendant rules of social decorum (see Merriam 1964:193). A further extension of this principle is found in Hmong secular instrumental music in which a performer too shy even to sing transfers his or her words to an instrument.

Another hypothesis is that singing is more formal and more artistic than normal speech discourse. The Hmong are well known for their artistic expressive forms. Song, like textile work, is another realm where women as well as men may display personal skill and artistry. Like textiles, song functions as a symbolic system of communication that sets the Hmong apart from other groups and that sets a talented individual above others within the group. Both are solo art forms and they attest to the importance of individualism even within a socially cohesive group and to the possibility of affecting one's marital fate despite the equally accepted convention of arranged matches.

Several middle-aged male Hmong consultants interpreted the videotaped performance to mean that the singer was inviting the boy to elope with her from her parents' house immediately, following one traditional Hmong method of betrothal that has become socially controversial and legally problematic in their new context. Young adult Hmong men and women felt that she was expressing only moderate interest in her partner, perhaps indicating the loosening of constraints on expression for Hmong-American youth. If nothing else, the example shows that these courtship messages are inherently ambivalent, deliberately left open to interpretation and speculation. The studied avoidance of looking at the ball in all the examples I have seen, the consistent coolness of the singers, seem to suggest that this ambivalence is a central dynamic in these courtship songs. Passionate and outspoken lyrics sung in a cool and casual manner create a powerful dynamic of opposition: fire and ice presented simultaneously for the listener to interpret the intended message—or at least decide which to accept and act upon.

But if the focused interaction provides an opportunity to evaluate mates, why could they not merely recite the words to poems rather than having to sing them? It might be much simpler and, in fact, most youths are unable to juggle the word tones and tunes acceptably. One explanation that seems to work is that the removal of the words from everyday speech through song functions in effect to absolve the singer from responsibility for their meaning, so that the masking of words through song serves to protect the singer from being taken too literally or even from being too easily understood. The process of singing distorts and rearranges the spoken tones of this tonal language, with regional substyles, so that many Hmong confess to difficulty in understanding singers from even their own regions. The framing of texts in melody sets the communication apart from normal discourse, causing the words to have a different significance than when spoken.

The interpretation of sung messages must rely not only upon the culturally defined cues that enhance the verbal message but also upon the sensitivity and personal and aesthetic tastes of the listener. One probable explanation for the use of the singing voice is to challenge and enhance the sensitivity of the listener and to arouse the feelings of love which might lead to marriage. The quality of the arousal intended is not overtly erotic or sexual, judging from the verbal content of the even their own regions. The framing of texts in melody sets the communication apart from normal discourse, causing the words to have a different significance than when spoken.

The interpretation of sung messages must rely not only upon the culturally defined cues that enhance the verbal message but also upon the sensitivity and personal and aesthetic tastes of the listener. One probable explanation for the use of the singing voice is to challenge and enhance the sensitivity of the listener and to arouse the feelings of love which might lead to marriage. The quality of the arousal intended is not overtly erotic or sexual, judging from the verbal content of the songs and the formal, restrained vocal style of Hmong singers. Rather, it combines the romantic, with many images from nature embellishing rosy pictures of happy lovers and animals mated for life, with the pathetic, in which the sympathy of the listener is sought.

The following is an example of the latter in which one of the three most highly regarded singers today, the newly bereaved Pa Shua Her (a White Hmong from Sayaboury Province, Laos) sings alone of her plight in order to attract a new spouse and protector. At the level of firstness, her expression is a self-description functioning to alert her community of her recent widowhood and mourning. She sings here without a partner, symbolically holding the courting ball, but shrouding it in a black cloth. Instead of a flowery parasol, she holds a black umbrella over her head.

Verbal Text #2. *Kwv Txhiaj Ntsuag* (Widow's Song)
Videorecorded in Fountain Valley, California December 31, 1984
Transcribed by Shur Vang Vangyi; translated by Shur Vang Vangyi and Amy Catlin

1. *Ua ciav...kwv tij Hmoob los lawm neej tsa es.*
Tawg paj rau tom tag es
Txi txiv los rau tom txuas
Xyoo no kwv leej tub leej roog ces tsis yog tuag mob los tuag nrag es
Tuag poj mab yawm lis suav tus hniav vuas nis
Kwv tij hmoob los lawm neej tsa....om.

Ua ciav tawg paj rau tom txua es
Txi txiv rov tom tag
Xyoo no kuv leej tub leej roog ces tsis yog tuag mob los tuag nraj es
Tuag poj mab yawm lis suav tus hniav ntaj ni...im.

2. *Cas leej tub leej roog cev ntaj tuag tas nrho es*
Muam Nkauj See xeeb tub yuj ywm rau nruab xub ntxha es
Tsis muaj txig rov los muaj nkawm yuav ua tshav los mus ua nag nga nis
Kwv tij Hmoob los lawm neej tsa...om.

Ua ciav leej tub leej roog cev ntaj tuag tas nrho
Muam Nkauj See xeeb tub yuj ywm los rau nruab xub puab es
Tsis muaj tsig rov los muaj nkawm yuav
Ua tshav los mus ua nag sua
Nis kwv tij Hmoob los lawm neej tsa...om.

3. *Cas qaib tsis muaj nkauj es*
Qaib nrhiav chaws ya
Muaj Nkauj See tsis txawj tus tub xyoo no

4. *Ua ciav muam Nkauj See tsis txawj*
Mus ua nyab yuav yug kooj los rawg es
Yog muam Nkauj See tsis ploj tsis tuag los tseg
Ploj tuag tas tes thov qhua tauj qhua yas ob cag
Hlub Nkauj See tub ntawm Nkauj mus See taw os
Kwv tij Hmoob los lawm neej tsa...om.

Cas muam Nkauj See tsis txawj mus tu tub es
Yuav yug kooj los yug yiag
Yog muam Nkauj See cev ntaj duab tuag
Tas ces thov qhua tauj qhua yas ob
Cag hlub Nkauj See tub ntawm nkauj mus see ntiag nis
Kwv tij Hmoob rov los lawm neej tsa...

5. *Tsis muaj tsag rov los lawm muaj nkawm es*
Seev yuv yeeg hais tias yuav zoo puab tam tim lub tsho yaj
Txheej raus dej saib dej puas ntub

Xyoo no tsis muaj tsag rov los muaj nkawm es
Yuav ua siab dawb puj paug mus qhia saib nus tij puas yuav yuav es
Saib nus kwv los puas yuav hlub os
Kwv tij Hmoob es...om.

Ua ciav tsis muaj txis rov los lawm muaj nkawm zoo puab tam tim
Lob tsho yaj txeeg raus dej saib dej puas duav es

Seev yuj yug tias tav ntuj li no tsis muaj tub muaj roog es
Ua siab lawb puj paug mus saib nus tij puas yuav hlub
Nus kwv los puas yuav yuav nis kwv tij Hmoob los lawm neej tsa...om.

6. *Cas nus tij siab tsis zoo nus tij seev*
Yug yeeg hais tias tu qaib ntsuag ces tau nqaij puab es
Tu tub tu kiv ntsuag yuav ciaj lawm yeeb ncuab...

Nus kwv siab txhooj tsis zoo es
Nus kwv yuav seev yug yeeg tias tu qaib ntsuag ces tau nqaij noj es
Tu tub ntsuag ces tau yeeb ncuab coj ni...im.

7. *Cas muam Nkauj See yuav tu siab lawm nrhuj nrho*
Hais tuas kuv yaj nyog los txia tau txia lis nrhis
Ua dab moj lis kawm ncig lis yeev rau toj lug lis
Taim toj roob zeb txho es
Nim yog phau ntaub coj los phau ntawv es
Kwv leej tub leej roog nyob tsab teb rov los ntuj twg yuav nyeem ntawv
   lawm tuj taws mus hais qhia leej tub leej roog rov qab los ro nis
Kwv tij Hmoob los lawm neej tsa...

Muam Nkauj See seev yuj yeeg tias chim siab ua luaj no yaj nyog los txia tau txia lis nrhis
Ua niam dab roj yig lis tsua ncig yeev rau toj lug lis taim toj roob zeb ntsuab es
Yog phau ntaub coj los phau ntawv

Kuv leej tub leej roog nyob tsab teb rov los ntuj twg es
Yuav nyeem ntawv lawm tuj taws mus hais qhia leej tub leej roog rov los **muab** *ces*

Paj lag hnub qub nras es
Leej twg ncauj npliag lim liag
Ho txai coj mus qhia
Leej twg ntxhais nis
Kwv tij Hmoob los lawm
Neej tsa...om.

1. Oh!
My Hmong brothers and relatives...
It flowers in the living room
And bears fruit in the **side room** (**txuas**) (women's room, kitchen)
This year my husband did not die from illness
But he died from the foreign woman's and Chinese people's
Teeth of the **tile** (**yuas**)

Oh! My Hmong brothers and relatives...
It flowers in the side room
And bears fruit in the **living room** (**tag**)
This year my husband did not die from illness
But he died from the foreign woman's and Chinese people's
Teeth of the **sword** (**ntaj**)

2. After my husband's death
I carried his son in my **bare** (**ntxha**) (smelling) bones
But I did not have my husband
To **hold** (**nqa**) me in the rain and sun

Oh! My Hmong brothers and relatives...
After my husband's death
I carried his son in the bones of my **groin** (**puab**)
But I did not have my husband
To **join** (**sua**) me in the rain and sun

3. Oh! My Hmong brothers and relatives...
When the chicken (**qaib**: junglefowl) does not have a roost
It will find a place to **fly** (**ya**)
I do not know how to raise my son
I raise him around the other people's **wall** (**nra**)

Oh! My Hmong brothers and relatives...
When the chicken does not have a roost
It will find a place to **sleep** (**ncooj**)
I do not know how to raise my son
I will raise him around the other people's **table** (**rooj**)

4. Oh! My Hmong brothers and relatives...
I did not know how to be a good bride
I raised the grasshopper (*kooj:* grasshopper, locust), my son
But I raised him too **little** (*rawg*)
If I do not die, it will be alright
But if I die
I must ask the people from another clan
To love my son
As a son born at their own **feet** (*taw*)

Oh! My Hmong brothers and relatives...
I do not know how to raise my son
I raised a grasshopper
But I raised him too **straight** (*yiag*)
If I die, I must ask the people from another clan
To love my son as their own in their **arms** (*ntiag*)

5. I do not have my husband
I am like the shirt which will be tested
To see if it becomes **wet** (*ntub*) in the water

This year I do not have my husband
I will show my good liver (heart)
And tell my older brother
To see if he will **take** (*yuav*) me
And my younger brother
To see if he will **love** (*hlub*) me

I do not have my husband
I am like the shirt which will be tested
To see if it becomes **covered** (*duav*) in the water

Let me go to show my good liver (heart)
To my older brother
To see if he will **love** (*hlub*) me
And my younger brother
To see if he will **take** (*yuav*) me

6. But my elder brother's liver (heart) is bad
He sighs longingly and says,
"If I raise an orphan chick
I will get its **legs** (*puab*) to eat
And if I shelter a widow
I will get an **enemy** (*ncuab*)."

But my elder brother's liver (heart) is bad
He sighs longingly and says,
"If I raise an orphan chick
I will get its meat to **eat** (*noj*)
And if I shelter a widow
I will get an enemy to **keep** (*coj*)."

7. I feel hurt If I could change my form
I would change into the Devil
And do spirit rites all around
To circle around the **blue** (*txho*) rocky hill
And if it were a story in a book
And if I knew which country or world
My husband has gone to
I would read the story to my husband
And ask him to come back to **release** (*ro*) us

My Hmong brothers and relatives...
The young girl, Moua Ngau Sheng, sighs longingly
I am very angry
If I could change my form
I would change into the Devil
To circle around the **green** (*ntsuab*) rocky hill
And if it were a story in a book
And if I knew which country or world
My husband has gone to
I would read the story to my husband
And ask him to come back and **take** (*muab*) us

The flowers are brilliant
Like the sky full of stars
Whoever can speak correctly
May learn this song
To teach to her daughter
My Hmong brothers and relatives...

The melody used for this performance, sung in a recitative-like syllabic pulsing manner often heard in *lus taum* or didactic narrative songs, contains a unique lower note which is always sung in a "creaky" or glottalized slide from a step above. It begins as follows:

Example 2:

Actual pitch is perfect fourth lower.

ua   ciav   kwv   tij Hmoob los lawm neej tsa es

At the level of secondness, or reception, her performance met with quiet tears to match her own. She was encouraged by the listeners to sing other songs and continued with a description of their courting days, and of her understanding of their early mistake at the gates of heaven: the issuing of improper soul visas by the Chinese gatekeeper, which led to the untimely death of one without the other.

Our interpretation of the song text required lengthy explanation of Hmong customs and beliefs. The singer alludes to the traditional Hmong taboo against cutting the body, symbolized in the "teeth of the tile," as tiles sometimes fall from Chinese roofs with fatal results; this suggests that she believed that it was the foreigners' invasive surgery that caused her husband's death in America. Another interviewee interpreted the song to mean that her husband had been killed by a non-Hmong thief; in her ensuing song she describes his lengthy illness. Next she alludes to the painful process of childbirth after widowhood, the difficulty of survival as a single parent, leading perhaps to her own death and and the necessity of giving the child to another clan for adoption as an orphan, the most pathetic position possible in Hmong society. She points to the socially unacceptible position of widowhood with children, feared by even close relatives as a harbinger of ill. Finally she threatens to become an evil spirit which circles around a blue or green hill, signifying her husband's burial ground, as the Hmong traditionally bury their dead on the side of a hill. Her recourse to the image of written books symbolize the inferiority and frustration the Hmong have felt for centuries as a preliterate people dominated by literate civilizations around them. (Smalley 1990:15) In closing, she reaches out first to all Hmong women, asking that they teach their daughters to sing, and finally to all the Hmong, who believe themselves to be related as kinsmen.

At the level of response, Pa Shua Her clearly inspired sympathy in her listeners, as one gentleman offered to sing with her in dialogue. She accepted only on condition that they not face each other, but instead sing back-to-back in observance of her period of mourning. Thus, a first step in courting the widow was taken.

The appeal of Pa Shua Her's poetry is undeniably strong, but without singing, we are told by the Hmong that it would not exist. Because of its very complexity, which renders it inimitable by all but the most talented Hmong, it functions as an ethnically-specific form of mating behavior. The songs also function as a tool for asserting ethnic identity which cannot be duplicated by outsiders. Indeed, despite general similarities, the song styles of other hilltribes of Southeast Asia would never be mistaken for Hmong kwv txhiaj, and like variations in dress and social structure, these expressive forms function to differentiate the many endogamous ethnic groups of the region, binding together the members who share the same cultural traits.

By extension, as virtually all the general characteristics of sung expression, reception, and response delineated here have parallels in most cultures, perhaps we can speak, in the tradition of *homo hierarchicus* (Dumont 1970), *homo ludens* (Huizinga 1950), and *homo ridens* (Milner 1972), of *homo cantens*: humans who share the practice of singing their verbal and nonverbal messages in order to arouse feelings of connectedness in their listeners and in themselves—and through that link, to express emotions beyond the means of mere linguistic communication.

NOTES

1.   For further study, both performances are available on the audio cassette entitled *Virgins, Orphans, Widows, and Bards: Songs of Hmong Women* (Van Nuys, Ca.: Apsara Media 1991 [1987]).

REFERENCES

Beeman, William O.
    1981   "Why Do They Laugh? An Interactional Approach to Humor in Traditional Iranian Improvisatory Theater." Journal of American Folklore 94:506–526.

Bender, Mark
    1990   "'Felling the Ancient Sweetgum': Antiphonal Folk Epics of the Miao of Southeast Guizhou." *CHINOPERL* 15:27–44.

Blackburn, Stuart H.
    1981   "Oral Performance: Narrative and Ritual in Tamil Tradition." *Journal of American Folklore* 94:207–227.

Blackburn, Stuart H. et al., eds.
    1989   *Oral Epics in India.* Berkeley: University of California Press.

Catlin, Amy
    1982   "Speech Surrogate Systems of the Hmong: From Singing Voices to Talking Reeds." In *The Hmong in the West: Observations and Reports*, eds. Bruce T. Downing and Douglas P. Olney, 170-197. Minneapolis: University of Minnesota Southeast Asia Refugees Studies Program.

    1985   "The Hmong and their Music. . . . A Critique of Pure Speech." In *Hmong Art: Tradition and Change,* ed. Joanne Cubbs, 10–19. Sheboygan, Wisc.: The John Michael Kohler Arts Center.

Catlin, Amy and Shur Vang Vangyi
    unpubl. "A Musical Notation System for Hmong *kwv txhiaj.*"

Dumont, Louis
    1970   *Homo Hierarchicus: The Caste System and Its Implications.* Translated by Mark Sainsbury [French edition published in 1966]. Chicago: University of Chicago Press.

Dundes, Alan, Jerry W. Leach and Bora Özkök
    1972   "The Strategy of Turkish Boys' Duelling Rhymes." In *Directions in Sociolinguistics*, ed. John J. Gumperz and Dell Hymes, 130–160. New York: Holt, Rinehart, and Winston.

Freeman, Eugene
    1934   *The Categories of Charles Peirce*. Chicago: The Open Court Publishing Company.

Goffman, Erving
    1974   *Frame Analysis: An Essay into the Organization of Experience*. New York: Harper Colophon Books.

Hartshorne, Charles and Paul Weiss
    1963   *Collected Papers of Charles Sanders Peirce*. Volume V: *Pragmatism and Pragmaticism* [Reprint of 1st ed. 1934]. Cambridge: Harvard University Press.

Heimbach, Ernest
    1969   *White Hmong-English Dictionary*. Ithaca: Cornell University Press.

Huizinga, Johan
    1950   *Homo Ludens: A Study of the Play Element in Culture*. Boston: Beacon Press.

Kirschenblatt-Gimblett, Barbara
    1975   "A Parable in Context: A Social Interactional Analysis of Storytelling Performance." In *Folklore: Performance and Communication*, ed. Dan Ben-Amos and Kenneth S. Goldstein, 105-130. The Hague: Mouton.

Liang, Yuanrong
    1987   "Miao Dances." In *Flying Dragon and Dancing Phoenix: An Introduction to Selected Chinese Minority Folk Dances*, ed. Chen Weiye, Ji Lanwei, and Ma Wei, 80–93. Bejing: New World Press.

Mareschal, Eric
    1976   *La Musique des Hmong*. Paris: Musee Guimet.

Merriam, Alan P.
    1964   *The Anthropology of Music*. Chicago: Northwestern University Press.

Milner, G.B.
    1972   "Homo Ridens." *Semiotica* 5, 1-30.

Mottin, Jean
    1980   *Fetes du Nouvel An Chez les Hmong Blanc de Thailande*. Bangkok: Don Bosco Press.

Proschan, Frank
    1985   "Love Dialogues in Asia and the Pacific." Unpublished paper presented to the California Folklore Society, University of California, Irvine.

Schechner, Richard
    1979   *Essays in Performance Theory*. New York: Drama Book Service.

Schechner, Richard and Mady Schuman, eds.
    1976   *Ritual, Play, and Performance: Readings in the Social Sciences/Theatre*. New York: The Seabury Press.

Smalley, William A.
    1976   *Ethno-Zoology of the Green Miao (Mong Njua) of Naan Province, Northern Thailand.* Napa: Napa College Graphics Department.

Smalley, William A., Chia Koua Vang, and Gnia Yee Yang
    1991   *Mother of Writing: The Origin and Development of a Hmong Messianic Script.* Chicago: The University of Chicago Press.

Wadley, Susan S.
    1989   "Choosing a Path: Performance Strategies in a North Indian Epic." In *Oral Epics in India,* ed. Stuart H. Blackburn et al., 140-154. Berkeley: University of California Press.

LEXICAL TONE AND MUSICAL PITCH IN AN IU MIEN YAO WEDDING SONG

Herbert C. Purnell

INTRODUCTION

One question about tone languages which has interested linguists and musicologists alike concerns the relationship or interaction between words (where pitch is used to distinguish meanings) and vocal melody (where pitch is used to distinguish notes). That is, in a tone language when a person sings a song, does he/she preserve the linguistic tones of the words while producing the melody? If so, what is the relationship between word tone and melodic pitch? If not, how can the listeners understand the lyrics? Also, how do the tones and the melody interact so that both word meaning and musical variety can be maintained?

This paper is part of a larger study dealing with the relationship between song texts and vocal melody in Iu Mien Yao.[1] It will examine the relationship between words and music in one genre of secular songs. Specifically, it will look at a twelve-line wedding song and attempt to show that there is a definite and regular relationship between linguistic tones and melodic pitch. Although the present study is limited to the particular text under consideration, it is nevertheless anticipated that the findings can be generalized to cover a large number of songs in the same genre. By way of background, the paper will first look briefly at the Iu Mien language system, tones, and the metrical structure of secular song texts before dealing with the wedding song and its melody. The relationship between lexical tone and musical pitch will then be presented.

THE IU MIEN

The Iu Mien Yao are one of the highland minority peoples found in northern Southeast Asia (Thailand, Laos, and Vietnam) where they probably number under 100,000. Traditionally slash-and-burn agriculturalists, they have, at least in Thailand within the last fifteen or so years, been persuaded or forced to move down to the foothills, into government self-help areas, or into towns for a variety of political, economic, and security reasons. There are now some 14,000 Iu Mien living abroad as political refugees from Laos: France 1,000; Canada 100; and the United States 13,000.

The Iu Mien were originally from China, where most of the remaining half million or more still live in Guangdong, Guangxi, Hunan, and Yunnan. Those in Southeast Asia share with their closest relatives, the Gem Mun Yao or Lantien, a special treasure not possessed by other minorities in the area: the extensive use of Chinese characters in their literary and ritual languages.

The Iu Mien language system

The Iu Mien possess a complex language system which consists of three core languages (or repertoires): a vernacular language ($mien^2 waa^6$), a literary language ($nzung^1 waa^6$), and a ritual language ($zie^2 waa^6$). The vernacular language is the basic or original language and is one of the main constituents of the Yao branch within the Miao-Yao family.[2] The other two languages and their accompanying forms were borrowed from two different types of Chinese and are written with Chinese characters. The literary language, together with poetic forms similar to Tang dynasty "Old Style" poetry,[3] was apparently borrowed from a type of Southwestern Mandarin and the ritual language, together with the use of Taoist ritual books, from a type of Cantonese. (For a more extensive discussion of the Iu Mien language system, see Purnell 1989.)

Of the three languages, the literary language (and thus the traditional singing of secular song-poems) is being most affected by education, urbanization, westernization, and other pressures or attractions which are part of culture change. For example, knowledge of the literary language and the characters needed to write song-poems is decreasing rapidly among refugees living in Western countries and in the camps in Thailand. The literary language is now preserved primarily by middle-aged and older men and women, especially by male ritual experts who, even though the literary and ritual languages are pronounced very differently, must maintain their knowledge of characters in order to have continued access to the books they need to perform traditional cermonies.

Iu Mien tones[4]

The same inventory and phonetic quality of tones is used in both the vernacular and the literary language. Six phonetic tones, numbered 1 to 6, occur with "live" or unstopped syllables (e.g., $dong^2$, wei^6), whereas only two phonetic tones, 7 and 8, occur with "dead" or stopped syllables (e.g., fat^7, $ziep^8$). They can be described as follows:

1. Mid level	3. High rise or rise-fall	5. Low-mid rise	7. High level
2. Mid-low fall	4. Low rise-fall	6. Low level	8. Low level

Although tones 7 and 8 are considered to be nonphonemic and included in tones 3 and 6, respectively, they are kept separate for the purposes of this paper. Tones 3 and 7 have slightly different tone shapes, and part of the current investigation is to see whether this difference has an effect on melodic pitch.

A BRIEF OVERVIEW OF THE METRICAL STRUCTURE OF SONG-POEMS[5]

In the literary language, a typical line of poetry consists of two vertical half-lines of seven characters/syllables each. These half-lines, separated by several spaces, are called "upper" and "lower" to reflect this traditional manner of writing characters. (For typographical convenience, however, lines will be written horizontally here.) Each half-line forms a complete syntactic unit having a fixed internal structure comprised of three subgroups as follows (with vertical lines separating the subgroups):

Upper half-line:	1a	2a	|	3a	4a	|	5a	6a	7a
Lower half-line:	1b	2b	|	3b	4b	|	5b	6b	7b

In addition to its syntactic structure, a line of poetry must also follow several patterns of tonal placement. These patterns are based on a two-way division of the tones, following Chinese usage (Downer and Graham 1963), into what are known as "level" tones (1 and 2) and "oblique" or "deflected" tones (3 through 8) as follows:

(Level)   (Oblique)
1 | 3 5 7 (=3)
2 | 4 6 8 (=6)

The first and most important of the tone patterns is that the tone on syllable 7a must be from the oblique category, whereas that on syllable 7b must be from the level category.[6] Overall, this pattern has very few exceptions.

The second pattern involves the preferred tonal relationships among the even-numbered syllables (2, 4, and 6). As described by Downer and Graham (*ibid.*) for Chinese Regulated Verse, there should be an alternation of the two major tone categories. An ideal alternation can be seen in the following formula, where "X" represents either set of tones, level or oblique, and "Y" represents the opposite set. Thus, the formula

	1	2	3	4	5	6	7
Upper:		X		Y		X	
Lower:		Y		X		Y	

can be read in two ways; either as

	2	4	6
Upper:	level	oblique	level
Lower:	oblique	level	oblique

or as

	2	4	6
Upper:	oblique	level	oblique
Lower:	level	oblique	level

This system of alternating tone categories was perhaps too complex or too restrictive for the Iu Mien since the pattern is regularly followed only in lower half-lines. Less than half of the upper half-lines observe the rule.

Downer and Graham (ibid.) also mention two additional patterns which place even tighter restrictions on a poet. The first of these requires that syllables 1 and 3 must be from the same tone category as syllables 2 and 4, respectively. The second pattern requires syllable 5 to be from the opposite tone category from syllable 7. In an examination of a number of Iu Mien song-poems, only a loose preference, just over 50 percent, for the first pattern was found. The second pattern occurred more frequently but was significant (about 80 percent) only on lower half-lines (Purnell 1989).

A WEDDING SONG AND ITS MELODY

The text used for analysis here is a complete song with six couplets, e.g., twelve full lines, and its own title: "A section singing about the creation of heaven and earth by Fu Hei."[7] The song is typical of other wedding songs in that each line begins with a repetition of the syllable cen^3, has fourteen full syllables in each line, and follows the metrical system of secular poetry. This text, an example of a formal song, also has end rhyme within a couplet (i.e., on the final syllables (7b) of a pair of lines), five couplets ending with -ing/-ing and one with   -ien/-ien.

In the following text a comma indicates the end of a half-line and a full stop the end of a full line. The slash (/) indicates where the singer paused to take a breath. In addition to the full syllables shown, the singer added a number of "padding" syllables. The variety, consistency, placement, and role of these extra vocalisms has been dealt with elsewhere (Purnell 1990). Although a full description of Iu Mien songs must account for them, padding syllables have been omitted in the transcription here because the primary focus in this paper is on the relationship between the linguistic tones of the full syllables and the notes on which they are sung. The numbering of the lines follows the numbering used for the entire wedding book. This song was recorded at three separate times: in 1972 in Laos, and twice in August 1984 in California. The version used here is the first 1984 recording. The Chinese characters are taken directly from the book itself and therefore may contain nonstandard or modified characters. A translation of the song follows the song text.

The melody (or range of melodies) in this version of the Fu Hei song is based on a pentatonic scale: C,D,F,G,A (do-re-fa-sol-la).[8] E^b (mi-flat) occurs fourteen times, but only five of these are basic notes on full syllables. The others are all passing notes. In fact, the overwhelming impression is that E^b is deliberately avoided, even in glides. G and A also occur an octave lower as part of descending glides at the very end of eight of the twelve lines, but this is treated here as voice decay indicating completion of the line.

As mentioned in the discussion of Iu Mien tones above, the final syllable in an upper half-line must have an oblique category tone (i.e., 3– 8). This syllable is followed by an ascending glide in the melody, indicated here by a plus sign (+). The final syllable in a lower half-line, on the contrary, must have a level category tone (i.e., 1 or 2) and is preceded by a descending glide, indicated here by an asterisk (*). The final syllable itself is sung on a low C. These same ascending and descending glides are found on the two introductory syllables cen^3 and producing the melodic equivalent of a lead-in line. Thus:

Lead-in: Cen^3 +, cen^3 *.

Upper: 1 2 3 4 5 6   7 (oblique) +,
Lower: 1 2 3 4 5 6 * 7 (level).

In the transcription which follows, upper case letters above the syllables indicate full notes of the musical pitch, whereas lower case letters indicate passing or ornamental notes. An ellipsis (...) is used to eliminate all except the beginning and ending notes of a contour glide, with the implication that the omitted medial notes do not appear to be significant.

Yiet[8] gin[6] ciang[5] koi[1]-tin[1] liep[8] dei[6] Fuq[7]-Hei[1] nzung[1] (1984A)　　一析昌開天立地伏儀歌

205.

A +	FCfGC *					
Cen³,	œn³. /					

A	F...G	f...C	DC	F	agA	f#G +
Biu3	zoi5	laang2	yin2 /	sei5	kiq7	sin5,

C	C	F	F...G	FGFC	DCF *	C
Ziq8	dau2 /	ziq8	muei4	sei5	yiem1-	sing1.

烏 在远逞世起扇
席头席尾世掩嘸

206.

A +	FGF *
Cen³,	cen³. /

A	A	FDC	EbDC	FG	G	C +
Siou3	zip7	ging1-	sou1	sei5	faat7	hin6, /

CDC	AF	C	FDC	F	fEbFG *	CDC
Daai6	daam3	ziq8	duang1	yiem5	zuang5	zing2.

手接京書世發現
大胆席中撬眾情

207.

A +	FGFC *
Cen³,	cen³. /

FD	CF	fDC	fDC	F	A	A +
Ging1	ding6	yun2	nin1 /	hong2	sui3	faat7,

A	F..C	A	FDFGA	FG..CG	dC *	C
Ciet7	ziu1 /	ciet7	ie5	yiem5	tin1-	ding2.

京是元年洪水發
七朝七夜淹天廷

208.

fG +	FGFC *
Cen³,	cen³. /

D	DC	DCfG	CEb	C	C	C +
Ha2	lou2	mbuei5	zang6	tin1-	dorng2 /	noi6

DFGCD	dfG	DC	C	F	CF *	C
Faan2	dong4	luei2	ding2 /	fiem1-	bin6	ging1.

竻箴浮上天堂肉
煩動雷庭心便京,

209.

fG +	FGFC *
Cen³,	cen³. /

F	FDCG	F	GDC	C	FDC	A +
M1	luei2	do5	buon3	njie6	dong1 /	koi3,

A	D...A	FDC	C	Eb	EbG *	C
Bin3	mbuo5	luang2	hung2 /	koi1	sui3	zing2.

五雷倒本下東海
穀票龍王開水情

210.

fG +	FDC *
Cen³,	cen³. /

fG	FDCG	A	FDC	G	DC	FGF +
Zing5	daai2	daa3	nqoi1	u3	hu2 /	hai3,

正東打開五湖海

FDC U^2	FD guei^1 /	fA tui^5	CDC bou^6	A sui^3	FDC * tui^1-	C ging^1.	烏龜退步水推京
211. A + Cen^3,	FGF * cen^3./						
A Yiem^5	DFG zien^4	FDC tin^1-	DC ding^2 /	F dei^6	A bet^7	AF + gorq^7,	淹尽天庭地八谷
F Yiem^5	AF fei^3	DC baam^2	FDC gen^1 /	C mou^6	CFG * maan^6	C nyien^2.	淹死尼間号萬人
212. fG + Cen^3,	FGFC * cen^3./						
CF Zong^6	FDCG liou^2	C Fuq^7-	FDC Hei^1	F liang^6	AGA zei^3	CG + mui^6,/	童晋伏儀兩姊妹
FD Tin^1	CG njie^6	DC mou^6	C nyien^2	F zei^4	FG * gap^7	C cien^1.	天下無人供合親
213. fG + Cen^3,	FGF * cen^3./						
fD Laau^2	C..G luoq^8	A yiet^7	FDCD ziu^2	dF lo^4	CDC you^6 /	A + biu^3,	劳禄一期老幼鳥
A Ndap^7	E$^{\flat}$FG zang^6	C ziq^8	C dau^2 /	DF ziq^8	DF * muci^4	C kung^1.	踏上席头席尾空
214. fG + Cen^3,	E$^{\flat}$FGC * cen^3./						
fD Nyien^2	C...G waa^6	FE$^{\flat}$DC sing^1-	FDC sing^1 /	D daai^2	AG yiem^3	A + diu^3,	人語哆哼素飲酒
A Duq^7	DFG gor^5	DC meng^2	C dau^2 /	A dou^3	dFG * lei^4	C kung^1.	得个名头肚里空
215. fG + Cen^3,	FGF * cen^3./						
fD Haeng^2	C...F hor^6	F zie^5	FDC nyien^2	FA kung^5	GA siou^3	FC + wei^6,	行賀已人空守位
FDC Zou^2	#fC jien^1 /	CF mben^6	A siou^3	A juoq^7	dC * mou^6-	C ding^2.	尉官辦手脚务庭

fG +	fG *					
216.
Cen^3,	cen^3./					

CF	G	e^{b}FDC	DC	dF	AGA	fG +
Jiem^1-	nyiet^7	laang^2	yin^2	yaam^6	jou^3	nzaan^5,

今日退選不失散

FD	CG	F	FDC	FD	G *	C
Yien^4	yuoq^8	fei^5	bin^1 /	nzoi^2	git^7	zing^2.

引若四处脊結情

A Section Singing About the Creation of Heaven and Earth by Fu Hei

205. I am at the wedding feast, trying to get my voice going;
To both ends of the table I am trying to make its sound rise.

206. Holding in my hands the wedding book, and trying to produce something,
I've gotten up my courage here at the table to try to flood your hearts.

207. In the first year of that reign, the flood waters rose,
Rose for seven days and nights until they reached up to heaven.

208. The gourd floated up into heaven,
Banging into Thunder's dwelling, filling his heart with alarm.

209. Thunder sent a message down into the Eastern Sea,
Telling the Dragon King to open the water drains.

210. So the drains were opened in all five parts of the sea,
And as the turtles moved out of the way the waters receded.

211. Since the flood covered the eight corners of the earth,
It drowned everyone; no people were left.

212. The only ones remaining were Fu Hei, the brother and sister,
With no one else under heaven whom they could marry.

213. All you friends, old and young alike, have suffered great inconvenience,
For you have stepped up to a bare table.

214. The call went out to come have a drink,
But you've gotten only the host's reputation—your stomachs are empty.

215. We called you to come, but have left you waiting in your seats;
The cooks have produced only their own busy hands and moving feet.

216. Now the wedding feast before long will end,
So I urge all sides to love each other.

ANALYSIS

Leaving aside for the moment the two *cen*[3] syllables at the beginning of each full line, there are several observations which can be made about the relationship between linguistic tones and musical notes. References to the text will be made by line and syllable number, "a" indicating upper half-lines and "b" lower half-lines. For example, 206:3b will refer to the third syllable of the lower half-line in line 206.

1. The final syllable in every full line, which must have one of the level category tones (1 or 2), ends on the lowest note of the scale: C (do). Since this is a special musical feature required by the genre itself, it is not of further relevance to the the present discussion.

2. The highest linguistic tones occur on the highest musical notes. There do not appear to be any significant functional difference between tones 3 and 7. Both occur on the highest notes: most often on a level A (la) and G (sol) sometimes preceded by an ornamental rising note or glide, or followed by an ornamental falling note or glide (e.g., 206:1a, 2a, 6a, and 2b; 209:6b; 211:7a and 2b).[9]

3. Likewise, the lowest linguistic tones occur on the lowest musical notes. Again, there does not appear to be any significant difference between tones 6 and 8, though six exceptions out of 31 occurrences have been noted. Tones 6 and 8 typically occur on the note C (do), sometimes followed by an ornamental rising glide (e.g., 206:7a, 1b, and 3b; 208:4a, 7a, and 6b).

4. The two linguistically simple contour tones, 2 (falling) and 5 (rising), occur, respectively, either on the same type of falling and rising musical glides or on low and mid/high notes, the end points of downward and upward glides. As with the previous tones mentioned above, they sometimes have additional ornamental notes. In this case the ornaments sometimes go in the opposite direction from the primary glide; for example, for tone 2 see 205:3a, 4a, and 2b; 208:1a, 2a, 1b, 3b, and 4b; 214:1a, 5a, 3b, and 4b. For tone 5 see 205:2a, 5a, 7a, and 5b; 207:4b and 5b; 211:1a and 1b.

5. Tone 4 has a linguistic low rising-falling contour. In music it loses the final fall, occurring with rising or mid pitches, similar to those of tone 5 but distinguished from 5 by most often starting a bit lower, on D (re) rather than on F. For example, see 205:4b; 208:2b; 211:2a; 212:5b; 213:5a and 6b; 214:6b.

6. The musical pitches on tone 1 are very similar to those on tone 2, primarily mid or low falling glides. On the one hand, this is surprising and highly irregular since linguistic tone 1 has a mid or mid-high level pitch, whereas tone 2 has a mid to low falling pitch. On the other hand, in the vernacular language tones 1 and 2 have very similar pitches when the intonation of both yes/no and information (WH-)

questions falls on them (Purnell 1965). Both 1 and 2 have a falling pitch in yes/no questions and a mid rising pitch in information questions. Even there, however, they can be distinguished. In the former type, there is a difference according to whether the breath pressure is toward the beginning of the contour (tone 2) or toward the end (tone 1). In the latter type, tone 1 has a simple mid rise, whereas tone 2 has a slight fall before the mid rise.

Based on this similar-but-different relationship between tones 1 and 2 in question intonation, the musical pitches will be distinguished by taking the first part of the tone 1 pitch as its basic note(s) and the second part of tone 2 as its basic note(s). That is, notes at the middle of the scale, F (fa) or the rare E-flat (mi-flat), which occur at the beginning of the musical pitch will be taken as basic for tone 1. This statement covers 21 of the 25 occurrences of tone 1. As for tone 2, notes at the lower end of the musical scale, D (re) and C (do), will be taken as basic. In fact, all but one of the 34 occurrences of tone 2 end on either D or C. Thus, although both tones 1 and 2 occur primarily on falling glides in this wedding song, the starting note of the glide will be taken as basic for tone 1, and the ending note of the same type of glide will be taken as basic for tone 2.

7. To return to the two lead-in syllables, both of which have tone 3, it is clear that the first occurrence of *cen*[3] maintains its linguistic tone since it occurs on the notes A or G, both of which are appropriate to that tone. The second *cen*[3], on the other hand, begins lower in pitch and often rises slightly before falling. Since, as was mentioned above, these two syllables carry in compressed form the musical pattern of an entire metrical line, in which the upper half-line ends in an ascending glide (+) and the lower half-line ends in a descending glide (*), it can be seen that the first of the lead-in syllables maintains its basic tone before the upward glide, whereas the second syllable is modified as the singer prepares for or actually begins the downward glide.

CONCLUSION

This paper began with the claim that in Iu Mien songs there is a definite and regular relationship between linguistic tones and melodic notes. By looking at the lexical pitches on which syllables occur in a twelve-line wedding text and comparing them to the musical pitches on which those same syllables occur when the text is sung it was shown that to a great extent there is clear and systematic correspondence between the two.

There are exceptions, of course. Although most of these are beyond the scope of this paper, tentative explanations can be offered for at least some. First, tone 7, a high tone which nearly always occurs on high notes (G or A), is found on a low note, C, in 212:3a. However, tone 7 here is followed by a hyphen which indicates that in normal speech it undergoes tone change and becomes phonetically tone 8.[10] Since tone 8 normally occurs on a low musical note, this seeming exception actually follows a regular phonological pattern.

But tone change rules will not always provide such a ready explanation. For example, in 208:5a, tone 1 undergoes tone change, becoming phonetically tone 2, and it thus has one of the musical pitches characteristic of tone 2:C. However, in 208:5b, where tone 1 also undergoes tone change, it maintains a mid-high level musical pitch: F. Perhaps a lexical tone change can be disregarded under pressure from the musical requirements.

Another exception which might be explained is in 205:6b where tone 1 again undergoes tone change to tone 2. This is reflected in the music as a low downward glide: DC. However, the direction of the glide changes from downward to upward and thus the whole pitch movement is DCF. Why should the glide shift upward? A possible explanation is that the singer wanted to get into position for the long descending glide which occurs in every lower half-line between syllables 6 and 7. While entirely plausible in this instance, the explanation does not account for the low pitch on tone 1 in 207:6b or in 210:6b. A similar situation seems to hold for tone 6. In 208:6b, the pitch terminates in a rise to F perhaps in order to anticipate the coming descending glide, but in 215:6b there is no such rise.

Although, as shown above, there is a definite relationship between linguistic tones and the musical notes they occur on, the whole process of producing and performing a song is an art form and thus is characterized not only by regularity but also by individuality, creativity, and variation. One must undoubtedly recognize "melodic license," departures from the usual or expected correspondences of tones and notes in order to produce a certain melodic effect or to resolve a musical or poetic problem. Some departures from the norm might be explained by an investigator, but others might make sense only because they intuitively "feel right" to the singer at that particular moment in the performance. This lack of consistent fit between tones and music has been examined, for example, by Catlin (1982, 1986) for Hmong, by List (1961) and Mendenhall (1975) for Thai, by Yung (1983a) for Cantonese, and by Chao (1956) for several types of Chinese.

As mentioned at the beginning, this paper is only one part of a larger study of Iu Mien song texts and vocal performance which is still in progress. A large piece of the picture which was ignored here in order to simplify the discussion but which will need to be taken into consideration in a more complete analysis is the inventory, placement, and function of the "padding syllables" which often occur between the full syllables of a poetic line.[11] Do these extra vocalisms provide a way to bridge the competing needs of lexical tones and melodic pitch, or are they simply vocalic embellishments which are not really integrated into either the poetic or the musical structure?

There are several other questions of interest for further research. First, does the particular syntactic grouping of syllables (1-2, 3-4, 5-6-7) in the upper and lower half-lines exert an influence on melodic pitch comparable to that exerted on the linguistic tone sequences preferred in the metrical structure (Purnell 1989)? Second, is it possible, even with the correspondence between tones and melodic pitches, to detect an overall (though perhaps abstract and not totally consistent) pattern of higher and lower musical notes, such that one could speak of a general melody which is found in one form or another in every line of a particular song? Third, are there identifiable musical figures, formulae, or chunks which can be considered the structural blocks by means of which melodies are produced and manipulated within the rather limited number of recognized secular song categories? Fourth, to what extent can the analysis of the cen^3 song presented in this paper be extended to cover not only other wedding songs but also songs in the other two major secular performance categories which use the literary language, doq^8 and $baau^5$? And finally, what range of variation is found in a particular song when performed by the same singer on different occasions or by different singers of both sexes (Catlin 1982:176–177)?

The present paper has attempted to take the first steps toward dealing with these and other questions by providing evidence of the basic relationship between linguistic tones and musical pitch. Obviously much more remains to be done in order to better understand this rich area of Iu Mien culture.

APPENDIX 1

IU MIEN WEDDING SONG

(Transcription by Guangming Li)

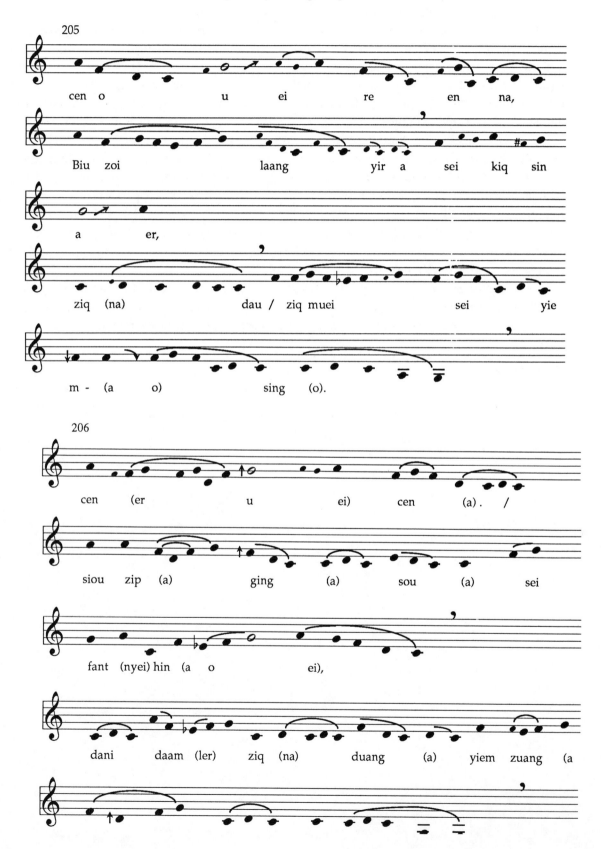

211

cen (o u ei), cen (a). /

Yiem zien (a) tin (o) ding (a) / bet (nyei)

gorg (o),

Yiem fei (yei) baam (ma) gen / mou (m) aan (o)

nyien (na).

212

cen (o a). cen (a). /

Zong liou fug - hei (a) liang zei mui (a u

ur),

Tin njie (zei) mou (lo) nyien (a) zei gap (o er)

cien (lo)

213

cen   (o   u),   cen   (a). /

Laau   luoq   yiet   ziu   (a)   lo   you /   biu   (o   o

ur),

Ndap   zang   (a)   ziq   (lo)   dau /   ziq   muei   (o   er)

kung   (er).

214

cen   (o   a)   cen   (a). /

Nyien   waa   (wei)   sing -   (a)   sing   (a) /   daai   yiem

(nyei)   diu   (la   o),

Duq   gor   (zei)   meng   (a)   dau /   dau   lei   (o   er)

kung   (lo).

215

cen   (o   a),   cen   (a). /

Haeng hor   zie nyien   (da)   kung siou wei   (ler   u

Zou   (na)   jien /   mben siou   (ler u) juoq   mou   (o)

ding   (o)

216

cen   (o),   cen   (a). /

Jiem - nyiet   (a)   laang   yin   (a) yin   Jiem - nyiet

(a)   laang   yin   (a)   yaam   jou   nzaan (o   er)

Yien   yuog   fei (na)   bin /   nzoi   git   (o)

zing   (o).

NOTES

1. This paper is a revised version of that originally presented at the 23rd International Conference on Sino-Tibetan Languages and Linguistics in Arlington, Texas, in October, 1990. I am grateful for funding by the Ford Foundation Indochina Studies Program (1972–1975) and the National Endowment for the Humanities Summer Stipend (1984).

2. Some scholars now refer to the Miao-Yao family as Hmong-Mien after the native terms of the two most prominent members. For an extensive classification of the Miao-Yao (or Hmong-Mien) languages, see Strecker 1987.

3. For a description of the main features of Chinese Old Style poetry and how it differs from Recent Style (or Regulated Verse), see Stimson 1976.

4. A full presentation of Iu Mien phonology can be found in Purnell 1965. The "unified" or standard practical orthography used in China and Western countries, along with a review of the phonology, is described in Purnell 1987.

5. For a detailed examination of the Iu Mien metrical system, see Purnell 1989 and 1991.

6. In older, more formal poetry in which there is a quatrain structure (four half-lines), however, the tone of 7a in the first full line may also be from the level category.

7. The song used here is taken from a wedding book which is the property of Mr. Fou Vang Tang, formerly of Laos and now living in Oakland, California, who also sang all the songs in the book and made extensive comments on their meaning. Work on the character text, Romanized transcription, and English translation of the entire book is currently in progress.

8. I am indebted to Mr. Guangming Li, a doctoral student in ethnomusicology at the University of California at Los Angeles, for a transcription of the music. The interpretations and analysis of his notation, however, are my responsibility.

9. It is interesting that the musical/metrical evidence independently supports the combining of linguistic pitch 7 (occurring on syllables having final stops) with pitch 3 into the same tone phoneme, indicated as -v in the standard orthography which uses certain consonants at the ends of words to mark tones. Theoretically at least, pitch 7 could have been combined with pitch 1 (both are high and level) or even with pitch 5 which ends high, but 3 and 7 are both oblique category tones for metrical purposes (1 is a level category tone) and both occur on the same musical notes. Similar evidence can be used for the combining of the low linguistic pitches, 8 and 6, into the same tone phoneme. Those who devised the various orthographies proposed for the Iu Mien (see Purnell 1987 for a survey) appear to have been unaware of this supporting evidence.

10. Tone change in the Thailand/Laos dialect of Iu Mien is described briefly in Purnell 1965.

11. See Yung 1983b for a discussion of padding syllables in Cantonese opera. Purnell 1990 discusses those found in Iu Mien songs.

REFERENCES CITED

Catlin, A. R.
1982   "Speech Surrogate Systems of the Hmong: From Singing Voices to Talking Reeds."
In *The Hmong in the West: Observations and Reports*, ed. B. Downey and D. P.
Olney, 170–197. Minneapolis: The University of Minnesota Southeast Asian
Refugee Studies Project.

1986   "The Hmong and Their Music: A Critique of Pure Speech." In *Hmong Art: Tradition
and Change*. Sheboygan, Wisconsin: John Michael Kohler Arts Center.

Chao, Y. R.
1956.   "Tone, Intonation, Singsong, Chanting, Recitative, Tonal Composition, and Atonal
Composition in Chinese." In *For Roman Jakobson,.* ed. M. Halle. The Hague:
Mouton.

Downer, G. B. and A. C. Graham.
1963   "Tone Patterns in Chinese Poetry." *Bulletin of the School of Oriental and African
Studies* 26/1:145–148.

List, G.
1961.   "Speech Melody and Song Melody in Central Thailand." *Ethnomusicology* 5/1:16–32.

Mendenhall, S. T.
1975   Interaction of Linguistic and Musical Tone in Thai Song. *Selected Reports in
Ethnomusicology* 2/2: 17–23.

Purnell, H. C.
1965   *Phonology of a Yao Dialect*. Hartford, Connecticut: Hartford Seminary Foundation.

1987   "Developing Practical Orthographies for the Iu Mien (Yao), 1932-1986: A Case
Study." *Linguistics of the Tibéto-Burman Area* 10/2: 128–141.

1989   "Tone and Meter in Iu Mien Yao Poetry." Paper read at the 22nd International
Conference on Sino-Tibetan Languages and Linguistics, Honolulu.

1990   "Observations on Padding Syllables in Iu Mien Song Texts." Paper read at the 23rd
International Conference on Sino-Tibetan Languages and Linguistics, Arlington, Texas.

1991   "The Metrical Structure of Yiu Mien Secular Songs." In *The Yao of South China:
Recent International Studies,* edited by J. Lemoine and C. Chen, 369–398. Paris:
Pangu, Editions de l'A.F.E.Y.

Stimson, H. M.
1976   *Fifty-five T'ang Poems*. New Haven, CT: Far Eastern Publications.

Strecker, D.
1987   "The Hmong-Mien Languages." *Linguistics of the Tibeto-Burman Area* 10/2: 1–11.

Yung, B.
   1983a   "Creative Process in Cantonese Opera I: The Role of Linguistic Tones."
            Ethnomusicology 27/1: 29–47.

   1983b   "Creative Process in Cantonese Opera III: The Role of Padding Syllables."
            Ethnomusicology 27/3: 439–456.

KHMER CLASSICAL DANCE: PERFORMANCE RITES OF THE GODDESS IN THE CONTEXT OF A FEMININE MYTHOLOGY

Paul Cravath

Today in both East and West a significant reexamination of traditional gender roles has brought a new refulgence to the timeless images of the Great Goddess archetype. In the search for new compatibility between male and female, the essential nature of the feminine principle has become both a touchstone of awareness and a fundamental source of empowerment. One important model of goddess veneration available to such contemporary scrutiny is the living tradition of Cambodian classical court dance performance which embodies numerous images of feminine potency. The following discussion of female figures appearing either in Cambodian mythology or in the repertoire of Khmer dance will collectively reveal four protean images of the feminine: the Goddess as primordial consort, the Goddess as beneficent warrior, the Goddess as contested wife, and the Goddess as celestial dancer. This survey will conclude with a brief examination of the Khmer dancer's ritual function within the traditional performance and social context.

The Goddess as primordial consort

Given the preponderance of the oral tradition over the written in Southeast Asia generally, textual documentation of early Khmer mythology or performance is extremely limited. The image with which we are first concerned is that of the half-human, half-earth spirit consort of an eminent man. Its earliest appearance in the area of Cambodia is in a Sanskrit inscription from Champa dated A.D. 657 recounting an origin myth associated with the city of Bhavapura.

> Kauṇḍinya, foremost of the brāhmaṇs of this city, planted the javelin that he had received from the eminent *brāhmaṇa* Aśvāttaman, son of Droṇa. There was a daughter of the king of the Nāgas . . . who founded on the earth the race which carried the name of Soma; having adopted this state, remarkable thing, she lived in a human dwelling. The foremost of the Manis named Kauṇḍinya married her for the accomplishment of the rites. (Finot 1904:923)

This legend of a *nāgī* ancestress is widespread in both mainland and island Southeast Asia as well as in parts of India (Przyluski 1925:265). In this case her name, Soma, establishes an identification with the moon. As daughter of the subterranean *nāga* king, her serpent form is that of an earth spirit, and her marriage to a human priestly figure is the archetypal "sacred marriage" from which so many races trace their mythic origins.

This serpent spirit, certainly vital for centuries prior to the establishment of the Angkor kingdom in A.D. 802, maintained a powerful position at Angkor. In 1296, Zhōu Dáguān, an envoy from the Mongol emperor Timur Khan, wrote that in the Royal Palace of the great city of Angkor

> there is a gold tower at the top of which the king sleeps. All the natives claim that there is a spirit in the tower, a serpent with nine heads, which is the master of the soil of the whole kingdom. It appears every night in the form of a woman. It is with this spirit that the king first sleeps and unites himself. . . . If one night the spirit of this serpent does not appear, then the moment of the king's death has come. If the king fails to come a single night, some disaster is inevitable. (Zhōu 1902:12)

The total welfare of the kingdom was dependent upon this ritual union between its preeminent male and an androgynous serpent—a figure associated throughout much of Southeast Asia with agricultural rites to assure an abundant rainfall. Indeed, this deification of earth energy is held to be the fundamental principle in the prehistoric "religion of monsoon Asia" (Mus 1933:374).

A protohistorical legend provides a more detailed view of the same figure and is still included in the Khmer dance repertoire as the story of Neang Neak (Lady Serpent) and Preah Thong. According to an oral tradition recorded in eighteenth-century Cambodian chronicles, Preah Thong was the son of a north Indian king who was banished and came to the area of Cambodia where he drove out the Cham ruler prior to his courtship of the beautiful daughter of the king of the nāga, Neang Neak.[1] Following a grand marriage, the nāga king manifested a kingdom for his son-in-law by drinking the waters covering a vast area on which he then created houses and a palace. This kingdom took the new name of Kambuja, and Preah Thong was the first Khmer king (Moura 1883:9–10).

Another version of the Preah Thong–Neang Neak legend says that growing in the area where Preah Tong landed was a "wonderful Talok tree."

> He ascends its branches to look about him, but the tree grows . . . and he fears he shall never see his mother earth again. In descending, however, he finds himself in a wonderful grotto in the hollow of a tree, where he meets with the dragon king's daughter, and marries her. (Fergusson 1971:50–51)

The most popular variation, and the one performed in the dance drama, tells of Preah Thong's excursion after conquering the Cham king, when he found himself on a sand dune of recent alluvion surrounded by the rising tide on "a day of the full moon in the month of *visākh*."

> The daughter of the underworld king, with a suite of a hundred nāgī, slit open the earth and came into the world of men. Swimming from island to island, she arrived with her following at a larger island isolated in the sea which is the one where Preah Thong and his court found themselves. Then, because destiny wanted the nāgī to marry Preah Thong, they all fell asleep, except him. The nāgī and her followers transformed themselves into human beings, forming a royal procession. Preah Thong heard their rustling, saw the woman in the moonlight, approached them. . . . They made each other's acquaintance and Preah Thong asked for her hand. She replied that she must first ask the consent of her father. (Porée-Maspero 1950:242–43)

The nāga king consented and the elaborate marriage was celebrated.[2]

After some time the new nāgī wife gave birth, surprisingly, to an egg. Furious, the king ordered that it be buried in the sand west of Angkor. The ambassador from Sukhothai of the kingdom of Bangkok, coming to offer the annual tribute for the Cambodian king's birthday, found the egg and took it back with him to Bangkok where it eventually became Phra Ruang, the legendary Thai king. Having given birth to the egg, the queen desired to return to the kingdom of her father, but her husband begged her to stay.

> Ashamed and homesick, the queen went to bed. The king returned to her chamber and saw with horror a serpent on the bed. He retreated, ran into the door, and his blood spurted out on the ground. At the commotion, the queen woke up, hastened to take the king in her arms, asked him what had happened and then assured him that it was not to amuse herself that she took her serpent form again but rather that she was in a deep sleep. (Porée-Maspero 1950:243–44)

In the dance drama, the events subsequent to the marriage are not performed.

Neang Neak's association with both earth and water, with a magical tree, the moon, and a serpent body, with the birth of a special son, and with the origin of the land itself are the distinguishing features of her image as primordial consort.[3] From the contemporary, psychoanalytic point of view, however, the greatest significance of this figure who enjoyed neither motherhood nor life in the human palace—longing instead to return to her simpler, earthy, "hidden" form—lies in the possibility that her serpent form represents the human unconscious, a representation substantiated by an early Buddhist text which says that while nāga appear to be human, "their serpent nature manifests itself on two occasions, namely, during sexual intercourse and in sleep" (Vogel 1926:3). Indeed, as in the myth of the Angkor king and the earth serpent, the story of Neang Neak seems to suggest that it is through communion with the unconscious that man will flourish.

A final image of the Goddess as primordial consort is found in the single most popular dramatic dance in the Khmer repertoire, the story of Sovann Machha. Her form is a variant of the half-serpent motif since she is "Queen of the Fish," and the dancer portraying her wears a large, highly ornamented fish tail suspended on her hips. While she is seductive and benign, Sovann Machha is also identified with a more fierce or wrathful aspect of the Goddess because she is said to be the daughter of the demon Rāb, analogue to the Sanskrit Rāvaṇa.[4]

The episode usually performed on the Khmer stage depicts the seduction of Sovann Machha by Rām's white monkey general Hanumān in order to stop her from dismantling the causeway he is building to Lanka for the purpose of rescuing Sitā. As fast as Hanumān's monkeys lay the stones, Sovann Machha's fish remove them to the shore. The monkey king finally turns from force of arms to arms of force, and Sovann Machha eventually yields to his seduction (Fig. 1). Ironically, however, even then the wishes of the Goddess prevail and her own interests are served, at least temporarily, because while Hanumān is sexually involved, no bridge building occurs.

The Goddess as beneficent warrior

The element of conflict in the Goddess-consort relationship is the predominant feature of a second Khmer image of the Feminine, the Goddess as warrior. The oldest text to characterize this aspect dates from the third century A.D., 600 years prior to the establishment of Angkor, and was composed by Kāng Tài, an envoy from the Chinese court of Emperor Wú (222–252) to Fúnán, a kingdom in Southeast Asia occupying territory in the area of present-day Cambodia. Kāng Tài's *Wú shī wài guó chuán* (*Account of Foreign Countries*), no longer extant, was the probable source for all subsequent Chinese historians' commentary on early Fúnán. Kāng Tài reported that

> at Fúnán's beginning, a woman served as ruler. Her name was Liǔ Yè. In the country of Mō Fū was a man named Hùn Tián who served the spirit with all his heart, unceasingly. He dreamed about a bow and was instructed to load a boat with merchants and set out to sea. The next morning Hùn Tián went to the temple and found a divine bow under an old sacred tree. He loaded a large boat. The spirits ordered the winds to turn and blow him to Fúnán. Liǔ Yè wanted to rob him so he picked up the bow and shot it, penetrating her boat. He had safe passage through and she fearfully submitted. Thereupon, he arrived at Fúnán. (Lǐ Fǎng 1963: j347, 1599)

In a later version "Hùn Kuǐ" only raised the bow without shooting it and when "Yè Liǔ" became afraid and surrendered, "he took her as his wife and occupied the country" (Fáng 1974: j97, 2547).

In the *Nān Qí shū*, or *History of the Southern Qí* (479–501) compiled in the sixth century, Hùn Tián from the country of Jī—following his dream and departure—met Liǔ Yè who had collected her soldiers to resist him. Hùn Tián shot an arrow through her boat, hitting one person. She surrendered in fear, and Hùn Tián made her his wife. To cover her nudity, he folded cloth and passed it over her head (Xiāo Zixiǎn 1936:j58, 1014).

Finally, the *Liáng shū*, or *History of the Liáng* (502–556) records that Liǔ Yè was young and strong, resembling a man. Hùn Tián from the "bordering country" to the south came to Fúnán as in the other accounts, whereupon Liǔ Yè's people saw his boat and planned to rob him. "He picked up his bow, shot an arrow through the side of her boat striking one person, and fearfully she surrendered with all her soldiers. Hùn Tián instructed her to cover herself. He ruled the country, married her and had posterity including seven sons" (Yáo Sīlián 1936:j54, 4).

The female figure in this origin myth has strong affinities with the Goddess as primordial consort because in light of her meeting with Hùn Tián surrounded by water, Liǔ Yè is an echo of the androgynous underworld nāgī, despite the absence of a serpent form. Liǔ Yè is also associated with a mystical tree since her name appears to be the Chinese inscription of a word for coconut (Christie 1970:8). To bear the name of a tree—capable of self-reproduction, having both male and female organs—adds a further dimension to the image of her androgyny.[5] Like the nāgī Somā she also marries a man of spiritual accomplishment.

Here the similarities end, however, because the marriage of Liǔ Yè was clearly accomplished under duress, and it is that fundamental conflict between male and female, however mutually dependent they may be, which defines the Goddess as warrior-like in her independence. While the outlines of Liǔ Yè are vague, her essential nature takes powerful dramatic form in one of the most popular stories in the Khmer dance drama repertoire—the archetypal conflict between Mani Mekhalā, "Goddess of the Waters," and Ream Eyso, the Storm-Spirit.

Figure 1. Sovann Machha and Hanumān, performed in the Royal Palace, Phnom Penh ca. 1937.
Photo: Musée Economique

Mani Mekhalā, holding in her hand a glittering crystal ball, emerges from her Kingdom of the Sea to go and pay her respects to Preah Vorachhun, "King of the Divinities" who entreats her in vain to give him the jewel. The giant Ream Eyso, dazzled by the flash of the magnificent jewel which he has attempted to wrest from her since "the beginning of time," now appears and engages and defeats Vorachhun in battle. When Ream Eyso now pursues Mekhalā, beseeching the Goddess to give him her magic attribute, his honeyed words (chanted by the accompanying chorus) are met with mockery (Fig. 2). He rushes at her in a rage, brandishing his magic axe, but Mekhalā merely tosses her crystal in the air and, blinded by the dazzling light which emanates from it, Ream Eyso collapses on the ground. Time and again he picks himself up for a new assault but finally must retreat with threats of future vengeance.

Khmers say that Mekhala's ball represents the lightning and the falling axe of Ream Eyso the thunder, with rain the result of their timeless conflict. On the mythological level, however, the crystal ball symbolizes the moon. The belief that the moon is the source of all fecundity is very widespread and for traditional Cambodians the moon literally caused the rain, fertilized the rice fields, and was responsible for all growth (Porée-Maspero and Bernard-Thierry 1962:263). Significantly Mekhalā leaves behind the earthly waters where she and Vorachhun perform the "Dance of the Makara," a mythical creature, half-fish, half-snake. With her ascent into the sky she becomes the Moon/Warrior, an elemental force.

Figure 2. Mani Mekhala and Ream Eyso.
Photo: Colin Grafton

Mekhalā's nature conforms to a fundamental image of the Goddess in world mythology. Whether in Europe, Asia, or the Americas,

> the Moon Goddess belongs to a matriarchal, not to a patriarchal system. She is not related to any god as wife or "counterpart." She is her own mistress, virgin, one-in-herself. The characteristics of these great and powerful goddesses do not mirror those of any of the male gods, nor do they represent the feminine counterpart of characteristics originally male. Their histories are independent and their functions, their insights, and their rites belong to themselves alone, for they represent the essence of the feminine in its sharpest contrast to the essence of masculinity. (Harding 1971:123–24)

In Liŭ Yĕ's loss of power to Hŭn Tián we see the demise of matriarchy, but in Mekhalā's unrelenting maintenance of the dynamic tension between female and male, with nothing taken for granted between them, we experience an image of the Goddess from whose pure beneficence all life emanates.

The Goddess as contested wife

As noted previously, the oldest Khmer myths concern the union of a female-male pair of progenitors. The contemporary repertoire of the dance drama adds pair after pair of characters to this list. Beneath the refined veneer of their stories and in the almost domestic, though always royal settings, the Khmer court dance repertoire dramatizes the eternal struggle for control of the feminine (Cravath 1985:289–343). This struggle exists on two levels—the realistic and the archetypal.

On the realistic level the struggle concerns the timeless, painful passing of the female from father to husband. The hero-husband requires magic power and help from animal energies to wrest his beloved from her father, who is in most instances in Cambodia a *yakkha,* or ogre. The yakkha does not represent evil but rather the older order with an incestuous aspect. This can be seen clearly in the prototypical struggle between Rām and Rāb for possession of Sitā since many versions of the Rām story, including Tibetan, Khotanese, Indonesian, Malay, Thai, and Lao claim that Sitā, like Sovann Machha, is the daughter of Rāb and, hence, a yakkha princess (Sachhidanand 1971:220).

On the archetypal level, however, Sitā maintains a more profound identity, as attested by numerous claims to her parentage. In the Cambodian *Rāmker,* the Cambodian story of Rām, Sitā "the white" is not born but, rather, is taken from the water of a river where she reposed in an open lotus floating on a golden raft. In other versions of the epic Sita is born from a plow furrow and is the daughter of the earth. At the end of the *Rāmker,* in an accommodation to her past conflicts with Rām, and unique to the Cambodian form of the epic, Sitā returns to the world of the nāga while Rām remains on the earth. More than likely, then, Sitā is a Sanskritized form of the ancient mythologems of the nāgī Somā and Neang Neak. In the latter case, this possibility is further supported by a legend in neighboring Laos that Sitā—not unlike Neang Neak—was born from a tree (Sachhidanand 1971:221).

What becomes apparent in this view of Sitā is not only her great value as the perfectly devoted wife, but also as the incarnation of the water and land, the control of which Rāb, the father, refuses to relinquish. Since it is by the action of the male upon the female that fertility is achieved—in the face of all opposition—Rām must retrieve his wife in order to attain fertility in a new generation. To do so he utilizes his own instinctive self in the form of Hanumān and eventually triumphs, regaining Sitā as the symbolic source of fertility, the land, and its people. This three-way struggle of hero-heroine-yakkha, or husband-daughter-father, is universally recurrent, and is the purest form of the Goddess who in Cambodian myth is who ends the contest between father and husband by resolving in her mind any confusion she may harbor as to their mutually exclusive roles.

The Goddess as celestial dancer

The fourth and final aspect of the Goddess is mentioned only briefly in classical epigraphy, but her image is proliferated in the thousands of dancers and myriad bas-reliefs from the Angkor period; this is the form of the *apsaras* or celestial dancers. An incomplete tenth-century Khmer inscription has been interpreted as reporting that "the origin of the kings of Cambodia goes back to the union of the hermit Kambu Svāyambhuva . . . with the celestial nymph Mera" (Coèdes 1968:66). In Angkorean mythology the apsaras were the sole fruit of the churning of the ocean by the gods and ogres using an enormous nāga to rotate a mountain as pestle. The mountain represents the king and ancestral power; the nāga represents earth energies. At the turbulent point of their union—where the hard rock of the masculine most stimulated the primordial ocean of the feminine—infinite hosts of apsaras dancers emerged, like the Greek goddess Aphrodite, from the foam.

Since the king of Angkor was maintained in the center of enormous man-made reservoirs from which all water for a great area was dispersed, and since the long nāga balustrades which bridged this "ocean" were symbolically churning the entire kingdom, Angkor may be viewed as a vast, generative *mandala*, an architectural metaphor of the process whereby earth energies are transmuted into both a refined spiritual consciousness and general prosperity. Thus, the apsaras leave all chthonic forms behind and represent the supreme symbol of transcendance in Khmer mythology.

While this image appears on stage in numerous pure dance pieces of the Khmer repertoire, the single "Apsara Dance" is considered its most perfect embodiment (Fig. 3). The chorus chants the words of the dancers entering the stage with slow, restrained movement. They have descended to earth to gather flowers in a garden to make a garland for their queen. They are dressed in gold and white and move with exquisite grace; by their presence the dancers transform the world into a garden in which they are themselves the fairest flowers.

On the mundane level the apsaras represent the welfare of the kingdom; until 1970 royal dancers were an important adjunct of the Cambodian kings' potency. Their ritual function in that context has received only limited documentation, but, in brief, the all-female troupe functioned as a national offering to the spirit world, particularly to invoke the rains by a royal ceremony known as *buong suong* (Cravath 1986:195–99). Seven "sacred dances" including the story of Mani Mekhalā, Vorachhun, and Ream Eyso could be performed in a ritual context to end drought or other calamitous circumstances within the kingdom.

Figure 3. Dance of the Apsaras.
Photo: Colin Grafton

In the sense that a rite is any ceremonial action to invoke and embody the presence or assistance of divinity, the most important traditional rite performed by the royal dancers was, thus, rain-making. A second rite was the channeling of the Goddess' fertilizing power to the earth, achieved mystically through sexual union with the king; historically, the royal dancers—who lived exclusively within the confines of the palace—fulfilled the function of a harem. A third rite was the making of offerings which included not only flora and fauna placed on well-tended altars, but the dance performance as well. Above all, the dancers themselves were an offering since their lives were consecrated to the dance. Their continual cultivation of beauty and ornamentation was a daily rite whereby they made themselves fitting vessels for the manifestation of the apsaras.

When speaking of the apsaras' dance as a rite of the Goddess, we see the highest function which dance can fulfill, namely the embodiment of wisdom. In the apsaras we move beyond the aspects of the Goddess discussed earlier—the self-indulgent usury of the female and male in competition; the aloof, self-contained, all-powerful image of the Goddess as bestower of life, or even the "perfect" woman in harmony with man as daughter, wife, and mother. Rather we sense in the apsaras' dance not only the internal psychic balance of the feminine with the masculine, but also a profound transcendence of all life's dualities. Watching the apsaras we feel somehow able to put aside all that is distracting and, in a meditative moment of hypnotic beauty, experience the dancer's inner stillness as profound harmony within our own mind and world.

The relevance of the Khmer mythologems of the Great Goddess archetype thus examined may be seen not only on the psychoanalytic plane as a series of gender role models, or on the purely aesthetic plane as meditation in motion, but also on the physical/metaphysical planes as guides to the protection of the earth itself. With Sovann Machha, "Queen of the Fish," we see that when man's construction on the earth is opposed, new life emerges from the conflict. With Mani Mekhalā, "Goddess of the Waters," we see that when man's desire to control the Goddess is thwarted, perpetual balance and creative tension result. Finally, with the apsaras we see that when the earth is treated as a garden, this human dwelling becomes sanctified by the presence of celestial divinity dancing therein. It is to this harmonious and productive dance of life on earth that the Goddess directs our attention in her timeless appearance on the Khmer stage.

NOTES

1. This legend was obtained by Moura from a manuscript of the royal annals prepared for him by King Norodom.

2. Porée-Maspero credits the source of this tale as Document 40008 in collections of the Commission des Moeurs et Coutumes au Cambodge.

3. It is worth noting that these features, for the most part, coincide with those of better-known goddesses from the ancient near East, Greece and elsewhere as delineated in such studies as Harding's (1971), Robert Briffault's *The Mothers* (New York: MacMillan, 1927), and Mircea Eliade's *The Myth of the Eternal Return* (Princeton: Princeton University Press, 1971).

4. In fact, the story of Sovann Machha does not appear in the Sanskrit Ramayana epic and her paternity appears to be an instance of late Sanskritization of a much older indigenous myth.

5. Christie's persuasive argument for "coconut" rejects earlier translations of the name as "willow leaf," a tree unknown in Southeast Asia. When the masculine quality of the Khmer goddesss became differentiated in the form either of husband or *nāgarāja* father, the androgynous coconut, both milk containing and phallic, was replaced in later myths by the more leafy and feminine *thlok* (often "talok") tree in which the feminine serpent (e.g., Neang Neak) resided.

REFERENCES CITED

Christie, Anthony
    1970   "The Provenance and Chronology of Early Indian Cultural Influences in South East Asia." In *R. C. Majumdar Felicitation Volume*, edited by H. B. Sarkar, 1–14. Calcutta: Firma K. L. Mukhopadhyay.

Coèdes, George
    1968   *The Indianized States of Southeast Asia*. Translated by Susan Brown Cowing. Honolulu: East-West Center Press. (Originally published 1944).

Cravath, Paul
    1985   "Earth in Flower: An Historical and Descriptive Study of the Classical Dance Drama of Cambodia." Ph.d. diss., University of Hawaii.

    1986   "The Ritual Origins of the Classical Dance Drama of Cambodia." *Asian Theatre Journal* 3/2 (Fall):179-203.

Fáng Xüánlíng, ed.
    1974   *Xìn shū*. Beijing: China Book Store.

Fergusson, James
    1971   *Tree and Serpent Worship*. Delhi: Oriental. (Originally published 1868).

Finot, Louis
    1904   "Les inscriptions de Mi-son." *Bulletin de l'École Française d'Extrême-Orient* 4:897–977.

Harding, M. Esther
    1971   *Women's Mysteries*. New York: Putnam.

Lǐ Fǎng, ed.
    1963   *Tài píng yù lǎn*. vol. 3. Beijing: China Book Store.

Moura, J.
    1883   *Le royaume du Cambodge*. vol. 2. Paris: Leroux.

Mus, Paul
    1933   "L'Inde vue de l'est: Cultes indiens et indigenes au Champa." *Bulletin de l'École Française d'Extrême-Orient* 33(1):367–410.

Pascalis, Claude
　　1931　　"Maṇimekhalā en Indochine." *Revue des Arts Asiatique* 71(2):81–92.

Porée-Maspero, Eveline
　　1950　　"Nouvelle étude sur la Nāgī Soma." *Journal Asiatique* 233(2):237-67.

Porée-Maspero, Eveline, and Solange Bernard-Thierry
　　1962　　"La lune, croyances, et rites du Cambodge." In *La lune, mythes et rites*, 261–87. Paris: Editions du Seuil.

Przyluski, Jean
　　1925　　"La princesse à l'odeur de poisson et la Nāgī dans les traditions de l'Asie orientale." In *Études asiatiques* 2, 265–84. Paris: G. Van Oest.

Sachhidanand Sahai
　　1971　　"Study of the Sources of the Lao Ramayana Tradition." *Bulletin des amis du royaume Lao* 6:219–32.

Vogel, Jean Phillippe
　　1972　　*Indian Serpent-lore.* Varanasi: Prithivi Prakashan. (Originally published 1926).

Xiāo Zīxiǎn, ed.
　　1972　　*Nán Qí shū.* Beijing: China Book Store.

Yáo Sīlián, ed.
　　1936　　*Liáng shū.* Shanghai: China Book Store.

Zhōu Dáguān
　　1902　　"Memoires sur les coutumes du Cambodge de Tcheou Ta-kouan." Translated by Paul Pelliot. *Bulletin de l'École Française d'Extrême-Orient* 2:123–77. (Originally published 1297).

MUNI MEKHALA:

THE MAGIC MOMENT IN KHMER COURT DANCE

Chan Moly Sam

Like other traditional arts, Khmer court dance has been trasmitted orally from master to student. A lifetime of training from early youth in a strict disciplinary milieu and a close relationship between master and student ensure a high standard of dance performance, its authenticity as well as its flow and continuity. Despite the difficulties experienced under different political or cultural contexts, there is an enormous effort and consciousness to keep the high standards of our forbears by the Khmer of all generations everywhere. The focus of this article is on the *Muni Mekhala* dance. The dance movement and its rhythmic pattern will be treated as magic in textual analysis. The ritual part of the dance in general will be considered as context, but the emphasis will be on *Muni Mekhala*.

Dance and dancer played an important role in the animistic cult of the indigenous Khmer people. Early Khmer music and dance functioned prominently in the ritual of animistic cults to ensure harmony, fertility of the soil, and prosperity for the country. Although he did not mention dancers, Pelliot (1903:303) noted that one of the earliest Chinese records tells of a group of musicians sent as a present from the Khmer king of Founan to the Chinese emperor in the year A.D. 243. From at least the sixth century onward, dance and dancer came to be associated with temple services, a tradition which eventually spread throughout the kingdom whenever temples were consecrated. Epigraphic studies of early inscriptions verify that dancers, musicians, narrators, and clowns were listed along with sacred objects as necessary to the maintenance of each temple.

The Angkor Era (802–1432) marked the zenith of Khmer civilization in which the arts—music and dance, among others—were highly developed. Inscriptions from the reign of King Jayavarman VII refer to a total of 1,622 dancers at Angkor. Thierry (1963) suggested that these dancers were identified hierarchically, a first order group of "sacred dancers" being assigned to the priests and performing in a strictly religious function and a second order being assigned to the public and performing in a less sacred, more entertainment-oriented function. Thierry surmised that the sacred dancers and the court dancers were not interchangeable and played different roles. The sacred dancers would have performed in the temple sanctuary where the *linga* phallus was installed as a symbol of the divine kingship and its creative power, the power that was endowed by the king through the mediating link of ancestral spirits to his own ascetic practices. Through the sacred dance and dancers, the god-king placated the celestial powers in order to ensure the safety and glory of his subjects. The sacred dancers secured the perfect harmony between the supernatural and natural forces and symbolized the welfare of the empire. According to Cravath (1986:199) the evidence suggests that dance was associated with funeral rites, with large bronze drums, with ancestor worship involving sacred stones, with a fertility cult, and with a pattern of kingship enabling communication with the ancestor-spirit realm in order to assure sufficient rain for earth's fertility.

If our ancestors had high regard for dancers as votive objects and as a medium for worship, then the whole complex of movement, gesture, posture, choreography, and soul was a source of interaction with the natural and supernatural forces. The sacred dancers of Angkor certainly bore forth this concept. Through ritual chanting and praying the temple dancers created heaven on earth, making direct contact with the spirit world and thus becoming themselves *apsaras*, the celestial dancers who were depicted in great plenitude on the exterior temple walls of Angkor.

The temple dance tradition subsequently vanished following the downfall of the golden era of Angkor, while the Khmer court dance maintained its continuity until early 1970. It was known as the *lakhon preah reach trorp* (theater belonging to the royal family) until March 18, 1970, when the monarchy was overthrown by the republicans. Under the new administration this dance form was called *robam kbach boran Khmer* (Khmer traditional dance). Despite the political upheaval during the past decade or so, Khmer court dance has managed to maintain and retain its status and form, although several aspects in the dance have been changed to suit the political situations of the country. Royal terms, titles, and some characters have been changed—e.g., princes to men, princesses to women, gods to people. It is important to note that the new political context gives no importance to dance as a function in the ritual context and as a result dance plays no role in it. Instead, efforts toward the cultural and artistic preservation center on secular contexts. And while many dance schools and dance companies have been established, the court dance tradition is principally preserved at the University of Fine Arts.

KHMER DANCE TRADITION AND ITS CONTINUITY

Kbach is literally translated as "design." Kbach may have been derived from the verb *kach* which means "to break" or "to pluck." Kbach may also describe the dance metaphorically as a breaking of stems (bending of limbs) and plucking of flowers (formation of hands) to create a floral arrangement (a standardized dance posture) (Lok Kru, personal communication, 1989). However, in the dance context, *kbach roam* is used as the configuration of hands, feet, and head that form a standardized posture. *Roam* is a verb which means "to dance" and in this case it signifies the dance movement, posture, and gesture. Kbach roam is used to differentiate it from kbach the architectural term. In addition to meaning a specific dance posture in its static attitude, it also indicates a dance movement that sequentially and rhythmically involves locomotion as a dynamic in swimming, flying, strolling, drifting, and so on. On the other hand, it could refer to any independent unit, for example, a hand gesture or a foot position, both of which are used in either a static or dynamic fashion. In the traditional teaching method which, in place of verbal instructions uses body contact to shape the apprentices' bodies and limbs to form a specific posture, it was common for the dance master to simply call out a name identifying a gesture or a posture, like *lear, stuoy*, etc., omitting the prefix *kbach*.

Kbach came to be known for its ornamental and geometrical features that characterized a foliage motif. It is important to note that in the dance structure, kbach that are geometric or ornamental become expressive. Among eight basic hand gestures, five are of foliage motifs; namely *lear* (leaf), *chip* (flower), *khuong* (fruit), *chang-oll* (the index pointing) and *bogna* (flower in cluster). However, the group of three—flower, leaf, and fruit—form a core of the dance repertory. Importantly, when adding five foot positions to the first group of hand gestures, hundreds of kbach, the "mother of postures," or the dance alphabet, originated. This dance alphabet is technically a pure dance, containing a geometrical composition. Nevertheless, a kbach is denotative or decorative based on the context used.

In Khmer choreography, there are many kbach which are treated in three essential groups:

1a.   Symbolic: An abstract form which can only be understood through song texts.
1b.   Realistic: An expressive and dramatic form which can immediately be recognizable due to its human behavior.
2.   Kbach that are set to musical repertory.
3.   Transitional: A connective kbach is an important form which is richly treated in accordance with the song texts. It serves to fill the music and to bridge other kbach (Sam 1987:93–94).

A dance choreography, or "text," has a built-in set structure that changes the dance alphabet (or ornament) within the musical accompaniment context into a dance statement created to suit the narrative song text within the dramatic context. The change, however, is made possible through the theatrical conventions that shape things according to tradition. The conventionalized method is used to build a theatrical idiom, achieved with the use of gestural kinesphere idioms and movement articulation.

The concept of multi-level presentations of a kbach includes vertical and horizontal planes which are divided into three locations: high, medium, and low in relation to the dancer's body. On the vertical plane, the high level is between the head and shoulders, medium ranges between the sternum and the chin and abdomen, and low level varies from the abdomen to pelvic area. The horizontal plane, however, ranges from the point of the sternum with hands in the body center, then opens up halfway to fully stretch out like wings. Within this framework, the change from one plane to the next also changes the meanings and ideas. The high level is used to express ideas concerning gods, supremacy, prosperity, etc., whereas the low plane signifies just the opposite. For instance, the double leaf placed across the chest signifies "love," whereas "grief" is at the lower abdominal area. Another example is the double flower which means "glory" or "the sparkle" when rising up from the sternum to open at the chin or facial area, but "separation and destruction" or "death" when the movement opens out from the abdominal or lower body part.

It is interesting to note that this gestural orientation essentially and symbolically replicates a basic principle of Khmer social behavior. That is to say, good is conventionally conferred a high spatial position and bad is given low spatial orientation.

On the other hand, the way in which a hand articulates with a rotation of the wrist from clockwise to counterclockwise can effect a change in meaning as well. A *lear*, the "leaf" position, drawn inward to the dancer's body to form a flower motif, indicates the action of calling "come in here." In contrast, reversing from *chip* back to *lear* means "leaving" or "going."

TEXTUAL ANALYSIS OF MUNI MEKHALA DANCE [1]

This dance is acclaimed as one of the most ancient and the most sacred for its characteristic essence and is fundamental to the Khmer court dance tradition. The characters can be portrayed by only the highest calibre performers who possess not only high technical skills but also physical beauty and a profound mental attitude, attributes which are the unique traits of the *Muni Mekhala* dance. It contains elaborately intricate dance sequences combining the melodrama between good and evil and, at times, a humor that is appreciated by royalty and commoners alike.

It was a very rewarding and moving experience for me to have had the opportunity to learn the Muni Mekhala dance with dance master Chea Samy in 1970. In this technical context, as a text, I choose the kbach diev presentation with its significance varying from flying to the celestial walk. Characteristic of this dance is the inclusion of many kbach diev, as does the *Suvann Machha* dance which we shall examine later.

Kbach diev or kbach hah

Foot positions and their movements primarily function ornamentally in completing the plastic harmony of a kbach, as well as providing variations and timekeeping in the general dance context.

Among the five foot positions, the *diev* position is preeminent, the prototype of the flying posture. Bending either foot backward high up, its heel almost touches the waist while the other foot remains on the ground. In fact, another variation is executed directly low, right on the ground in a kneeling position reminiscent of the apsara's original flying posture as carved on the wall of many temples centuries ago. Like other goddesses and celestial dancers, Apsara and Muni Mekhala strike this pose; Muni Mekhala's variation is to hold the powerful gem in her right hand. However, in the dramatic performing context, *diev* conventionally illustrated an imaginary entrance and exit from one dimension to another, from heaven to earth. In the dance context Muni Mekhala flies from the underworld, her oceanic palace, through the earth and up to the sky. Both the earthbound and the skybound aspects are demonstrated through an analysis of a spatial and temporal orientation.

Prior to the demonstration, it is necessary to look briefly at all three components—music, singing, and dance—and how they work holistically together, such that the whole is more than the sum of its parts.

The *pinn peat* ensemble accompanies the dance and the choir uses a poetic text to sing, explaining the situation, the feelings of the character, and the plot in the manner of a song-narration. There are hundreds of musical and singing tunes, each employed for distinctive situations such as weeping, fighting, or procession to suit the story. Whereas the singing tunes express all the basic human emotions, the dancer remains silent, visually making use of dance kbach and miming the sung text in the language of dance. The kbach are strung together in such a way that they illustrate the storyline, but they are choreographically prescribed, based primarily on the dictates of the narrative poetic text.

The continuous melody constitutes a free-flowing motion that influentially and intrinsically establishes the fluidity of movement of the dancer's body. This body movement in space is in perfect harmony with the musical tune suggesting timelessness, but the punctuation stressed by the *sampho* (small barrel drum) and the *chhing* (small cymbals) or the *krapp* (bamboo clappers) signals the ending or opening of each new kbach. In effect, each stroke of the *sampho* or *chhing* changes the shape of the dancer's body in space from one configuration to the next. For instance, from the body's center the head tilts horizontally, the head and body sway or glide to draw a subtle figure eight or a circle in response to the rhythm of the *sampho* or *chhing*, as does the articulated hand movement when stretched or flexed.

Pulsation is the key element serving to lock a dance kbach in place upon its completion by descending. The ascending motion is to let go or release an old kbach in order to reform a new one. Timekeeping is the function primarily of the foot, though the arm, too, flexed and stretched through the arch of the elbow, articulates rhythmically. The knee is flexed deeply and is extended in full standing position. Foot tapping is an important cue in dramatic expression to signify the take-off; more generally, it simply precedes lifting the foot to achieve any posture. In addition, footwork also carves a ground plan like the hands do in space. In place, the dancer faces the audience from either the left or right side. In locomotion, elaborately carved circles or spirals are used to shift from center to the front or back, or to the right and left again.

KBACH ROAM AND ITS MAGIC MOMENT: POSITION IN SPACE

For comparative purposes, I have chosen as models three dance performances of varying duration presented by master dancers of three generations. Two are videotape recordings produced in the 1970s and 1980s and the last is a motion picture produced in the 1960s.

The focus of the discussion centers on the *kbach diev* and *kbach hah* in the Muni Mekhala dance context.[2] I pick up the story at the commencement of the dance/mime when Muni Mekhala dresses up, after which she holds her crystal ball and takes her leave to the sky to pay homage to the gods and goddesses.

Description: At the center stage, upstage, a *kre* (bed) symbolizing Muni Mekhala's oceanic palace is set up. After the end of her toilette, there is a two-second pause. Poet Text of Narrative Chant (in slow tempo):

Ke kâ
(Rising)

kann kaev
(holding the crystal ball)

ritthi krai
(very powerful)

srey thlai
(the dear woman)

char chenh
(leaves)

chak vimean.
(the palace)

Frame one:	On the kre (bed) facing the audience, Muni Mekhala dances. In standing position, feet together, both hands are placed at the right side of the waist, to signify waiting.
Singing	(*chhrieng reay* in narration fashion): *Ke kâ* ("The Goddess").
Music:	Only sampho tapping continuous pulse tip, tip, tip, tip. Kbach: Corresponding to the word "the goddess"; she strikes a diev posture, shifting her body to the left.
Foot:	Shifting the left foot sideways with the whole body, tap right foot, then bending up to achieve kbach diev.
Left Hand:	Extending out to the back in chip motif, resting directly on the sole of the bending right foot.
Right Hand:	Folding in an angle in lear motif, placing it at the body center.
Head and Torso:	Tilting to the right as one whole unit, looking possibly in the same direction—right to the audience.
Dancing:	In this static kbach hah, the movement of lowering down is done on one foot, gently descending in very slow motion. Harmoniously, the rippling voice of the lead singer and the tapping sound of the sampho creates a sense of timelessness, setting the feeling and mind of the dancer and the audience in a new dimension. The landing is achieved when she sits on the *kre* and it becomes breathtakingly imaginable that the goddess possesses the magic power to fly down to earth with greatly sumptuous grace.
Singing:	*Kann kaev* ("Holding the crystal ball").
Dancing:	Lowering diev in slow motion, more than halfway.
Music:	Continuous sampho pulse: tip, tip, tip, tip. Upon the touchdown, she picks up and holds her crystal ball with her right hand.
Singing:	*Ritthi krai* ("Very powerful").
Dancing:	Holding up to head level, corner of the eye. Looking proudly at her attribute, the jewel. Left hand bent in lear, placed at the body's center. Alternating from right bent foot to the left.
Music:	The same pattern.
Singing:	*Srey thlai* ("The dearest woman").

Dancing:	Remaining at this posture, both hands from the body's center assume chip., raising, opening up like a flower blossom. This is done by drawing both hands simultaneously in a circle in a complete lear in the gesture, ascending, and then descending to lock in this posture. The head draws a subtle figure eight.
Singing:	*Char chenh* ("Leaves").
Dancing:	This gesture indicates the symbolic opening of the palace door, achieved from a closed or "circle" position, then opening both down, in withdrawal gesture, while the body is about to turn. From the early latest posture diev in sitting at left.
Singing:	*Chak* ("From the palace").
Dancing:	Change movement (kbach) from left, turning to the right hand side.
Foot:	Bring the left foot from diev side by side, with the right bending foot, weight shifting. Initiated by the right bent knee, turning to the right hand side, with all the weight on the right leg, then bring the left leg forward, diagonally to the right knee. With all the weight on the left leg, the right foot bends into diev.
Hands:	While making turn, both arms turn slightly the direction of the body movement. Energetically, the body movement sways as if drawing a half circle in space, and the ground plan is carved into a half circle as well.
Head and Torso:	Move in one unit in concert with the body movement.
Singing:	*Vimean* (pause) ("Palace").
Music:	Up to the word "palace" (sampho sounding a strong loud stroke—tip).
Dancing:	The kbach diev and hand position are compelled with a punctuation of ascending and descending to lock the posture in place—static.
Head:	Tilt to the right with the body. Look to the extended left arm. Right arm bent in an angle placed at the head—corner of the eye.

At this sequence, the energy charging technique is rather exciting in rhythmic pattern, singing, and dance action. The left hand uses two opposite motions, extending and flexing. This unique convention, performed in place, represents and functions as energy charging prior to take-off and is used mainly by gods and goddesses. The rhythm established by such a precise pattern sets a time passage, rendering a moment of magic cut from its normal context. The dancer's upward movements through space mark spatial change and the formation of kbach in which the passage of time projects three different dimensions: the underworld (ocean), earth, and sky-heaven.

Out of its context the kbach diev is a decorative element, but in the new context its transformation into the magic position of "flying" is achieved. This is done precisely, however, within the temporal orientation of the musical framework. It is explained vocally through the poetic text in which the melodious voice is significant in setting the perfect harmony.

From the *stuoy veng* in the diev attitude, the goddess is poised and gay, flying among the clouds in an imaginary sky. Simultaneously, the musical tune of Choeut Chhing picks up at the last word indicating *"vimean."*

PLAN I
Singing: *"Ke kâ"* (The Goddess)
Music: Sampho - tip
                Chhing - chhing
Dance: Right foot - diev
                Right and left hands/arms - flexed

PLAN II
Singing: *"Kann kaev"* (Holding the crystal ball)
Music: Sampho - tip
                Chhing - chhepp
Dance: Right foot - diev
                Left hand/arm - extended
                Right hand/arm - flexed

PLAN III
Singing: *"Ritthi krai"* (Very powerful)
Music: Sampho - tip,tip
                Chhing - chhing, chhepp
Dance: Right foot - diev
                Right hand/arm - extended
                Left hand/arm - flexed

PLAN IV
Singing: *"Srey thlai"* (The dearest woman)
Music: Sampho - tip
                Chhing - chhing
Dance: Foot - diev, then bring right knee together with left knee
                Right hand/arm - flexed
                Left hand/arm - move up a little fast within one beat

PLAN V
Singing: *"Char chenh chak vimean"* (Leaving the palace)
Music: Sampho - tip, tip, tip
                Chhing - chhepp, chhing, chhepp
Dance: Left foot - slowly bring left foot up to kneeling on one knee position, and bring the
                whole body into standing diev (right leg in diev position)
                Right hand/arm - flexed
                Left hand/arm - move up (like Plan VI)

PLAN VI
End of Music
Dance: Left foot - on the floor
                         Right foot - flexed
                         Left hand/arm - extended
                         Right hand/arm - flexed

The celestial walk

Another hallmark of the Muni Mekhala dance is the celestial walk. In her journey to meet with the other gods and goddesses in heaven, Muni Mekhala makes use of this dance sequence, the spatial kbach, with the music Cheut Chhoeung. Again in the diev motif, she walks gracefully and celestially. Performing in place, the dancer operates in superbly slow motion, in which she switches horizontally from side to side. This directional change could suggest the winding walkway that calls for the change from one kbach to the next in relation to these course changes. Each change from one kbach to the next is done at each side. Turning is marked by the rhythmic change delivered by the cue of the sampho stroke. In this way, the indication of such an arranged passage explicitly symbolizes the celestial walk. The melody of the Cheut Chhoeung tune provides such feeling, and exhibits a smooth and continual flow, free enough to allow maximum time for the character to best perform each kbach.

Kbach diev as drifting in the Suvann Machha Dance context: The mermaid

The following section examines the contextual change that adds a new meaning to the same basic text kbach. In this case, the text changes from flying in the Muni Mekhala dance to the drifting in the Suvann Machha dance. These two dance sections bear the same technical features in kbach and music. Only the dance costume and Muni Mekhala's crystal ball differentiate these two excerpts. It is possible that to the Khmer these two elements of air and water are compatible energy sources.

Therefore the kbach of the two dances, which represent Muni Mekhala's flying and Suvann Machha's drifting, are interchangeable. In practice, the music, Cheut Chhoeung, and the kbach have several variations in kbach which are designed specifically for each character and the situation that is to be highlighted in the story. The hallmark of the Suvann Machha dance is this kbach signifying drifting which highlights the mermaid's essential characteristic (Figure 4). Again, only a leading dancer would be chosen to portray this role.

Despite the passage of time, kbach roam have been preserved virtually intact. Many of the *kbach* are direct copies of the positions that are immortally carved in stone on the temple walls, providing an inexhaustible source of knowledge for the Khmer over the past ten centuries. Over time, a high degree of refinement may be achieved by the dedicated dancer, but above and beyond this technical world another new dimension of spirituality is important in attaining the totality of performance. Only through this manifestation of the spiritual characteristic in performance do *kbach diev* texts become *kbach hah* or flying movements with an aura of divinity. This aspect of performance is what transforms the dancer into a goddess with the power to fly.

THE MYTH OF MONI MEKHALA

Once upon a time, there was a ghost named Ream Eyso and a witch named Mekhala. Both of them had served a magical and powerful hermit in order to learn magic spells. Both pupils were bright and talented and each had worked very hard to please their teacher, who also loved his pupils equally. After he had taught them all the subjects, he wanted to test them to find out who was smarter, saying, "Whichever of you can bring me the first glassful of morning dew, I will make that dew into a *kaev monorea* (magic crystal ball) and with the possession of that ball the owner can have everything he or she wishes."

Ream Eyso took a glass to gather the dew which hangs on leaves and grass. He patiently did this every morning with no good result. Mekhala, who knew how to think better, took an inner part of a branch which was like a sponge to absorb the dew on the leaves and grass until it was fully soaked. Then she squeezed it into the glass and gave it to the hermit. The hermit then created a crystal ball and gave it to Mekhala, telling her, "This crystal ball is very powerful. If you have a wish, you simply toss the ball and at once your wish will come true. Moreover, this crystal ball can make you fly." Mekhala got the crystal ball, tossed it, and flew into the sky.

Ream Eyso, after much patience, brought a glassful of dew and handed it to the hermit. The hermit then told Ream Eyso, "You bring this dew to me too late. I have already given the crystal ball to Mekhala and I can perform the magic to make the crystal ball only once." Upon hearing the bad news Ream Eyso was very upset and wept. The hermit then consoled him by saying, "Don't worry! I will give you an axe. With this axe you can go and fight with Mekhala to get the crystal ball from her. When it rains, Mekhala likes to fly in the sky and take a rain shower. So, when it rains, you throw this axe at her; then she will throw that crystal ball. But during the antagonism, when you see her toss the crystal ball, you must close your eyes before you throw the axe."

After taking the axe, Ream Eyso looked for Mekhala in an attempt to possess the kaev monorea. But when Mekhala saw Ream Eyso, she anticipated bad deeds from him, tossed the crystal ball, and flew away up high into the sky. Seeing the glitter of the crystal ball, Ream Eyso closed his eyes and then threw his weapon. The weapon flew extremely fast, with an enormous sound and noise, but did not hit Mekhala. Ever since, when it rains, there is lightning and thunder as the result of the everlasting antagonism between Ream Eyso and Mekhala. (Sam 1988:250–251)

Myth as oral tradition

In the *Preah Chonuok*-based legend, Muni Mekhala appears as the goddess of water, or the Water Guardian. Like other goddesses, Muni Mekhala had the power to fly. Her role was to rescue good people from drowning. After a shipwreck the surviving Preah Chonuok met with the Water Guardian Muni Mekhala. After his boat and his men's lives were lost in the middle of the ocean, her powerful possession was the crystal ball, given to her after the completion of her study with the hermit. This jewel was her life-protective weapon to be used in life threatening situations. Its glitter would cause her opponent temporary blindness, or allow her to escape to safety.

Ritual dance and context

The explanation of the myth of the Muni Mekhala and Ream Eyso dance originates in the indigenous Khmer society's practices centered on agriculture in which men and women took part.

> An alternative explanation might emphasize magico—religious means by which women gain and maintain title to control. For example, women might gain power and authority in societies where maternity was viewed as a sacred or magic function. (Sanday 1974: 203-204)

This may have occured in early agricultural communities where there was frequently an association between maternity and fertility of the soil. In the context of this value system, Muni Mekhala represents this dichotomous view clearly symbolized by vitally multiple roles as the water guardian, guardian of life and her personal attribute—the magic crystal ball. This precious attribute in its original form was a result of the combination of the collective dew and the magic formula created and given to her by the hermit. On the other hand, the magic axe came as a second attribute, and both the first and last derived from the same common origin given to Ream Eyso by the same hermit the teacher. According to Mrs. Chea Samy, the hermit teacher loved both apprentices equally, but since Muni Mekhala gave him the dew first, and because she was female, the crystal ball was made especially for her. As for Ream Eyso, who came last with the dew collection and was male, it was appropriate that he received the magic axe (personal communication, 1989).

The symbolism and meaning of ritual objects in the Muni Mekhala Dance

The following are various representations of the meaning and symbolic rendering in the ritual dance objects, the crystal ball and axe. In the aforementioned process of power-making and its origin, explained in the myth, these two objects come from common derivatives. From the dew or water which is natural, and the magic formula which is acquired, the two powerful attributes are brought into existence. Nonetheless, the objects' key symbol and ritual ideology vary not only in form and power but also in gender property; that is, objectively, they serve and fulfill specific functions and missions. First, the crystal ball is endowed with such power that when maneuvered its glitter causes blurriness to others. Apparently it is made from the concentrated dew symbolizing water, and combined with the feminine provides dual life-giving and life-sustaining functions. In contrast to the life-giving power, the axe comes as a second award from the dew-collecting contest, representing the masculine. Consequently, death will result when struck by it. However, the symbolic function of life and its meaningful value seems to suit the pattern of agrarian society, where subsistance is based on water, which is viewed as a powerful and influential energy source. At one level, from an agrarian society's traditional point of view, it reflects the important role of men and women. It is clear, however, that men and axes go together. With that implement, they clear the forest to prepare soil for planting, while, women role care for and nurture the crops. Here, we see two separate functions, one a life-destroying and the other a life-giving or life-regenerating force.

As a female, the goddess Muni Mekhala's role is related to matriarchal notions of the guardian of the ocean and the guardian of life. She is the guardian of the magic crystal ball (kaev) symbolizing rain as fertility, in which it is the powerful source of life as well as life-sustenance. Ream Eyso is a male ogre armed with his magic axe—the agricultural tool representing life destruction and sterility. The central point in the dance illustrates power and power acquisition. The male ogre's attempt to track down the fertility charm in order to acquire its potent power leads to a celestial fray. Only through interaction is the tension created, producing lightning and thunder, which results in rainfall as a release. The thunderstorm pouring upon the earth to nourish the crops is analogous to the release of sexual tension. Out of this opposition it significantly features a complementary aspect of polarity—the good and bad, fertility and sterility. Although the ogre is physically ugly, evil, and psychically hideous, he has the potential of being good in that he produces good things, as exemplified in the dance, because of his interplay with goodness and beauty when he creates rainfall. In brief, the goddess' magic and sacred function, coupled with her attribute expressed in the ritual dance, is the corporeal notion of women's role in the matriarchal world.

MEKHALA DANCE AS FERTILITY

As discussed earlier, the function and intention of presenting dances is important, but that is the demonstration of a purely conceptual idea and belief. Therefore, it is of particular interest here, to further examine the ritual symbols and meaning in the dance itself as the expression of physical transformation. It is important to bear in mind that the dances seen today preserve as much of the true originality in their form as their content. Despite the fact that some of their meanings may have been forgotten and that minor reconstruction has been necessary, due in part to the oral transmission process over generations, certain characteristics such as the floor pattern, to a great extent, remained intact, said Mrs. Chea Samy (personal communication, 1989). Through close examination of the ancient dances that are characteristic of the planting culture, we find a number of them that are closely related to the modern Khmer court dance, the floor pattern, for instance. Among others, the zigzag and the circular are two specific floor patterns found. Both the Muni Mekhala and Suvann Machha dances contained these two types of patterns which depict the chase and pursuit of opposite sexes. This occurs when the demon (male) is trying to catch the goddess, and Hanuman also tries to do the same to the mermaid, but she dodges, creating the sequential dance movement called zigzag. Under Sachs' classification of fertility dances, he described dances as rain charms (1937:114).

One of Sachs' examples was the scooping motion of water executed by women, then later on, he remarked: "But there is a new crossing in the scooping motif: the conception of religious fertility power in the chaste maiden" (ibid.). Elsewhere he provided another example: "In the rain charm of Mallorca, the Ball de la Xisterna, the girl skips backwards in zigzag from the mountain" (ibid.: 152). Relating to the circular pattern despite its diverse interpretive meanings, it is relevant to the ritual dance context of Muni Mekhala. Sachs again explained the circle with its center as a hole or pit in the earth, where in early form there was a fireplace, and then later on, without a fire it becomes round. Then in the predominantly feminine cultures with leanings toward the matriarchal the pit in the ground is given a clearly defined magical significance as a symbol of the generating bosom of the fruit-bearing earth itself (ibid.:146).

This courtship dance episode, Hanuman (white monkey) chases the mermaid and following behind her closely, they dance in a circular pattern. In the chase and persuit theme, Ream Eyso and Muni Mekhala engage in an interplaying act. They dance while exchanging places in opposite direction to form a round three-circle floor pattern. The song text explains: "They are encircling the zodiac."

The last phase underscores the emergence of the Muni Mekhala Dance. A certain power is presumably drawn from it, and because of that power this Muni Mekhala Dance is considered sacred. However, it is important to keep in mind that the dance's aim is to obtain rain when rain is needed, and so we learn that the crystal ball's symbolism is life-giving water—rain, that is desired by the demon in the myth. In this last phase the only focus is the crystal ball, the fertility charm. This kaev is still held firm in the goddess' right hand, and for the first time the long-wanted jewel is just within the demon's reach. Therefore, the dance passage is the focal point to determine the synthesis of the ritual ending in the myth, and resolution in the rainfall symbolically produced in the dance. The hand manipulation of this kaev as a ritual object becomes a dominant symbol in the entire dance, involving the use of spatial and temporal effects.

As the two dancers move from stage right to stage left hemisphere and vice versa, the movement of the goddess' hand holding the crystal ball lures the demon. Most important conceptually, these four lures connote forces of the cardinal points, so that the forces of high and low terrestrial and celestial alike are to be summoned to manifest their power. Positioned in place at this time, right at the center stage, the touchdown enfolds. Focusing on the kaev manipulation motion three times, a slash then crosses his face, instantaneously flinging up into the air, and the kaev releases its glitter signifying the symbolic release of power—rainfall—and simultaneously the demon's collapse. Mookerjee wrote: "As crystallized products of invisible rays, gems have the magnetic power to transmit cosmic rays through space, and in this way, they are on a par with the planets. Gems are regarded as reservoirs of energy concentrated from cosmic rays" (1977:120).

THE MANIPULATION OF THE RITUAL OBJECT "GEM" AND THE MAGIC MOMENT

The action of shooting the gem into the air conjures magic and power. However, it is essential to view all aspects in the dance and its symbolism, in order to give meaning to the entire picture.

Power is charged into the crystal ball, and the densely accumulated cloud is analogous to the built-in tension in the dance. When the right moment arrives, the shooting action commences right in the center of the dance stage. When the *kaev* is flung up into an upright position high in the sky, suggesting the piercing action of breaking up a cloud, the gem releases its powerful forces, causing rainfall. Meanwhile, this power also brings the demon's downfall. This collapse parallels the rainfall that pours high from the sky down to the earth, and the shooting of the kaev low from the earth into the air is just the opposite. The sky-earth presentation is viewed as the magic position in space and the releasing of tension in the dance is seen as the cloud-breaking in which the rainfall reckons with the magic moment.

In conclusion, though the mythic narrative has no resolution, we know for certain that despite the conflict and life threats both the adversaries and their magic attributes are safe from destruction. The endlessness of the myth has far-reaching significance that epitomizes the continuity of life where these two living forces—lightning and thunder—ensure rainfall for the annual, or seasonal cycle of plant life. Rainfall is vital as a life-supporting function, and this sacred dance is believed to fulfill the fertility function by imploring for rain. In brief, the Muni Mekhala Dance is the fertility dance that is meant to go on for an eternity, as long as there is life.

PERFORMANCE CONTEXT

From the Sihanouk period onward, Khmer court dance increasingly gained widespread popularity through frequent international touring and nationwide performances. For that reason, the old practice of an all-night dance drama has undergone curtailment to merely two hours for a stage performance. New choreographed dances are also constrained to last from five to ten minutes maximum. While expanding on this secular performing context as a tool for political campaigns to gain foreign attention, the tradition of ritual practice is perpetuated. Even in modern times, under the king's orders, astrologers determine the day and hour auspicious for certain rites and ritual dances to be initiated, on which the welfare of the country depend. For both contexts, secular and ritual alike, the same dance repertory normally serves. However, despite accommodations to a modernized context that to a certain extent involved modification, specific changes in characteristics of the rituals are kept to the minimum.

MAKEUP APPLICATION AND MASK

Prior to Sihanouk dancers wore white powder on exposed areas like arms, feet, and face. Eyes and eyebrows were blackened with lampblack mixed with oil, and the dye from Chinese red paper was used to tint the lips, according to master dancer Mam Kany (personal communication, 1987). A wide range of characters in the myths and legends, all except the demon and monkey, had white painted faces. Masks worn by the demon and monkey were composed of elaborate patterns, and were rich in colored designs and specific attributes accompanied by fangs for the giant and teeth for the monkey. Whether a real dancing mask or a chalk-white application, both contained meaning, amplifying a spiritual dimension. However, at the stage when the makeup was being applied, it symbolically signified the transformation process from profane to sacred dancer and to the character in the myth, whom she was to embody.[3] Sisowath's dance company touring in France maintained traditional makeup. Prince Sihanouk's dancers used, in contrast, the conventional cosmetic products of the present, but masks were maintained for demonstration roles only.

The modern dancers' access to cosmetic products may in a way seeming to materialize the spiritual nature of the dance. Nonetheless, it is the principle of ideal beauty that consciously governs the disciplined dance technique. The court dance tradition demands that the dancer's face should remain neutral and that the emotion and expression are to be conveyed by the hands. The passive attribute gives the impression of projecting a mask-wearing effect, where oftentimes a subtle smile may appear as enigmatic. Mara put it: "Undisturbed by dancer's ego, the audience can meditate on the beauty of the line" (1953:52).

Dance has been extolled as a sacred offering expressed in the royal term as *dangvay*. *Dangvay Preah* means the offering for the Buddha. The Buong Suong Dance text demonstrates this context.

Re roam buong suong
(Sway in dancing to pray)

tvay daoy pitt
(truly offer)

dall ang Sorarith
(to King Suramarith)

krup tih ti.
(in all the directions).

In this vein, the dance was directly connected to a sacred location such as the royal palace. In the presence of a statue, in the throne hall wherein dwelled the defunct monarch's power and soul he was manifested as the protector of his kingdom. At the temple courtyard of Angkor Vat, there is another. The shimmering, flickering light of the torches of the past and the electric spotlights of modern times highlighted the legend of Preah Ket Mealea. The legend retold the founding of the Angkor era and its civilization—presumably Jayavarman II in 802 A.D. Other legends and myths, including Buddha's life stories—the *jataka*—were reenacted in dance. In this respect, the ritual performing context established the sacred link that bound the historical past to the present, to open up contact mediated symbolically through the *dangvay robam* (dance offering). The spirit of the ancestor was thus fed and placated and only then, in return for the wish, boons and happiness were granted and insured as a reciprocal gesture. The temple and the royal palace were alike, for they were the divine king's abode, where his soul and power after death rested. Phnom Daun Penh, or the hill of Grandma Penh, marked the axis of the capital city, Phnom Penh, considered, too, as a sacred place for ritual. Frequently, one heard the sound of music dedicated by a worshiper. Each annual performance honored the newly presiding guardian divinity of the year and, of course, the wish that the country would be blessed under his protection. At the east side of the foothill, out in the open, a specially built dance stage was shaded by tall trees, walled by spectators. This was a prominent celebration of the year, in addition to the king's birthday. Originally, on only these two occasions the ritual dance was presented to the general public. It is noteworthy that regardless of the context of the performing location, stage, or space, it is a tradition to begin with a simplified ritual offering of music, incense, and candles to sanctify the area prior to the opening (curtain). Significantly at the time of the performance, all the power of the spiritual teachers (*krou*) is invoked to manifest itself. They are, namely, the holy hermit, the deceased dance master, and also the living ones.

In the Khmer dance performance context, the ritual begins backstage at least three hours prior to curtain. This tradition of preparation is meticulously observed under the dynamic control of the dance masters. Dancers put on ritual gear that are hierarchically composed in elaborate order and design specific to each role, which requires assistance from wardrobe mistresses.[4]

At the same time, the offering of candles, incense sticks, and flowers is conspicuously made in front of the head gear, and dancing masks, along with other objects such as the crystal ball, magic axe, etc. These are all set on a raised platform, apart from the activity. During the last stage, these headdresses will also have to go on the dancer's head, placed by the dance master of that role. It is important to note that the dancer pays high respect to those headdresses. Before, during, and after they go on the dancer's head, they *sampeah* (join both palms in prayer). From this moment on, the dance becomes unified as one with the spirit of the character she portrays, according to the Khmer belief. One by one in hierarchical ranking, the star dancer is, first, to pay respect to her dance master by giving her the offering of five incense sticks and a candle. The dance master receives, and in turn, gives her the blessing. Then the dancer receives it in *sampeah* fashion with great reverence. Then they are ready for the curtain to open. All lengthy preparations create a harmunious environment and mood setting, as if to transform the dancers into the mythical beings of the dance, marking the transition from the exit to the stage.

RITUAL IN PERFORMING CONTEXT

As the candle and incense smoke float up in the air, the ritual time and space is marked outside normal time, as it transforms the bare stage into a new dimension. The first stroke of the sampho regulates the rhythmic tempo, expelling a dynamic flow of energy produced in music and singing, summoning those mythological beings to enter onto their natural habitat, "the stage."

THE CONCEPT AND CHARACTER TRAITS

This abstract feature of Ream Eyso is clearly depicted in the physical feature: the mask. His aggressiveness characterizes his evil quality. These negative qualities constitute the concept of out of order, or out of proportion to the point of exaggeration, as they are represented in the dance through movement, gesture, and posture. In contrast, Muni Mekhala, the goddess, has beauty that shines internally and externally. Her unmasked face and subtle smile are the reflection of her passiveness or good quality, compared to Ream Eyso's mask, which is composed of complex lines, with two fangs, expressing his threatening nature. Therefore, a subtle smile and serenity in passive behavior is the reflection of idealness. Simplicity is beauty, and that beauty comes from harmony; thus harmony grows in proportion. Oftentimes the Khmer compare these artistic qualities to real human quality. For instance, someone who is physically ugly is evil as well. Similarly, walking abruptly and heavily as a giant walks, even gesticulation or temptation, is considered an evil attribute of a demon. The proper human characteristic is "humbleness and modesty."

THE PERFORMANCE STRUCTURE

On the level of cultural understanding, these messages are communicated in the presentation of dance. On stage, two protagonists take their roles which are artistically set into motion. What makes this dance unique is the music and sung melody that is remarkably beautiful and full of dramatic features suited to the situation and progress of the story line. The sound of music and the singing voice had a built-in structural power to invoke, while dance is a medium through which mental images are visually projected. In this sense, the artist creates an artistic product, with its structure that builds on the original internal model—the structure of the human body and spirit.

And it, too, moves the audience, even a non-Khmer viewer. At another level, through the same fundamental units of music, singing, and dancing, a new dimension is created appropriate for the goddess and demon. They are made coexistent in the single and continuous flowing motion of music and dance. From the onset of the sampho's stroke followed by other instruments, to the last stroke of *skor thomm* marking the end of the performance, for the dance involves dramatic expression that is being experienced and continuously absorbed by the audience.

The dance was performed by life-trained dancers, either at the palace, or at the School of Fine Arts, and the high degree of refinement in the dance style was exemplified in the sumptuous costume and jewelry.[5] With little or no knowledge about the dance, the point of dance kbach might at times appear abstract, or simply to make or add ornaments to beautify the dancer. But the dramatic or expressive category of dances are the favorites.

DRAMATIC DANCE EXPRESSION

Expressive gestures, in the mocking situation, are another favorite form of dramatic expression. The crystal ball is held in her right hand while her left hand forms a pointing motif. Both hands are placed in front of his face as close as possible to his eyes. She teases him by twisting her hands. Advancing and stepping towards him, the demon backs off. This is done simultaneously and rhythmically, the singing says, and she jests him.

From this part onward, the audience will find the dance action rather appealing and engaging even without the support from the singing-text explanation., because the action itself is heightened through the continuous build-up until it reaches its climax. Enraged, his footstamping trembling the floor, the demon points to Muni Mekhala's face. Swiftly she turns away and never does she change her attitude or speed. She does this twice. The second time around, like the heart beat racing—motion, but consistently paced, the intensity of the struggle between the two opponents is musically accelerated by the switch to the faster tempo marked in the big drum and sampho.

He threatens her with his axe when she doesn't give him the crystal ball. In this situation, he points to his magic axe, she remains placid, responding in gesture signifying "No, no fear." He raises it high and twirls. The goddess escapes death. The clash sounds when his axe hits the floor, instantly producing a thunderbolt, accentuated by the strong and loud strokes of the big drum. This time, his rage is at its peak, and the story reaches its climax. After the pursuit and escape, they once again meet. He darts at her, but she dodges. At her last round turn, gracefully she exposes her jewel close to his reach.

This dance segment serves to puzzle Ream Eyso, as well as the audience, but not Mekhala; thus, this creates tension. Opposite each other, with his front facing in, and her front facing out to the audience, the precious gem is held in her right hand, extending out to the demon. His right hand is positioned to reach at approximately two inches distance, side to side. First advancing to his side, he retreats. Then she retreats, he advances, in the fashion of giving and taking. At this very moment, the attention is focussed on the crystal ball, that is being lured gracefully up and down. His hand never fails to track it. To the right and back to the left, up and down, lastly right at center again, still up and down. In just a split second, across his face flits one last teasing, and swiftly she flings her jewel into the air. The glitter from the crystal ball turns into lightning that dazzles the opponent's eyes, and instantly causes blurriness. He loses his balance. Muni Mekhala, the goddess, catches the jewel, passive as always in her subtle smile. Meanwhile, Ream Eyso collapses. One last strong blast as he hits the ground, creates a thundering sound. She pauses for a few seconds, looking at the demon, then leaves the scene to proceed on her journey. From the artistic point of view, the releasing of the crystal ball flying high into the air, is done with skill, especially catching it back. This in itself is breath-taking as well as surprising to the audience, causing powerlessness to the demon. From the last resounding to the fading away, the goddess exits, her both hands joined in gratitude to the spirit of her role. This symbolic act is therefore to signify the ritual spiritual exit that transports the mythological drama back to its normal position. The time changes at the end of the dance drama when the curtain closes. That also changes from the living natural habitat back into an empty stage or a dancing platform through the symbolically rhythmic ending of sound, voice, and movement. And backstage, dancers take off their ritual dance dresses, and change into their daily dress. What is left is the happy ending of the ritual dance drama, the feeling of relief on the audience's part that the conflict came to an end, bringing triumph to the goddess. Though these two prevail side by side, the malevolent demon is kept under control of the benevolent goddess according to Buddha's principal law of *karma*.

THE RITUAL END

The ritual dance of Mekhala concludes with a happy ending. The power is acquired from the magic gem when it releases the rainfall. The goddess retrieves her powerful possession for the next time, season, or when her power is needed and the dance will be initiated again. So the union of these two protagonists brings forth power in order to sustain the balance of the cosmic order perpetuating harmony and prosperity in life. Above all, the efficacy of providing a symbolic counteracting phenomenal force is used against threatening situations of supernatural forces like drought or flood.

In this most basic sense, the dance is a ritual offering and a visual sacrifice, in the way in which the dance action is similarly a magical trap to attract and allow the communion and harmony between the power of human forces and the supernatural to achieve good deeds.

Above and beyond the entertaining aspect, Khmer court dance had multiple ritual presentations—the function associated with the court ritual, ceremunies, and other festivities. This function is essentially the tradition that was maintained from the golden age of the Angkor era, which ranged from 802 A.D. to 1432 A.D. until the last decade in 1970. The purpose was to ward off the potential devastation of a catastrophe such as drought, epidemic, or famine. At the foot of the sacred temple hill lies the axis of the capitol city, Phnom Penh, where the ritual dance presentation was to be observed. This important event, however, coincided with the New Year celebration which significantly marked the life renewal cycle from the dry to rainy season. Originally, these dances were ritually intended to ensure the good crops and good life that the new season and year were hoped to bring. In addition, other major occasions are for example: the sovereign's birthday and the inauguration of a new sanctuary. Among the top selections is the Muni Mekhala Dance, one of the crowning masterpieces, which is still performed in Cambodia and elsewhere. Besides its standing reputation as sacred, it is believed to have some sort of magical power to hasten rain. Its technical execution is also what made this a premium dance on which the foundation of Khmer cultural artistry is laid.

In the new socio-political context, the pattern of kingship no longer exists, and thus no performance of the ritual is necessary. The idea and means to achieve prosperity and welfare of the country is no longer dependent upon the invocation of the divine king's power, and that of the supernatural forces, but it is through the idea and means of solidarity.

Art remains part of the Khmer expression and is expressed through a new channel of interpretation. In the most practical sense, the sacred dances expanded cultural horizons in a more egalitarian direction, and were best appreciated and supported for their versatile functions and values at several levels in the new society. Facing this new socio-political context, the art at home is both artistic and economic (Chheng Phon, Colloquium given at the University of Fine Arts, 1988). On the other hand, music and dance are viewed by the refugee camp (along the Thai-Cambodian border) leaders as therapeutic, and only through them can the lost soul and spirit of the Khmer during wartime be restored. Far away from home, in third countries, the attitude toward art preservation is different. In the cultural context, it is equally significant to all Khmer living among other minorities.

In sum, while fitting into various new contexts the same Muni Mekhala Dance text, among others, is still being performed for Khmer people everywhere. Although the dance may have lost its original ritual significance as a fertility dance and is no longer exclusively for the royal court, it has taken on new meaning in the transnational context as the true symbol of the Khmer soul and spirit.

NOTES

1. The entire Muni Mekhala dance described here has been issued on a video entitled "Khmer Court Dance," released by the Khmer Studies Institute, Newington, Connecticut.

2. This flexing and extending of the hand produces the impression of elasticity and is usually followed immediately by a circling in place pivoting before the actual flight, prior to the exit locomotion in the floor pattern as seen in the Apsara and Best Wishes dances.

3. Khmer court dance has been known to be a female tradition, at least since the 19th century. Now the form also includes male dancers to play the monkey roles.

4. The traditional dance costumes are composed of gold or silver and silk materials. The gold jewelries and gears are studded with precious gemstones of diamonds, emeralds, rubies, and sapphires for the star and leading dancers. At present, costumes, jewelries, and gears are made of paper mache, metal sheet, or leather, then decorated with filigrees, beads, sequins, and rhinestones.

5.   Among two or three leading dancers within a generation, only one could carry the principal role of Muni Mekhala, and another top dancer would be selected to portray the Queen Mera in the Apsara Dance.

REFERENCES CITED

Aschenbrenner, Joyce.
    1980   *Katherine Dunham: Reflections on the Social and Political Contexts of Afro-American Dance.* New York: Congress on Research in Dance.

Cravath, Paul
    1986   "The Ritual Origins of the Classical Dance Drama of Cambodia." *Asian Theatre Journal* 3(2):179–203.

Mara
    1953   "For Whom the Bells Tinkle." *Dance Observer,* (April):52–53.

Mookerjee, Ajit, and Madhu Khanna
    1977   *The Tantric Way: Art, Science, Ritual.* London: Thames and Hudson.

Pelliot, Paul
    1903   "Le Fou-nan." *Bulletin de l'Ecole Francaise d'Extrême Orient* 3:248–303.

Redfield, Robert
    1953   *The Primitive World and Its Transformations.* Ithaca: Cornell University Press.

Sachs, Curt
    1937   *World History of the Dance.* New York: W. W. Norton.

Sam, Chan Moly
    1987   *Khmer Court Dance: A Comprehensive Study of Movements, Gestures, and Postures as Applied Techniques.* Newington, CT.: Khmer Studies Institute.

Sam, Sam-Ang
    1988   "The Pin Peat Ensemble: Its History, Music, and Context." Phd diss., Wesleyan University.

Sanday, Peggy
    1974   "Female Status in the Public Domain." In *Woman, Culture, and Society,* ed. Zimbalist Rosaldo and Louise Lamphere, 189–206. Stanford: Stanford University Press.

Spence, Lewis
    1947   *Myth and Ritual in Dance, Game, and Rhyme.* London: Watts.

Spencer, Paul, ed.
    1985   *Society and the Dance.* Cambridge: Cambridge University Press.

Thierry, Solange
    1963   *Les Danses Sacrées.* Paris: Sources Orientales.

Turner, Victor, and Edward Bruner, eds.
    1986   *The Anthropology of Experience.* Urbana: University of Illinois Press.

THE FLOATING MAIDEN IN KHMER SHADOW PLAY:
TEXT, CONTEXT, AND PERFORMANCE

Sam-Ang Sam

This article will consider the performance genre of Khmer shadow play and within it the text called "Reamker," the Khmer version of the Ramayana, and in particular, the excerpt known as "The Floating Maiden."[1]

REAMKER AS TEXT

The Reamker, a tradition that has been transmitted from one generation to the next without interruption for at least 1,400 years, covers a vast domain from simple beliefs and the most elaborate art forms to the aesthetic, religious, and philosophical thought of the people and the history of Mon-Khmer civilization. The exact knowledge of the Khmer version of the Ramayana helps us understand the genre, origin, and evolution of each art form. From poetry, song, music and dance, to architecture and sculpture, it is rare not to feel a breath and whisper of the Reamker. To understand this is to possess one of the keys to the secret of the Khmer creative imagination, which allowed artists to create a purely national masterpiece from their foreign materials.

The Reamker has served as the main theme for all Khmer arts: literature, drawing, painting, sculpture, court dance, masked play, and shadow play. It appears in several versions, each adapted to the technical requirements of a particular genre or other art form. These versions, however, all are derived from the Indian Ramayana by Valmiki (Pou 1981:95; *Reamker* 1970: 1–2; *Ramker: Ramayana Khmer* 1969:a, 27).

The entire story of the Reamker is rarely performed.[2] Each and every Khmer performance genre has its favorite episodes. In court dance, for example, the typical episodes are:

- Battle of Lanka
- Chase of the Golden Stag
- Abduction of Seda
- Hanuman and Suvann Machha
- Seda and the Fire Ordeal
- Ream Leak Chup Leak.

In masked play the typical episodes are:

- Preah Ream in Search of Seda
- Battle of Kumphakar and Preah Ream's Army
- Combat of Veyareap and Preah Ream's Army
- Return of Kumphakar
- Kumphakar and the Water Barrage
- The Death of Kumphakar.

In the large-sized shadow play, the typical episodes are:

- Sukhachar
- The Death of Intrachit
- The Floating Maiden.

Seda, Preah Ream's wife, is often seen as the subject creating situations for the plot in the story to unfold. The Floating Maiden episode is a perfect example illustrating conflict between Reap (the demonic king)[3] and Preah Ream (Rama) over Seda. This article only discusses the Floating Maiden episode, whose synopsis is as follows.[4]

Seda was abducted by Reap (Ravana) and taken to the island of Lanka. Thinking to stop Preah Ream from fighting, Reap decided to trick Preah Ream into believing that Seda was already dead. To realize his plan Reap had his niece, Bonhakay (Bonakaya)[5] transform herself into the image of Seda's corpse floating in front of Preah Ream's camp pavilion. At first Preah Ream could not help but believe that it was the true corpse of Seda and was somber with sorrow and grief. But Hanuman (the white monkey and general of Preah Ream's monkey army) doubted the situation because the disguised corpse floated unnaturally upstream instead of downstream, and suggested to Preah Ream that the corpse be cremated. If it was not Seda's true corpse, then whoever impersonated her would not be able to withstand the heat, and the secret would be revealed. True enough, Bonhakay could not resist the heat and thus flew away. Hanuman saw the situation, pursued her and brought her back to Preah Ream, to whom Bonhakay acknowledged the trick. Preah Ream then ordered Hanuman to take Bonhakay back to Lanka, a journey during which Hanuman and Bonhakay fell in love with one another.

Knowing that the trick had failed, Reap ordered his army led by his son Intrachit to war with Preah Ream. Preah Ream responded to the aggression by sending his army led by his brother Preah Leak (Laksmana). In the confrontation Intrachit used the trick of hiding in the clouds and shot Preah Leak with his serpentine magical arrow. With help from Piphek (*vivek*, an astrologer), Preah Ream sent his arrow with a message to his foster father, Krut (Garuda) to save Preah Leak. Upon receiving the message and request, Krut hurriedly arrived at the scene and saved Preah Leak. Then Preah Ream ordered his army to return to the palace and brought the episode to its close.

The characteristic model of the *Reamker* demonstrates the originality of Khmer thinking. It has a spiritual force of divine essence, for Preah Ream is the reincarnation of Lord Visnu (Vishnu), and therefore represents the virtue of the good. In the collective consciousness of the Khmer the Buddha is venerated as the Teacher in religious thinking and practice, whereas Preah Ream is a precious source that nourishes Khmer culture (Pou 1981:98).

The Reamker has a dual function, artistic and therapeutic or aesthetic and magic. In lkhon khol, for example, the magic of Reamker helps solve the problems of practical social disorder, drought or epidemic. When there is a drought the Khmer believe that it is because Kumphakar (Reap's brother) sleeps, damming the flow from the sky.

The Reamker is considered a fundamental masterpiece of Khmer literature as well as a literary art of Cambodia. It can be classified into two distinct forms: the popular and the classical. The former is much longer (107 booklets) than the latter (20 booklets), and has survived in the oral tradition—recitation and declamation—which then serves as the basis for the performance of lkhon khol in Vat Svay Andet (Kandal) and Battambang regions and sbek thomm in Siem Reap. The popular form also appears in versified texts on *kraing* (manual) in Vat Svay, Battambang, and at the Royal Library. Another prose version can be found in Doeuk Keam's collection. It is in an accessible language and presentation that can be easily grasped by the masses, which cannot be forgotten. This popular form often stresses naivete and bad taste in the eyes of the elite. The classic form survives among the educated and the elite. It appears in poetic manuscripts written on leaves of Latanier (a species of palm), published by the Buddhist Institute in Phnom Penh, Cambodia. This, in turn, serves as the basis for the development of sculpture, bas-reliefs, and lkhon kbach, whose scenes contain a drama, and are successful in giving a complete idea of the action. These classic texts are characterized by unity, order and measure in conception, composition, and style.

The classicism of the lkhon kbach, for example, has imposed a definite Khmer style to the Ramayana which has been interpreted since the Angkor era and still holds true today. It is also this condensed and compact form of the plot—the most intense and dramatic—that was carved in scenes of the Khmer bas-reliefs. Beautifully versified texts of the Reamker are found either in songs accompanying the lkhon kbach or in declamation of the dramatic representation. The lkhon kbach includes in its repertoire, a vast number of scenes depicting life, love, and war of the hero, Preah Ream. The repertoire always stresses the most dramatic scenes of the Reamker, which are cut into tableaus—scenes and episodes—and never progresses from the beginning to end. Dance masters know the epic in its detailed development. Their knowledge is based either on the oral tradition or song texts and poems. Nevertheless, knowledge of the entire story is necessary for the realization, even for a very simple and short tableau.

There is evidence that a literary basis for dramatic performances of the Reamker existed in the Founan-Chenla period (first–ninth centuries A.D.). A sixth-century inscription found near the Khmer village of Veal Kantel, just below the border of Laos, listed gifts made by the brother-in-law of King Bhavavarman to a Shiva temple. Included were copies of the Mahabharata and the Ramayana from which daily recitations were instituted (Barth and Bergaigne 1885:30).

Scholars agree that many Khmer art forms were strongly influenced by Indian culture: architecture, sculpture, music, and dance as well as the Reamker. Traces of acculturation of the Indian Ramayana in Cambodia date back as far as the first carvings of the Rama legend, particularly on bas-reliefs. Studies of the literary texts of the Reamker confirm this point of view. A movement in Cambodia to make the Ramayana more Khmer produced the name Reamker, which means "the fame and reputation of Preah Ream, the protagonist" (Chuon 1967:1046) and which was depicted in sculpture, dance, and music. In adapting to the artistic and literary forms of the Khmer, some foreign characteristics of the Ramayana were dropped and local aspects adopted. In other words, the Indian epic underwent a complete mutation in contact with Khmer thought and aesthetics.

It is probable that the *Ramayana* was known to Khmer sculptors around the same time lkhon kbach was born. A rough sense of Khmerization of Indian cultural components was strongly felt already at the time of Banteay Srey (second half of the tenth century), as depicted on its pediments, and certainly appeared at the Baphuon (beginning of the eleventh century). For example, the meeting scene of three characters—Preah Ream, Preah Leak, and Sukrip—in tears is connected only to the reamker and not to the Ramayana of Valmiki (Groslier 1969:91). Again, the bas-reliefs of the Angkor Vat and Banteay Samre (twelfth century) manifest the Khmerization of the Ramayana along with the classic literary poetry, Reamker (books 1–10) (Groslier 1969:92). This notion of the Khmerization of the Ramayana is not new; Finot (1956), Coedes (1968), and Martini (1961) have all pointed out the differences between the Valmiki Ramayana and the Reamker.

Outside of India, as in Cambodia, the local adoption of the Ramayana ranges from simple translation, to adaptation, to a complete remodeling. Traces of the Ramayana have been identified in Tibetan, Chinese, Siamese, and Laotian forms. In Khmer and Indonesian, there exist complete versions of the epic.

The artistic and literary forms of the Reamker include: 1) recitation and declamation in the form of storytelling, 2) stage performance of the lkhon kbach, lkhon khol, and sbek thomm, and 3) art representation of sculpture and painting. Under a full moon on a bamboo bed surrounded by children of the village, a grandparent tells of the combats and the vivacious *yeak* (demons). Their counterpart, Hanuman remains vivid in memory and enchants the imagination of the Khmer. Reap, on the contrary, is hardly talked about, for it might attract misfortune and bad luck. The Reamker is popular and important in social life. For instance, each time a person in trouble seeks help from a fortuneteller whose art involves the reading of the future in the text of Reamker, he trembles when the card of an ill-fated personage is drawn. If it falls on Seda, it signifies bad things, such as separation or death. The Khmer believe that if the card of Reap is drawn, a catastrophe or death will surely happen.

KHMER SHADOW PLAY AS PERFORMANCE GENRE

Before movies and television the Khmer watched and enjoyed shadow plays, a performance genre related to shadow puppetry found in other parts of South and Southeast Asia. A group of researchers led by Mr. Chheng Phon has claimed, "Based on comparative studies among Khmer arts, we can assume that shadow play originated long before the Angkor period" (*Sbek Thomm Sbek Tauch* 1987:a). With the advent of modern forms of entertainment its popularity has dwindled, becoming a background art form, so that today it is unknown to many. There are two types of shadow play in Cambodia: the smaller known as *sbek tauch* (*sbek*, leather or skin; *tauch*, small) or *ayang* which presents local legends or current events of the country, and the larger *sbek thomm* (*thomm*, big or large) which presents excerpts from the Reamker. This article deals only with the latter.

In recent history there have existed two sbek thomm troupes in Cambodia, one in Battambang and the other in Siem Reap, both in the northwestern part of the country. The former was patronized by Lok Mchah.[5] Defeated by the French, Lok Mchah went west to Thailand, ending the life of the sbek thomm in Battambang, leaving only one troupe in Siem Reap (*Sbek Thomm Sbek*

Tauch 1987:10). After Lok Mchah left, the 130 life-size puppets were then kept in the attic of the Damrey Sa Pagoda (White Elephant Temple) in Battambang (Tauch 1974:155).

Preah Ream and Seda (Bonhakay disguised)

The sbek thomm troupe of Siem Reap was lovingly maintained in the village of Ta Phul under the direction of Master Chum Nap (reciter). The troupe possessed 150 puppets (Nuon 1973:8).[6] The sbek thomm puppets may be six feet tall and weigh as much as sixteen pounds (*Sbek Thomm Sbek Tauch* 1987:9). Unlike the small sbek tauch they do not have articulated arms or jaws. Each of them is handled by a puppeteer who is also a dancer. One dozen puppeteers hold the translucent puppets firmly against a white scrim lit by the flame of torches or dried coconut shells, which are preferable as they cast more shadows. Like other traditional arts, a sbek thomm performance in the village usually takes place at night when a traditional or religious ceremony is organized. Such a performance occurs only when commissioned locally since there is no system of sponsoring tours.

Although puppetry is a common artistic medium in many countries in the east and west, Khmer sbek thomm is quite distinctive, being most closely related to the Thai *nang yai*.[7] Having a style of its own both in the construction of the puppets and their manipulation, it is a unique expression of Khmer art and culture. The sbek thomm draws its performance scripts from texts of the *Reamker*. In villages across Cambodia performances of shadow theater often continue all night. The stage is illuminated by vast burning torches or dried coconut shells. Although contemporary performances have converted to electric lights, the puppet characters remain identical. This contrasts with *lkhon kbach* (court dance) and *lkhon khol* (masked play) in which dancers learn only the one role or character most suited to their personality and temperament (Sam 1987:24). Puppeteers must learn many roles, although they also specialize in a given role. Khmer sbek thomm puppeteers dance while manipulating the puppets, occasionally going away from the scrim and merely dancing with the puppets in their hands, or sometimes even without the puppets. The dance postures can be observed at all times, walking, standing, and sitting, even when they are behind the scrim performing. Therefore, puppeteers carefully study the traits of each character when acting, walking, sitting, and flying.

Whereas Khmer sbek thomm was originally an all-male tradition this was changed when it was brought to the University of Fine Arts in Phnom Penh in the early 1970s. In addition to employing female dancers, the university increased the number of puppeteers. This change in the tradition was evident, for instance, at the First Third World Theatre Festival and Conference in the Philippines in 1971, in which the Khmer sbek thomm performance included female dancers, among whom were Chan Moly Sam and Sokhanarith Moeur, both now living in the United States.[8]

TEXT, CONTEXT, AND PERFORMANCE OF REAMKER: THE FLOATING MAIDEN

Traditionally, before a performance, a ceremony called *hom rong* is conducted to appeal to the spirits to bless the stage and to concentrate the puppeteers' minds. Thus, prior to the action, the musicians and puppeteers solicit the protection of the great masters invoking the spirits.

After the curtain is raised, the audience sees the narrators and puppeteers *angkuy chong hong* (sit)[9] in front of the scrim, both palms joined together, then placed above the head to salute the spirits. Against the white scrim, the panel of Eysey (hermit) stands in the middle; to the right is Preah Neareay (Narayana), and to the left, Eysaur.[10] In front of the three panels votive objects, candles and incense sticks are arranged. After the curtain is fully raised, the *sampho* (horizontal barrel drum) player strikes the first few strokes to signal that the invocation of the spirits will now take place.[11]

1. *Ruo Samala*. (This piece has a magic power to put the puppeteers in the right mood for the ceremony.)
2. *Anhcheunh Krou*. (Invocation to the teacher or spirit, in two parts, Pali and Khmer, conducted by the leading narrator.)[12]

Namo tassa

phakava to

araha to

samma samputhasa.

Puthaing aratanaing karomi

Thormaing aratanaing karomi

Sangkhaing aratanaing karomi.

Tutiyampi Puthaing aratanaing karomi

tutiyampi Thormaing aratanaing karomi

tutiyampi Sangkhaing aratanaing karomi.

Tatiyaimpi Puthaing aratanaing karomi

tatiyaimpi Thormaing aratanaing karomi

tatiyaimpi Sangkhaing aratanaing karomi.

U ka sa yeung khnhomm taing lay Everyone of us	*saum krap thvay bangkum* wish to lie down and salute
krom preah boromaneath under your highness	*ney den phen phup preah thorani.* of the earthly world (and the goddess of the earth).
Yeung khnhomm taing lay Everyone of us	*saum on kay leuk anhcheali* wish to bend our body, raise our hands
bangkum kun krou ba achar krup preah ang to salute all the teachers	*del kung nea than soloah choan.* who reside in heaven.
Yeung khnhomm saum arathanea Everyone of us wish to invoke	*nimun sdech yeang anhcheunh* invite
krou kamnoeut the teacher	*del bangkoeut yeung khnhomm.* who gave us life.
Khnhomm saum anhcheunh I wish to invite	*krou sampho roneat sralai korng skor* the teacher of the barrel drum, xylophone, shawm, gong, drum
chaul mork prasithi por to come and bless	*oy kaun sih krup krup knea hong.* all the students sitting together.

The narrator calls the piece *Sathukar.*

3. *Sathukar* (*Chhak ho* three times). The narrators and puppeteers remove the Eysey panel and the votive objects, and slowly move themselves out of the stage. Two puppeteers, one taking the Preah Neareay panel and another the Eysaur, prepare for the next piece.[13]

4. *Cheut Chapp*, on the *sralai* (quadruple-reed shawm) and *skor thomm* (large barrel drums). A combat scene between Preah Neareay and Eysaur.

5. *Cheng Char/Phak.*

First Narrator:

Dang noh krong Reap asora
Once upon a time, Ravana, the demon

kung koal knong preah reach rong rum.
in the pavilion.

chuop chum ah puok pul sena
gathered all of his followers

[Followed by the sampho and skor thomm strokes]

Second Narrator:

Chum ah muntrey neamoeun tauch thomm
All the low and high dignitaries

chaim sdapp preah reach ongkar.
await his royal edict.

kung koal bangkum
attend to his presence

6.   *Cheng Char/Phak.*

First Narrator:

Preah chao krong Langka
The King of Lanka

chaul mork bangkum koal dauchnoh hoeuy
coming for an audience

ba euy! Bonhakay knuoy mear euy you
"Bonhakay, my dear niece

trauv neang pranhapp hiev hah
phlek   phlah
hurry up and fly

Bonhakay kmuoy mear.
Bonhakay, my dear niece."

luh sdech ban tort yul Bonhakay
upon seeing Bonhakay

preah ang ka mean preah ongkar tha
he ordered:

chaur neang komm bangkum koal ang anh oy loeuy
do not wait here too long

teou e ti utuok thearea chea
kar pranhapp choh na
to the sea

Second Narrator:

Bonhakay luh ban sdapp preah mear
Bonhakay, upon hearing

neang ka leuk kar pranamm
greets

hiev hah phlek phlah
and flies

mean damrah trah proeu dauchnoh hoeuy
her uncle's order

bangkum lea thay pi ti koal
says goodbye

samdao teou e utuok thearea
to the sea

oy ban dauch chea preah reach damrah trah proeu.
as ordered.

7. *Cheut/Ruo.* Bonhakay flies to the sea.

8. *Lo.* (Arriving at the sea, Bonhakay disguises herself into Seda and floats on the water in front of Preah Ream's pavilion.)

9. *Cheng Char/Phak.* (On his water pavilion, Preah Ream sees the disguised Bonhakay and thinks that she is Seda.)

First Narrator:

Sdech chaul knong preah punlea than	*boeuk preah kavtan*
His majesty enters the pavilion	opens his eyes
kamsan preah reach haratey.	
and relaxes.	

[Followed by the sampho and skor thomm strokes]

Second Narrator:

Sdech tort kiri voreak	*sak sapp yeak vea kala*
He sees	the disguised corpse of the demon
preah haratey ett sangka	*sman tha Seda mohesey.*
without a doubt	his wife Seda.

10. *Pol.* (Seeing Seda's corpse, Preah Ream takes her in his arms and weeps.)

Samdech preah phisovung pung krala	*ahchar luh sdech ban tort yul*
His majesty	upon seeing
sak sapp cheyea dauchnoh hoeuy	*preah ang ka yeang choh teou*
his wife's corpse	descends
op krasop bey bam thnakk thnam	*oy ban dauch chea preah reach haratey.*
to embrace her	as he wishes.

11. *Ruo.*

12. *Aut.* (Preah Ream weeps.)

13. *Pol.* (Finding out that Bonhakay cannot trick Preah Ream, Intrachit orders Virulmouk Kumar to lead his army to the battlefield.)

Intrachit asora Intrachit, the demon	*luh trung chreap tha* upon knowing
Bonhakay teou lor banhchhaot *baksvey monussa* that Bonhakay is not successful	*pum ban dauchnoh hoeuy* in deluding His Majesty
sdech ka proeu oy Virulmouk Kumar then orders Virulmouk Kumar	*leuk ah kang tuos yothea* to lead the ten armies
teou e ti somaraphoum chey to the battlefield	*oy ban dauch chett chenda.* as intended.

14.   *Krao Nai Muoy Choan.* (Intrachit's army marches to the battlefield.)

15.   *Cheng Char/Phak.*

First Narrator:

Dang noh Samdech Preah Neareay Reamea Once upon a time, Preah Ream	*kung knong preah punlea* resided in a pavilion
neou nea rosiel preah surya. in the late afternoon.	

[Followed by the sampho and skor thomm strokes]

Second Narrator:

Chum ah puok pul sena All the followers	*sdapp preah ongkar* listen to the edict
ang Preah Neareay Norupadey. of Preah Ream.	

[Followed by the sampho and skor thomm strokes]

[*Chhak ho* by the demonic army]

16.   *Pol.* (Hearing the demonic warwhoops, Preah Ream orders Preah Leak to lead the army to the battlefield.)

Samdech Preah Neareay Reamea Preah Ream	*luh sdech loeu samrek srek york chey khoh* upon hearing the warwhoops
krong asora dauchnoh hoeuy of the demons	*preah ang ka chatt proeu oy* then orders

Srey Leak anuchea
his younger brother, Preak Leak

leuk toap teou e ti somaraphoum chey
to lead the army to the battlefield

oy ban dauch chett chenda.
as intended.

17.   *Krao Nak.* (Preah Leak's army marches to the battlefield.)

18.   *Pol.* (Virulmouk Kumar orders his army to engage in battle with that of Preah Leak.)

Virulmouk Kumar
Virulmouk Kumar

luh ban leuk ah kang tuos yothea
with the ten armies

*chaul mork dall ti somaraphoum
chey dauchnoh hoeuy*
arriving at the battlefield

preah ang ka chatt oy puok pul sena yothea
then orders them

chaul thveu kar oy doeung dech dai dauch ta teou.
to engage in the battle.

19.   *Cheut.* (Both armies engage in battle)

20.   *Trakk/Ruo.* (Preah Leak is hit by an arrow.)

21.   *Tayay.*

22.   *Cheng Char/Pol.*   (Knowing that Preah Leak is hit with an arrow, Preah Ream asks Piphek, the fortuneteller, for advice.)

First Narrator:

Samdech Preah phisovung pung krala
His Majesty

ahchar luh sdech ban tort yul
upon seeing

*Srey Leak anuchea trauv sar Intrachit
dauchnoh hoeuy*
his brother Preah Leak hit by Intrachit's arrow

*preah ang ka mean preah
ongkar suor teou Piphek tha*
then asks Piphek:

ba euy! neak Piphek hora euy
"Piphek, my dear fortuneteller!

toeu neak kitt yang na teou vinh
what do you think,

na neak Piphek hora?
Piphek, the fortuneteller?"

Second Narrator:

Piphek hora luh ban sdapp
Piphek, upon hearing

preah reach damrah trah suor dauchnoh hoeuy
the question

asora ka leuk kar pranamm bangkum toul tha
"Your Majesty!

saum mchah chivitt leu tbaung serisey
greets and says:

thleng sar teou anhcheunh Krong Krut Baksa
send the arrow to invite the garuda

oy sdech mork chuoy york asar teup ban
to come for the rescue

saum trung chreap.
please."

23.   *Cheut Chhoeung/Ruo.* (Preah Ream sends his arrow to Krong Krut Baksa.)

24.   *Pol.*

Krong Krut Baksa chea preah thorm beyda
Garuda, the father

kampung te kung knong simpeali than
residing in his abode

*you bantech srapp te kheunh sar ampi
Preah Neareay*
then sees the arrow from Preah Ream

mork anhcheunh dauchnoh hoeuy
to invite him

sdech ka hiev hoh phlek phloh
and flies

*teou oy ban dauch chea preah reach damrah
trah hao.*
as called upon.

25.   *Phlek.* (Krong Krut Baksa on his journey to rescue Preah Leak.)

26.   *Ruo Samala.* (Krong Krut Baksa pulls the arrow from Preah Leak.)

27.   *Pol.* (Knowing that Preah Leak is rescued, Preah Ream orders his army to return to the palace.)

Samdech Preah Neareay Reamea
Preah Ream

luh sdech tort yul Krong Simpeali Baksa
upon seeing the garuda

*mork dak sar ampi Samdech anuch
dauchnoh hoeuy*
pulling the arrow from his brother

preah-ang ka leuk ah kang tuos yothea
leads the ten armies

chaul teou suvann preah punlea chey vinh
to return to the golden pavilion

oy ban dauch chett chenda.
as intended.

28.   *Punhea Doeur/Chhak ho.* (Preah Ream's army returns to the palace.)

Instead of being in an epic poetic form, the text of sbek thomm, as mentioned and presented above, is a popular version set mostly in prose, but sometimes in verse. In the latter, two meters are used: *pumnol* (sixteen syllables) and *prumakitt* (twenty-two syllables).[14] The former is used in dialogue or when showing anger, while the latter expresses sorrow and grief. The entire story is cut into small tableaus suitable for the performing art.

In the context of shadow play only the theme is preserved. The scenario, including performing elements of narration, music, calls for pieces, and plots are created to adapt to the stylistic requirements of the shadow play's form. It should be noted that the Khmer sbek thomm has a unique style that is easily recognizable. This unique regional style is reflected by the narration in Siem Reap accent (tonation), giving the sbek thomm its soul, which cannot be substituted or replaced.

The language employed in the sbek thomm performance is by and large vernacular, although royal language is used for characters of royal status. The use of speech and voice modifiers, or special voice quality and speech styles, is not found. Aside from music, there are four types of speech (recitation and narration): *phak, phdaim moeung, pol,* and *cheng char.*[15]

In terms of musical styles, percussion players use only hard mallets in the *pinn peat* ensemble that accompanies the sbek thomm performance. It is always the pinn peat, because in the ears of Khmer musicians and audiences, it has the strongest sonority of all their ensembles; a special sound quality and dynamic that can support the dramatic tension of the warlike story of *Reamker.* The musical pieces used in the performance of sbek thomm according to the characters, situations, and actions are *sathukar, cheut, cheut chapp, cheut chhoeung, krao nak, krao nai, trakk, tayay, lo, aut, phlek, prathum, khlomm,* and *punhea doeur* (Nuon 1973:9).

CONCLUSION

Like most Asian countries, Cambodia has received some form of Indian influence. For centuries the Khmer have localized and created a national version of the Indian classic epic Ramayana known as Reamker. It demonstrates the originality of Khmer thinking and is considered by them to be a fundamental masterpiece of their literature. In the arts the importance of the Reamker in the arts lies in the unique versions required by each particular genre: recitation/declamation (theater and shadow play), dance (pure dance and dance drama), and artistic representation (painting and sculpture).

In the social and cultural life of the Khmer the Reamker is both artistic and therapeutic. For instance, in times of drought the Reamker can be performed to attract rain by means of a masked play. Just as important the Buddha represents philosophy and religious teaching, Preah Ream (the protagonist in the Reamker) represents the virtues of Khmer culture.

With the destruction of Khmer culture attempted by the Khmer Rouge and with the advent of modern forms of entertainment, the life of the Khmer shadow play is dangerously threatened. It has become a dying tradition in Cambodia. Traditional performances of Khmer shadow play using the Reamker formerly lasted for several nights. Today the only performances to be seen are hour-long presentations by members of the University of Fine Arts and Department of Arts in Phnom Penh. The switch from the temple courtyard to the concert hall, the replacement of burning torches or dried coconut shells by modern lighting, and the senseless threat of the Khmer Rouge to Khmer arts have all contributed to changes in the life of the Khmer shadow play and the Reamker.

NOTES

1. Transcriptions of Khmer words in all literature in Khmer studies is inconsistent because the Khmer language has many more sounds than the English alphabet can accommodate. To provide readers with an indication of pronunciation, I have modified the usual transcription system and devised my own (see Appendix I). In this performance text of *sbek thomm*, the Khmer transcription is in italics, whereas the English translation underneath it is in Roman type. Readers will come across different spellings of the same words. For example, the word *Reamker* (my spelling) is sometimes spelled *Ramker* (original spelling of a book title). Be reminded that the titles of some musical pieces appear similar, viz. *Samala* and *Saloma*. This is not a typographical error. The translation of Khmer texts is not word for word but phrase by phrase. In some cases, I intend to provide readers with a general meaning of the sentences.

2. During the hair-shaving ceremony of his son, it is accounted that Lok Mchah had his lkhon khol (masked play) troupe perform the entire *Reamker* for fourteen consecutive nights (Tauch 1974:196).

3. Also known as Tossakann (ten-armed demonic King).

4. The Floating Maiden is better known in Khmer as *Sar Neakabah* (dragon-trapped arrow), *Sar Poan* (tangled arrow), or *Sar Prumeah* (a kind of special arrow). This episode is a unique branch story employed only in Khmer sbek thomm and Thai nang yai. (Note similarities in these names to Surpanakā, from which they derive. Ed.)

5. Bonhakay is the Khmerized form of Surpanakā ("having nails like winnowing fans")—Ed.

6. Lok Mchah was the Governor of Battambang Province during the late 1800s and early 1900s (Tauch 1974:185-186).

7. The book *Sbek Thomm Sbek Tauch* mentions 154 puppets were being used (1987:10, 39).

8. For further study of the Thai *nang yai*, see Mattani Rutnin (1975), Michael Smithies and Kerdchuay Chalermporn (1974), and Dhaninivat (1962).

9. The Sbek Thomm Troupe of the Department of Arts in Phnom Penh which toured Europe in October 1991 also included female puppeteer (Khuon Pok Nary).

10. To sit or squat by bending both knees, the buttocks above the ground, using both feet to support the whole body.

11. An audio recording of this item, entitled "Theatre d'Ombres Nang Sbek: Ream-ke (Ramayana)," recorded in Cambodia by the University of Fine Arts is available from Hanuman, P.O.B. 26017, Los Angeles, California 90026. This same item was performed during the Cambodian tour of the U.S. in 1991—Ed.

12. The beginning of the invocation is in very old and broken Khmerized Pali. It is typical of incantations by musicians and others, used for casting magic spells, as explained by Rev. Kong Chhean, Long Beach, California, June 9, 1992. Its approximate translation is as follows—Ed.

> I pay homage
> To the Buddha
> The saint
> The enlightened one
> I make the Buddha triple gem (sic)
> I make the Dharma triple gem
> I make the Sangha triple gem.
> A second time, I make the Buddha triple gem
> A second time, I make the Dharma triple gem
> A second time, I make the Sangha triple gem.
> A third time, (etc.)

13. Puppeteers sometimes use two panels of monkeys, one black and the other white, instead of the Preah Neareay and Eysaur panels.

14. These two meters were among the five meters dated back to the Angkor Period (Pich 1988:19–20; Sam 1988:181; *Sbek Thomm Sbek Tauch* 1987:28).

15. For further information see Sam-Ang Sam (1988).

REFERENCES CITED

Barth, Auguste, et Abel Bergaigne
    1885-1893   *Inscriptions Sanscrites du Cambodge et de Champa*. Paris: Imprimerie Nationale.

Brunet, Jacques
    1969   "Nang Sbek, Danced Theatre of Cambodia." *The World of Music* 11(4): 20–37.

Chuon, Nath
    1967   *Dictionnaire Cambodgien*, 5eme ed., 2 vols. Phnom Penh: Editions de l'Institut Bouddhique.

Coedes, George
    1968   *The Indianized States of Southeast Asia.* Ed. Walter Vella. Honolulu: East-West Center Press.

Dhaninivat (Prince)
    1962   *The Nang.* Bangkok: The Fine Arts Department.

Finot, Louis
    1956   *L'Origine d'Angkor*, 2eme ed. Phnom Penh: Editions de l'Institut Bouddhique.

Martin, Francois
    1961   "Quelques Notes sur le Ramker." *Artibus Asia* 24.

Nuon, Kan
    1973   *Le Theatre dans la Vie Khmere.* Phnom Penh: Universite des Beaux Arts.

Pich, Tum Kravel
    1988   *The Art of Writing Poetry.* Phnom Penh: Ministry of Culture.

Pou, Saveros
    1981   "Etudes Ramakertiennes." *Seksa Khmer* 4:91–126.

Ramker. Ramayana Khmer
    1969   Phnom Penh: Imprimerie Sangkum Reastr Niyum.

Reamker
    1907   7eme ed., 10 vols. Phnom Penh: Editions de l'Institut Bouddhique.

Rutnin, Mattani, ed.
    1975   *The Siamese Theater.* Bangkok: The Siam Society.

Sam, Chan Moly
    1987   *Khmer Court Dance: A Comprehensive Study of Movements, Gestures, and Postures as Applied Techniques.* Newington: Khmer Studies Institute.

Sam, Sam-Ang
    1988   "The Pin Peat Ensemble: Its History, Music, and Context." Phd diss. Wesleyan University.

Sbek Thomm Sbek Tauch (Large-Sized Shadow Play Small-Sized Shadow Play)
    1987   Phnom Penh: Ministry of Culture.

Smithies, Michael, and Kerdchuay Chalermporn
    1974   "The Wai Kru Ceremony of the Nang Yai." *Journal of the Siam Society* 72(1):143–147.

Tauch, Chhuong
    1974   *Battambang Samai Lok Mchah* (Battambang during Lok Mchah's Time). Battambang: Association of Documentation in Battambang.

CONTEXTS OF *DONTRII LAO DEUM*: TRADITIONAL LAO MUSIC[*]

Katherine Bond and Kingsavanh Pathammavong

INTRODUCTION

Musicians from the royal palace of Luang Prabang claim their tradition dates back 600 years to the Lan Xang period and has been passed on by trained musicians within the palace as well as from other villages under the patronage of Lao kings. The music found in Vientiane after 1954 played a role in the development of Lao nationalism. Initially performed by the Lao Radio Ensemble, the music expanded with the development of the Natasin School, the National School of Music and Dance. Because there has been very little contact between the two groups, they will be treated separately.

After 1975, many of the country's finest musicians and dancers fled to Thailand. Some faced political persecution whereas others realized that there was no future in continuing their tradition, which was marked by the new regime as "the music of the aristocracy." Following their escape to Thailand, two groups of musicians and dancers reunited in the Nong Khai refugee camp where they rehearsed, taught, and performed for other refugees.

In the early 1980s, the two groups were resettled in the United States under the sponsorship of American churches and families: The artists from the palace in Luang Prabang landed in Nashville, Tennessee and those from the Natasin School in Vientiane were resettled in Des Moines, Iowa. Many musicians and dancers arrived with hopes of performing full-time in their new home. However, the challenges of adaptation and survival in a new society have presented many obstacles to maintaining their tradition. The music, separated from its vital role of entertaining and establishing a ritual atmosphere, is less frequently performed within the Lao community in the United States.

It was our original intention to examine the social role of *dontrii lao deum* prior to 1975, focusing on musicians and contexts for performance. We expected to rely primarily on observations of performances at community festivals to gather data on performance contexts, and to interview key performers. As it turns out, most of our information was derived from interviews with musicians, dancers, and other community members. The informants were selected based on their roles in various music and dance groups, or their involvement with institutions that supported the tradition.

This methodology has presented several unavoidable problems. First, many of the informants are older and their memories have faded. Second, their present lifestyles have influenced their perspectives on the past. Third, the information presented by one informant sometimes contradicted that of another and some factual information was not in agreement. Finally, we were unsure how to distinguish what was said from what was actually done.

Our findings are a result of interviews with Lao who have resettled in the U.S., and to a lesser degree, in France. We have had to examine not only what we have been told, but the gaps in information presented. There was relatively little talk of war and politics, little knowledge of the history or story behind the repertoire, no interpretation of the stories and dances, and many missing details. What we are able to present, then, is a sketchy history of music in the palace of Luang Prabang, and the National School of Music and Dance in Vientiane and a picture of contexts and musicians of dontrii lao deum prior to 1975 as presented in oral histories derived from refugees who have been living in and adapting to a new society over a period of ten years.

* * * * * * * * * *

Dontrii Lao Deum, also referred to as lowland Lao classical music, was traditionally performed in state and court ceremonies, rituals, as accompaniment to theater and dance, and as entertainment in the homes of the Lao aristocracy and in villages. Translated literally as "traditional Lao music," other terms ascribed to this music include "court music" and "ceremonial music." Related to the Khmer *pin peat* and *mahori* ensembles (Sam 1988), and Thai classical music (Morton 1976), dontrii lao deum is a distinct genre of traditional lowland Lao music that has developed within the context of Lao history, culture, and ceremony.

Historical accounts of dontrii lao deum refer to it as "royal Lao classical music." Danielou translated the Lao *pi phat* and *mahori* ensembles as the classical orchestras of Cambodia and Laos (1957:6). Referring to Thai music, Morton described the "classic" period of the late nineteenth and early twentieth centuries as creating a high-art music that evolved into a guild system under the aegis of royal patronage and support by the aristocracy (1976:15). Due to political turmoil and slower economic development in Laos, however, this type of patronage did not last long enough and was not extensive enough to call it a "classical" period.[1] Thus, the standard "folk-classical" definitions seem out of place in the Lao context. In the case of Laos, the musicians who performed in the courts and for the aristocracy were originally villagers and could be commissioned to perform at temple ceremonies for the general public. While it is true that the court musicians were more skilled than those in the villages, and the ensembles were complete, the interaction between village and palace performance continued until the mid-twentieth century.

The term "classical" seems inappropriate for a number of additional reasons. First, it implies that the music is performed primarily in a formal stage setting with an attentive audience, usually the elite, and less for ceremonial functions. Whereas the former implication is true in some cases, it does not encompass the full range of performance contexts of dontrii lao deum. Second, the term suggests an era during which the music was supported, developed, or refined with support from the aristocracy. Finally, it is used to distinguish certain genres from "folk," popular, or village music.

The Lao term dontrii lao deum includes the pi phat and mahori ensembles. Although it may officially include *mohlam*, a sung poetry/musical genre, it primarily refers to the music performed in ceremonies and as accompaniment to dance and theater. The term *mohlam* is usually used separately on its own to describe the sung poetry found in Lao villages in central and southern Laos. Other names include *natasin*, the spoken term used exclusively in Vientiane to describe the performing arts at the National School of Fine Arts, *sinlapakorn*, the formal, written term to describe the performing arts, and *sep ngai* and *sep noi* in Luang Prabang.

Dontrii lao deum is divided into two types of ensembles: pi phat and mahori in Vientiane, and *sep ngai* and *sep noi* in Luang Prabang. The pi phat ensemble consists of several percussion instruments: *ranat ek, ranat thoum, khong wong, kong taphone, sing* and *sap*.[2] In Laos, the *pi*, or oboe, after which the ensemble is named, is rarely used, and the *khene*, a reed mouth organ considered the Lao national instrument, is substituted. The pi phat ensemble is used for processions, funerals, and big events as well as for dance accompaniment. The mahori ensemble, found at smaller, indoor events, usually consists of ranat ek, *khoui, khene, so duang, so ou, kim*, sing and sap.

In Luang Prabang, sep ngai is comparable to the pi phat ensemble and sep noi is comparable to the mahori ensemble, although more stringed instruments are used and the khene is found less frequently. We must point out that whereas there are general guidelines for these ensembles, flexibility and practicality dictate the actual performance. Musicians play whatever instruments are available. In some cases, an ensemble may not have the complete set of instruments. Therefore, the term dontrii lao deum is more commonly used because it has, by necessity, a general and rather vague definition.

MUSIC OF LUANG PRABANG

Dontrii lao deum was found throughout the city and villages and within the palace of Luang Prabang. Many Lao believe that the music and dance tradition of the palace originated in Cambodia and appeared in Laos with Fa Ngum and the Khmer in 1353 as part of the ritual offerings to the gods. During the French occupation musicians were recruited from Ban Phanom, a nearby village, to perform in the palace. After independence young musicians were recruited from public schools to preserve the tradition. Isolated by mountains and difficult to access, Luang Prabang's tradition remained relatively unchanged until recently, when modern music reached the city.

The Harvard Dictionary of Music states:

> Over the past 100 years, the Lao courts at Luang Prabang developed *beepat* and *mahori* ensembles under the direction of court musicians from Thailand. Though the performers were Lao and some of the compositions were based on Lao melodies, the ensembles never took root in Laos, and it is presumed that they are no longer played there. (1986:791)

Based on our informants' reports, the author appears to have confused the music of Luang Prabang with that of Vientiane. We know that Luang Prabang was a vassal to Siam for much of the past century and that it is likely that the Siamese influenced court rituals. However, the former residents of Luang Prabang and employees of the palace prefer to look back to the Khmer influence during the time of Fan Ngum. Further, they describe the traditional music as distinctly different from the Thai. They acknowledge that cultural exchange did exist with Thailand, but explain the development of court music during the past century in three stages: 1) *sakdinaa* (feudal) labor, 2) patronage within the palace, and 3) preservation.

Approximately four kilometers from the city of Luang Prabang on the bank of the Nam Khan river is Ban Phanom, translated as "Breast Mountain Village," where two rocks shaped like a woman's breasts lie at the head of the village. The villagers' origins are Lao Lue who migrated from the northern region of Sipsong Panna and settled in Ban Phanom centuries ago. Predominantly farmers, carvers, blacksmiths, weavers, and other artisans, the villagers served the palace of Luang Prabang and thus were exempt from paying taxes or serving as transporters for the French. Ban Phanom was well known for its artisans, including musicians. Thongtanh Souvanaphanh, a reporter for the Voice of America who grew up in Ban Phanom, described the village as follows:

> One could say that Ban Phanom was directly under palace protection. During the French occupation, my uncle, Phia Vohan, was a very good friend of King Sisavangvong. He gave special rights to Phia Vohan and his followers not to pay taxes. These people were considered to belong to the palace. Before World War II the whole village was under the leadership of Phia Vohan. The king assigned him to be in charge of entertainment and cultural affairs. That's why almost everyone in Ban Phanom was able to play music and to dance. (Bounthan Xayprasith, personal communication, 1989)

Phia Vohan reportedly assisted Auguste Pavie, the French explorer who was appointed vice-consul to Laos in 1887, indicating that his involvement with the musicians of Ban Phanom occurred in the late nineteenth century.

Other village musicians could be found in and surrounding Luang Prabang. Sep ngai ensembles were found in Siang Maine, Houa Xieng, Sangkhalok, and Phan Luang. Bounthan Xayprasith, a so player from Luang Prabang, described the musical setting of Luang Prabang:

> I have reason to believe that Luang Prabang was the city where music was born. In Luang Prabang men, women and children all knew how to play instruments, like khoui, khene, ranat, so. Every village had its own music. During every season the wealthy people would have house fairs and would hire musicians to come and play at their homes. The host would invite all the people he knew to join him in making merit. (personal interview, 1989)

Musicians could not survive on music alone for their livelihood. Many were farmers and merchants who performed mainly during the festival season. Music was a part of their daily lives, though. Merchants who traveled to sell goods brought their instruments along.

> These merchants put two boats together and built a roof over the boat, like a house. There were usually eight to ten men with their musical instruments. When their boat began to pass by a village they started playing music, or when they stopped at the bank of the village where they stayed overnight, they would play for the villagers, and court the women of that particular village. Almost every man in Luang Prabang could play a musical instrument. (personal interview, 1989)

During French occupation, music was a daily part of life, with certain villages, like Ban Phanom, specializing in a particular tradition. In the late 1940s, the French began to nurture a sense of nationalism that was slowly beginning to emerge with the Lao Issara movement. This nationalism was intended to counter the pan-Thai sentiment that threatened the French occupation. King Sisavangvong increased his support of the Ban Phanom village musicians.

After independence in 1954 the villagers of Ban Phanom took on other occupations in the military, and as civil servants. King Sisavangvong hired the older performers as full-time employees of the palace, where they could work to preserve the music. Palace musicians were recognized as better musicians because they were able to develop their skills and expand their repertoire.

However, according to Mr. Bounthanh, not many people wanted to play in the palace because the pay was low compared with other occupations.

The Kounlavong family, now residing in Nashville, worked for the palace for four generations. Ekeo Kounlavong is currently the leader of the troupe in Nashville. His father was the leader of the palace's sep ngai ensemble. Three of his brothers studied with palace musicians. The family was trusted by the royal family and after the death of their father, the sons worked full-time in the palace.

In the late 1960s the older musicians taught a group of approximately ten young boys, all of whom were children of palace employees. Sisouphan Kounlavong, the seventh of nine children, started studying in the palace a few years before his father's death when he was eight years old. He attended music classes after regular school hours. He and the other young musicians started by learning *khong wong* and later progressed to other instruments. They were taught each song in sections, memorizing by rote. Students would perform next to the masters until they were confident the students had memorized the full song. They were then allowed to perform alone. Sisouphanh learned approximately sixty to seventy songs during his peak years as a student.

The palace musicians also learned two systems of musical notation, the numerical system and the Western scale notation, which Sisouphanh called "beansprout notes." We do not know how these systems were introduced to the palace, raising new questions about cultural contact.

During the period of independence, as Luang Prabang gained increasing exposure to Western music and dance, the palace saw a need to preserve the tradition and began a recruitment policy. Girls, aged fourteen to fifteen, were recruited from public schools each year to dance for the New Year's festival. Recruitment of dancers began in 1956, three years before the death of King Sisavangvong and continued until 1975, when King Sisavang Vathana abdicated the throne.

The repertoire of the palace included *Fon Nang Keo*, the Lao version of the Khmer Apsara dance, and segments from *Phra Lak Phra Lam*, the Lao version of the *Ramayana*, which is performed in various versions as as a masked dance drama, or *khon*, in Cambodia and Thailand, as well as Laos. Phra Lak (Laksmana) and Phra Lam (Rama) are the names of the epic's heros. The differences between the Lao *Phra Lak Phra Lam* and other versions is well explained by Sachidand Sahai (1980:67–83).

Fon Nang Keo is inspired by the Khmer Apsara dance, dating back to the period of Angkor. Apsaras, or celestial dancers, were "the embodiment of the life-creating energy resulting from a process for which Angkorean temples and entire cities were architectural metaphors," or symbols of the welfare of the kingdom (Cravath 1986:185). Before the period of preservation by King Sisavangvong, *Fon Nang Keo* was performed in villages. Wat Sene was famous for its rendition of Nang Keo. During King Sisavangvong's reign, *Fon Nang Keo* was designated as a royal dance and was later prohibited in the vicinity of the palace. The piphat ensemble accompanied *Fon Nang Keo* with pieces called *Nang Nak* and *Soybon*.

The palace musicians and dancers began to lose their status as traditional performers after the foundation of the Natasin School in Vientiane. However, the king still felt that they were authentic Lao dancers who remained relatively uninfluenced by other styles, and attempted to preserve the art with his recruitment policy.

MUSIC IN VIENTIANE

Since 1560 Vientiane has been the capital of the Lao kingdom. Vientiane, then called Vieng Chan, was seen as the center of Buddhist learning during the period of King Souligna Vongsa from 1627 to 1694. However, in the early nineteenth century Vieng Chan was sacked by the Siamese and claimed as a vassal state.

Due to the destruction of Vieng Chan again by the Siamese in 1827, no records exist of the musical activities in the kingdom. Several sources suggest that all arts and treasures, including performers, were captured and taken to Bangkok (Somboun Sounantha, personal communication 1989). Others suggest that artists fled to the other side of the Mekong River, near Ubon. Previously, the left side of the Mekong had been claimed by the Siamese, and although the borders were frequenty disputed with the French, it was given back to Thailand and is now referred to by the Lao of Vientiane as "Isan" or part of Thailand.

During the period of French colonization (late-nineteenth to mid-twentieth centuries), and later after independence in 1954, Vientiane was developed as the administrative capital. With assistance from France and the United States, administrative buildings were built, embassies were constructed, and the city was frequently visited by foreign dignitaries (Dommen 1985). Reports of music in Vientiane take us only as far back as the period of French occupation.

Khruu Ouane Southathamma's *Lykhee* Troupe

During the French occupation a troupe of *lykhee* performers traveled from northeast Thailand, around the southern and central part of the Lao kingdom, from Khorat to Pakse and Savannakhet, and then north, to Vientiane. According to Miller (1985:74), lykhee is a theatrical genre that traveled from central Thailand into northeast Thailand and Laos very recently. "Its language is not only Siamese but the musical instruments were also Siamese, principally the *ranat, kong wong, pi, ching* and drums." Miller cites James Brandon, who wrote:

> *Likay* was introduced into Lao early in the twentieth century. . . . *Likay* troupes, speaking standard Thai, played in Northeast Thailand for the Lao-speaking Thai people of that region. From there it was but a short trip across the Mekong River to play for audiences in Laos. (Brandon, cited in Miller, 1985:74)

During that period Siam had returned the land west of the Mekong to Laos, so it was still considered by the Lao to be part of Laos. The group's leader, Ouane Southathamma, was from Khorat, on the other side of the Mekong River. It is believed that Khruu (teacher) Ouane and his troupe introduced this genre to Laos. Sometime between 1947 and 1950 (stories conflict on dates), Khruu Ouane's troupe began performing in a theater in Vientiane, where they recounted stories from Lao literature and history.

Original members of the lykhee troupe, most of whom came from Khorat, later played a major role in the establishment of the Natasin School, the Lao National School of Music and Dance. They would go on to teach music and dance, and to choreograph and compose new pieces for the independent nation of Laos.

THE NATASIN SCHOOL

Foundation

Branchard de la Broche, a Franco-Lao known to the Lao as Papa Suphanh, conceived of the national school of performing arts because he loved Lao traditional music and wanted to support the arts. When the new nation began, he saw that a school could serve to preserve traditional music and dance. Lao officials felt it would be important to have a group of artists to present formally to foreigners and to represent the new nation. The Natasin School was founded in 1956 by de la Broche and Ouane Southathamma with funds from the United States Agency for International Development (USAID) through the Department of Education. Many former teachers and students did not seem to know about the purpose of the school. Others suggested it was formed to preserve the arts, and one suggested that it was a crucial element of any new nation.

> Every nation must have this type of school. [A nation] without the arts is like a nation without flowers to decorate it. Art is one of the most important representations of the nation. Lao music and dance were performed for their own sakes. Finally, the government tried to promote it on a national level. (Chandeng Pongphimkham, personal communication, 1988).

The school was also used to develop messages of a new nationalism promoting unity and harmony through performance.

In the early 1950s the demand for lykhee was in decline because of the introduction of the modern movie theater. We may suggest that the performers saw an opportunity in creating a national school of performing arts as a way to continue and even develop their performance careers.

Training

In 1955 the Lao government recruited ten elementary school teachers from across the country and sent them to study in Thailand. Between 1956–1959 the returning dance teachers taught students of the Chao Anou Elementary School. In 1959, when the school officially opened, they recruited students who had graduated from elementary school and then trained the Chao Anou students to become Natasin teachers. Betweem 1956–1958 the musicians and dancers held performances at the royal palace in Vientiane and at welcoming ceremonies honoring guests of the state.

In the 1960s students were awarded stipends that motivated approximately fifty to sixty of them to take entrance exams each year. The school selected the thirty most talented; students who could write, sing, or play instruments were given preference. In retrospect, many teachers felt that the selection discriminated against talented students who may not have been beautiful or who may have had some kind of handicap.

Of the thirty students admitted each year, many dropped out. They initially came because they received a per diem. According to Thongmouane Vilavong, "they tried it, didn't like it and dropped out. They registered because of the payments" (personal communication, 1989). Other informants suggested that students dropped out because their parents felt they were not gaining a good education and there would be no future in the arts.

> There was not a lot of interest in cultural activities on the part of the government. Look at the school next to Chao Anou. It looks like a chicken coop, an old barn, a shack! The people who went there could not study anything else, so they went to study Fine Arts. Their parents didn't support them because they believed that singing and dancing is not proper for females. (Seng Chitdalay, personal interview, 1989)

An average of only ten students graduated each year, most of whom were hired as teachers by public schools requesting teachers in other regions. Those teachers would be required to teach other subjects and to research the dance or music styles of those regions.

Natasin School teachers worked closely with administrators to develop messages portrayed through dance and song. Major adaptations from the Thai training included integrating the khene into the ensembles, choreographing dance, and composing music reflecting agricultural activities and ethnic diversity, as exhibited in *Fon Haa Plaa* (Fishing Dance) and *Fon Phao Lao* (Ethnic Dance). As an organ of the Lao nation the Natasin School produced performers who became the official representatives of Lao performing arts. Although many of the original teachers and students came from across the Mekong River and were considered Thai Isan, the suggestion that this art form replicates the Thai, as even those from Luang Prabang might imply, causes the troupe members to defend their art.

> We learned from them, but we were not supposed to imitate them. We established the school but couldn't even write a book about it. We received training from the Thai, but that doesn't mean that the Thai instructed us on everything. We developed our own style also. Laos, Cambodia and Thailand share the same kind of dance. The style is different. The Cambodian is very slow, the Thai is very fast and the Lao is in between, and nicer. Some people can identify the style. If we had written about it during Khruu Ouane's time, we would know what belonged to us and what didn't. (Chandeng Pongphimkham, interview 1989)

Another informant expressed appreciation of the Thai:

> We have to thank Thailand for training us because they developed their music and dance. They had all the opportunities and are a peaceful country, unlike Laos. We have had wars, revolutions and coup d'états all the time. Look at the differences in style between Thailand, Cambodia and Laos. (Sinouane Oudomhack, personal interview 1989)

While they acknowledge the Thai training and influence, their defensiveness appears to be more directed toward the government's inadequate support and education. They criticize the leadership, and feel regret that the young Lao nation did not experience a period of peace long enough to fully develop a Lao national art.

DONTRII LAO DEUM IN FESTIVALS AND CEREMONIES

Lao Buddhist religious holidays involved villagers going to the temple (*wat*) to make merit, or *boun*. Lao Buddhists believe that the accumulation of boun will result in good health and prosperity and will lead to rebirth in a higher order. The wat is the center of merit making in which the Buddhist monks receive donations and perform rituals and blessings to ensure the well-being of the community and its individual members. Most Lao Buddhist holidays correspond with indigenous ceremonies linked to the agricultural cycle.

Music is an integral part of the ceremonies and rituals that contribute to Lao Buddhism outside of its actual worship. It is found on temple grounds at funerals, weddings, temple festivals, and Buddhist celebrations throughout the calendrical cycle. Its primary functions are to establish atmosphere and to entertain. Musical performances also call to spirits and gods that may be considered animist or Hindu, but still fit into the Buddhist religious tradition in Burma, Thailand, Laos, and Cambodia. Bounthanh Xayprasith described how music was always found at ceremonies throughout the calendrical cycle:

> There were always festivals in the temple. Music had to be present so when people walked by they would hear it. Some people would sit and watch when there was a dance performance. Festivals were a time for socializing. There were no theaters, movies, or bars so people entertained themselves with music. When making merit, music was played to entertain the angels. Music could be played but dancing was not allowed. (personal interview, 1989)

Music had an important role in village and palace life. It was used in ritual offerings to the angels and spirits and supported the activities of making merit. It was also used to welcome important visitors to the palace and state, to entertain the king, his guests, and the villagers as well as to accompany dance. The two largest festivals of the calendrical cycle, the New Year's festival of Luang Prabang, and the That Luang Festival of Vientiane, are described below.

Music within the Calendrical Cycle of Festivals

Boun Pii Mai. Boun Pii Mai, the Lao New Year, was the most important festival in Luang Prabang and throughout the country. According to Nginn, the date was set to occur in mid-April, during the fifth month of the lunar calendar, when days get longer, symbolizing a period of brightness and prosperity. It was also a time of rebirth, like spring, when "the earth, lifeless and barren by many months of heat and drought, is reborn and turns green again under the first showers" (1959: 268).

In Luang Prabang, these festivities occurred over a two-week period. During the French occupation the *sa ban to* (sword) ceremony was performed for high-ranking officers, ministers, and administrators approximately one week before the designated New Year's day. The tip of a sword was put into an alms bowl of water blessed by monks and all present were required to drink the water. Officials thereby proved their loyalty to the country and their responsibility to their individual roles. The palace's sep ngai ensemble performed during this ceremony, creating a sense of excitement and drama.

The New Year's day celebration began in the morning with a *baci* ceremony for the royal elephants, followed by the baci for the king and queen (Chanthy Chanthasouk, personal interview, 1989). The baci ceremony is described by Abhay as "an expression of the Lao *joie de vivre* and warmheartedness, an expression of welcome that greets an official or sends off any traveller on his way" (1959:128). It was performed at weddings, births, greetings, and farewells to express wishes for good health and prosperity and to honor guests. Commonly called *soukhuan*, the baci ceremony was performed by a Brahman who invoked the soul to return to the body. Offerings placed in a centerpiece included rice, eggs, coconuts, alcohol, and other items to entice souls that may have strayed.

After the chanting, or calling of spirits, was finished, the guests of honor had white cotton threads tied around their wrists while receiving wishes. They, in turn, presented the offeror with threads and wishes. Music was always played while the threads were tied and wishes given, and contributed to an atmosphere of warmth and joy. In Luang Prabang, the music performed for the baci included *Khao Nai, Nangnak,* and *Sinouan* (Bounthanh Xayprasith 1989).

Following the baci ceremony, the king presented awards of honor to government officials, military personnel, and civilians. Every New Year, segments of the *Phra Lak Phra Lam* and *Fon Nang Keo* were performed before the guests sat down to eat. The most popular segments included *Fon Ling* (Hanuman, the monkey dance), and *Fon Yak* (Totsakan, the giant dance). The song that accompanied *Fon Ling* was *Kao Nok,* meaning "outside noise." According to Sam-Ang Sam, Kao Nok accompanied the march of human troops (1988:321). *Kao Nai* literally means "inside noise," and accompanied the march of the giants, or *yak,* as they prepared for battle. These two pieces were performed in the same contexts in Cambodia, and were transcribed by Sam (1988:318, 321.) Sam also referred to these selections as being particularly popular among the Khmer.

For several days after a number of processions occured involving first the monks and later the king, who was traditionally seated on a carrier perched upon an elephant. Musicians led the processions by playing pieces that had an exciting beat signifying the upcoming event. The songs signifying the king's procession differed from those of the villages. For the New Year's procession musicians in Luang Prabang and Vientiane played *pheng* (song) *Kao Nai* and *Kao Nok.* The song for the king's departure was *Pheng Phayadeum,* literally translated as "the king walks." *Pheng Phayadeum* was also performed in the Khmer *Reamker,* or *Ramayana* epic, to indicate the procession of the king (Sam 1988). These processions, along with the preceding rituals and social gatherings, provided the major opportunity for musicians in the palace of Luang Prabang to perform.

Boun That Luang, **That Luang** . Boun That Luang was the major festival of Vientiane, celebrated in the twelfth month. According to Abhay, That Luang, the royal stupa, was built in 1566 by King Setthathirath, over a small stupa said to contain a hair of the Buddha (1959:287). The stupa was spared when, in the early nineteenth century, the Siamese sacked the city of Vientiane; however, in 1873, it was virtually destroyed by Yunnanese pirates. The stupa was later restored with the support of the Ecole Francaise d'Extreme-Orient and completed by Mr. Fobertaux in 1931. Since then, the That Luang Festival became one of the most popular holidays in Vientiane.

The festival was celebrated over seven days, with the last day designated as the national day of offering alms to the monks. This took place on the temple grounds, with monks and citizens coming from around the country to participate. Officials and civil servants also confirmed their loyalty to the government. Led by the piphat ensemble, they proceeded to the royal palace, Ho Kham, in Vientiane. There, the *sa ban to* (sword) ceremony was performed, as during the New Year's festival in Luang Prabang.

Later, the Natasin troupe and royal palace musicians performed to entertain the guests of Ho Kham. One member of the palace ensemble claimed that the king invited the Natasin troupe to perform at the palace, but was disappointed when he saw them because they resembled the Thai style. The following year he invited his own ensemble and dancers to perform in Vientiane. Reports of Lao Natasin dancers contradict that story by claiming to have performed annually at Ho Kham, his palace. This story is one of a few indications of the lack of contact among, and slight rivalry between the musicians and dancers of Vientiane and Luang Prabang.

During the new era, the festival became an international "expo" where merchants, government officials, private citizens, and embassies exchanged culture and technology. The festival became the major opportunity for the Natasin troupe to perform for the public and likewise for the public to view the performers considered to represent the Lao nation. The audience consisted of everyone from farmers to high officials.

A large stage was set up in the area around That Luang. Students of all levels were allowed to perform, with the beginners performing the basic dance, those of mid-level performing *Fon Phao Lao* (dance of the ethnic groups), and the older group performing *kheuang ngai* and *lakhon* (theater). The dancers also performed segments from the *Ramakien*, or *Phra Lak Phra Lam*. The most common segment performed by the Natasin group was the Abduction of Sita. *Fon Hanuman*, the monkey dance, was also popular. This performance was the first opportunity many Lao had to see their national performing arts troupe. However, the audience at Boun That Luang was not always friendly. Several dancers, who wished not to be identified, complained of harassment by the audience that brought shame to the family.

> When my family went to watch me dance at the That Luang Festival, they observed that the dancers were insulted by young men who stood around the stage and shouted obscenities at us. The elderly people went there to see a beautiful performance and to support their granddaughters. Some people would say that we were just dancing for money [fon kin ram kin].[3] We had to go through a lot with the public. Sometimes their children saw the beautiful performance, the costumes, and later told their parents they wanted to be like us. Those children were told that it is a bad career to have. 'These dancers are just dancing. They cannot do anything else and will not get any better.' That's what most of the people in Laos would say about the Lao artists. (personal interview, 1989)
> We tried not to pay attention to them. They said 'fat one, skinny one, big breasts, small breasts,' and so on. Sometimes we couldn't concentrate on dancing. One dancer was angry so she pointed her foot at the audience.[4] (personal interview, 1989)

Despite the harrassment, many dancers and musicians were proud to have performed for the public.

In addition to festivals during the calendrical cycle, musicians and dancers were required to perform at other ceremonies. In the palace, musicians performed for weddings, births, funerals and royal audiences. "Every event had music. Without music it appeared to be sad" (Chanthy Chanthasouk 1989). The Natasin students and teachers were also commissioned to perform for the aristocracy.

Welcoming Ceremonies

When Laos began to establish diplomatic relations with Western countries, a formal welcome was given to state audiences. These ceremonies occurred whenever a foreign visitor or dignitary arrived. An important part of the welcome ceremony was the performance of the Welcome Dance. The dancers most frequently performed in the homes of Lao officials, at the U.S. embassy, and in the French compound. The welcome dance is *Fon Uayphon* or *Fon Pinihan*. A group of dancers wore the traditional lowland Lao dress including the *sin*, the traditional Lao skirt, a long sleeved blouse, and gold jewelry. They also carried a silver bowl containing flower petals. The dance exhibited the hospitality of the host, the grace, shyness, and beauty of Lao women, and expressed good wishes when the dancers sprinkled flower petals on the guests. The Welcome Dance for the king was reported as *Dao Vadeung*, a longer and more elaborate version.

Weddings

Many weddings in Laos were arranged by parents of the bride and groom. The wedding ceremony was preceded by a formal proposal and exchange of a bride price. In the evening before the wedding, a ceremony called *suat mone* was performed, during which the monks blessed the water that would be sprinkled upon the young couple the next day. On the morning of the wedding, the musicians comprising a small mahori ensemble began playing around 9:30. The actual ceremony, the baci, started at 11:00. Close family members and two attendants would conduct the ceremony, wishing joy and prosperity for the couple. The musicians stopped playing while the attendants called the souls. After the calling of souls, the musicians resumed playing while cotton threads were tied around the wrists of the bride and groom. The musicians described the wedding songs as joyous. They played favorite songs such as *Dok Mai Uayphon* (well-wishing flower), *Lao Longnam, Lao Kathopmai, Lao Khamhon, Lao Sieng Thian,* and fast and slow songs to extend or shorten the performance time. Musicians from the palace did not describe in great detail the weddings but merely stated that they performed *Lao Chaleunsy, Lao Somdet,* and *Khmen Bothisat.*

Funerals

Lao Buddhists believe that death will lead to rebirth into a higher order, and ultimately, *nirvana*, where the deceased will escape the suffering of worldly beings. Lao funerals, then, express joy for the deceased as well as sorrow and grief for the survivors. Lao funeral rites used to be practiced differently according to the cause of death. If a person died as the result of violence, he would be buried. Death by disease or another natural cause would result in cremation (Abhay 1959:145). According to Thongmouane Vilavong, a Natasin-trained musician, music began the moment the parents sprinkled the face of the deceased with scented water (personal interview, 1989):

> Songs would send a message to the deceased. The deceased would hear the music, hear that his house was so noisy with people, and he would not be able talk to anyone, because the dead can't talk back. The deceased would then realize that he or she was dead and would accept that he or she had to leave the human world to enter another world. Only the rich would hire musicians for a funeral procession. The reason behind the music of the funeral procession is to send the spirit of the deceased to heaven, to support the spirit of the deceased by showing that even though he or she passed away, there are a lot of people who care about him or her and come to proceed to the cemetery. For the survivors, such as the family members, having live music to accompany the funeral procession shows that they are wealthy, that they care about the deceased, and that they wish for the deceased to pass peacefully into heaven, or wherever.

Sad songs such as *Phakhom* and *Nang Hong* were played by the pi phat ensemble. *Nang Hong* is a sacred song performed only for funerals. Musicians believe that if *Nang Hong* is performed or even rehearsed during any other time, misfortune or death will befall the group. We were unable to hear or record *Nang Hong*, and question how musicians remember this sacred piece when they are unable to practice or perform it frequently.

THE *WAI KHRUU* CEREMONY

The *wai khruu* ceremony of worshipping ancestral spirits is found in many performance genres throughout Cambodia, Laos and Thailand. It can be performed annually, weekly, and regularly before each performance. Many performers believe that praying to the ancestors and teachers will help them to perform better. They also pay respects and gratitude to the teachers for passing on the tradition. Sam-Ang Sam (1988:268) referred to the *pithi sampeah krou,* as prescribed in the *kraing anhchoeunh krou* (invocation of the spirits manual), which tells how to practice the ritual. According to Sam the ritual is observed on a number of occasions, inluding prior to a performance, called *hom rong. Hom rong* is conducted to bless the stage and all the performance items, and consists of a series of twelve musical pieces, the first of which is *sathukar.*

Thongmouan Vilavong, a member of the Natasin troupe, also described *hom long,* as it is called in Lao, as a series of fifteen instrumental pieces performed to worship the ancestral spirits, and to provide a prelude for the audience. The prelude which precedes a stage performance will gather the audience together and excite them to see the performance. The first piece of the worship is *sathukan* (personal interview, 1989). According to Miller, the *"wai kroo"* ceremony was performed in northeast Thailand by mohlam and lykhee troupes. The offerings to the spirits were placed on a tray, and included candles and flowers, and egg, rice wine, and other items (1985:46).

Khruu Ouane Southathamma led the Lao Natasin troupe in this ritual, which he probably learned in Bangkok or Cambodia. It is described by Somlith Prasasouk, one of the original members of the theater.

> I don't know the history of why we worship Leu Si's head. It has been carried on for many generations. Why does our art respect Phra Phikhanet, that has four arms and an elephant head? That is the instructor of music, so they pay respects to it today. We had incense, candles and flowers. We worshipped and prayed, 'please let the audience like and enjoy me.' We provided fruits, sweets and alcohol. Every year in April they had a major ceremony with offerings consisting of a pig's head, banana, coconut and merit making. After the monks ate, they chanted and we received blessings. Khruu Ouane led the worship of the ancestors. Worshipping the ancestors is very difficult. The person leading the ceremony must wear white, and must know the right words. Over here there is no one to lead. (personal interview, 1988)

Lamse Trechanh's training in Thailand also consisted of the wai khruu ceremony, but she did not describe it in as much detail so we are unable to compare the Lao to the Thai ritual.

> Thursday was the day for everybody to worship the ancestors. The meaning of Wai Khruu is to pay respect to the teachers and ancestors who have left this art behind for us to carry on, and to ask for talent. They also had an annual worship day. (personal interview, 1990)

The weekly *tway kru* ceremony of the Royal Khmer dancers described by Paul Cravath was performed every Thursday also. "The musicians were required to play at least five specified pieces of music, four of which corresponded to the four role types: female, male, monkey and ogre" (1986: 197). The ritual in the Khmer palace had implications beyond wishing for a smooth performance when it was requested by the king to "create security for the country or to fulfill some national need" (ibid.). The wai khruu ceremony was an important part of all performances in Southeast Asia. Its ritual origins are most likely Khmer, but the practices have been adapted within the Thai and Lao traditions.

The wai khruu ceremony remains an important part of the artists' beliefs and practices. Chandeng Pongphimkham, a Natasin dancer, strongly believes in the Buddhist and animist religions. A room in her house is designated to worshipping Buddha images and ancestral spirits. She recounted several incidents when neglecting the ancestors cause problems for the performers.

> At the school, the annual worship ceremony is held in June. It is related to both Buddhist and Brahman religions, because before we started we had to invite the Buddhist monk to perform the chants, and make merit. After that, we had the spirit ceremony with the Brahman calling the spirits. We believed that the spirit of the ancestors could come into our body or soul to assist us in performing well. Before each performance we had to light candles and incense first. If we did not worship, we might have some misfortune. We worshipped the Thotsakan mask, the giant. It is believed that certain giants follow the Buddhist precepts and others do not. They will eat raw meat and food, alcohol and smoke tobacco. It has been said that in Pha Tho No Kham [located in the city of Vang Vieng, north of Vientiane] there are two giants. At the time one giant will eat raw meat and so forth, the other giant will eat only fruit and vegetables. Now, if we do something wrong, such as not worship to ask for guidance or permission before dancing, we will indeed make a mistake, get confused, not perform smoothly, or forget what we're supposed to do.
>
> Four months ago we were coordinating a performance here with one by the dance group in Laos. People over there prayed for us and for the performance to go well and succeed, and we, over here, were supposed to do the same thing, but we didn't do it. What happened was that we all went to Cedar Rapids to perform and somehow Mr. Thongmouane forgot to bring the bag of equipment. They also got a flat tire on the way there and back. It had never happened before. Also, something must happen to make you sick. One time in Laos, we were going to perform Thotsakan (giant) dance or *khon*. The person who was to dance Thotsakan could not be found and they switched a big tall woman to replace him. After the performance was over, several of our teachers got sick and had an accident. We later had to ask for forgiveness, because we weren't supposed to let a woman perform the role of Thotsakan at all. (personal interview, 1988)

Oulinh Manivong, another dancer, described feeling possessed by spirits.

> Somehow I felt like something came into my body and made me like to dance when the music started to play. It would be normal without music. They said that the spirit comes into the dancer's body to giver her inspiration. I do not believe in spirits at all, but everytime they played the *hom long* I felt goosebumps and it made me want to dance immediately. Ever since I've been in the United States I haven't felt that way. May be I don't worship enough. Maybe I work too hard. (personal interview 1989)

The wai khruu ceremony is one of the most important rituals for Lao performing artists. Without it, the feeling of being disconnected from the ancestors, from the roots of the tradition, and in an entirely different context, has left many artists feeling uninspired to maintain their tradition.

CONCLUSION

Dontrii lao deum is part of a larger Southeast Asian tradition of music shared by Laos, Thailand and Cambodia. Songs, dance repertoire, and ritual ceremonies such as wai khruu provide strong evidence of a tradition that transcended national boundaries. However, dontrii lao deum developed its own style and evolved within the smaller context of ceremonies, court performances and festivals, and the larger context of a nation divided by war throughout most of its history. In Luang Prabang, its initial role was to serve as an offering to the gods, to provide excitement and atmosphere while accompanying ceremonies, and to entertain the palace residents and guests. It was performed by musicians from a neighboring village and was developed and supported by the kings. During the French colonization it was supported in order to evoke a sense of pride in Lao culture, facing threats by a pan-Thai nationalist sentiment. This may account for the denial by palace musicians of any contact with the Thai. Thus, it took on an added role of preserving the French colony, and accompanying ceremonies showing allegiance to the kingdom. After independence, the shift in power and administration to Vientiane caused the music and dance traditions to be overshadowed by a new "national" art, and to be self-consciously preserved. The Lao Natasin genre was relatively young. It was created in order to show a "national art" to foreigners and dignitaries. Music and dance compositions reflected the lowland Lao lifestyle, distinct from its Thai and Cambodian neighbors. The khene, the Lao national instrument, was introduced into a traditional pi phat ensemble, which accompanied newly choreographed dances illustrating ethnic harmony, and the agrarian lives of lowland Lao farmers, thereby promoting a sense of Lao nationalism. In 1975, dontrii lao deum was further divided, along with the citizens of Laos. The performing artists, now Lao Americans, struggled during their initial years of resettlement to maintain their tradition while, at the same time, adapting and assimilating into a new society. The new context has yet to define a secure role for dontrii lao deum. It is found only occasionally to promote the preservation of "folk traditions," and is performed on a stage, separated from the ceremonies and rituals it originally supported, and apart from the nation it helped to legitimate.

NOTES

* The authors would like to thank the Social Science Research Council, Indochina Studies Program for providing a grant to support this research. Funding support for the SSRC ISP program came from the American Council of Learned Societies, the Ford Foundation and the National Endowment for the Humanities. The authors would also like to express their appreciation to the Smithsonian Institution's Office of Folklife Programs for logistical support and to the Lao musicians and other community members who generously shared their knowledge and experiences, and whose cooperation made this research possible.

1. The groups we interviewed include the term "classical" in their names; i.e. the Royal Lao Classical Dance Troupe (Nashville, TN) and the Lao Kingdom Classical Musician Troupe (Riverside, CA). These names were accepted by the groups at the suggestion of Western-educated Lao community members who had been living in the United States for some time, but seemed to have little significance for the troupes themselves.

2. For description of musical instruments, see Rattanavong's "Music and Instruments in Laos: Historical Antecendents and the Democratic Revolution" in this volume.

3. The expression *ten kin ram kin* is literally translated as "dance to eat." It implies a very low class female who cannot otherwise earn a living. In some cases it is analogous to prostitution.

4. The Lao believe in the hierarchy of the body, with the head being the most sacred part, and the feet being the lowest part. To point one's foot at someone is extremely insulting, indicating that that person's status is below the lowest part of one's own body.

REFERENCES CITED

Abhay, Thao Nhouy
    1959   "Marriage Rites, Death and Funeral Rites. The That Luang Festivities." In *Kingdom of Laos: The Land of the Million Elephants and of the White Parasol*, ed. Rene de Berval, 137–144. Saigon: France-Asie.

Archaimbault, Charles
    1964   "Religious Structures in Laos," *Journal of the Siam Society* 52:56–74.

Compton, Carol
    1979   *Courting Poetry in Laos.* De Kalb: Northern Illinois University Center for Southeast Asian Studies.

Cravath, Paul
    1986   "The Ritual Origins of the Classical Dance Drama of Cambodia," *Asian Theatre Journal* 32:179–203.

Danielou, Alain
    1957   *La Musique De Cambodge et du Laos.* Pondicherry: Publications de l'Institute Francais d'Indologie.

De Berval, Rene, ed.
    1959   *Kingdom of Laos: The Land of the Million Elephants and of the White Parasol.* Saigon: France-Asie.

De Gironcourt, Georges
    1942   "Recherches de Geographie Musicale en Indochine," *Bulletin de la Société des Etudes Indochinoise* 7:1–174.

Dommen, Arthur J.
    1985   *Laos, Keystone of Indochina.* Boulder and London: Westview Press.

Gerboth, Walter
    1963   *Music of East and Southeast Asia: A Selected Bibliography of Books, Pamphlets, Articles and Recordings.* Brooklyn, N.Y.: State University of New York Press.

Hafner, James et al.
    1983   *River Road through Laos: Reflections of the Mekong.* Asian Studies Committee Occasional Papers Series No. 10. Amherst: University of Massachusetts.

Kene, Thao
    1959   "The Khene-Maker," In *Kingdom of Laos: the Land of the Million Elephants and of the White Parasol,* ed. Rene de Berval, 217–220. Saigon: France-Asie.

Knosp, Gaston
    1912   "Rapport sur une Mission Officielle d'Etude Musicale en Indochine," *Internationales Archiv fur Etnographie* 20.

Lefevre-Pontalis, Pierre
    1896   *Chansons et Fetes du Laos.* Paris.

LeBar, Frank M., ed.
    1960   *Laos: Its People, its Society, its Culture.* New Haven, Conn.: Hraf Press.

Miller, Terry
    1980   *An Introduction to Playing the Kaen.* Kent, Ohio: Kent State University Press.

    1984   "Reconstructing Siamese Musical History from Historical Sources: 1548–1932," *Asian Music* 15(2):32–41.

    1985   *Traditional Music of the Lao: Kaen Playing and Mawlum Singing in Northeast Thailand.* Westport, Conn.: Greenwood Press.

Miller, Terry, and Jarernchai Chonpairot
    1978   "The Musical Traditions of Northeast Thailand," *Journal of the Siam Society* 66/67:1–41.

    1979   "The Problems of Lao Discography," *Asian Music* 11(1):124–139.

Morton, David
    1970   "Thai Traditional Music: Hot-House Plant or Sturdy Stock?" *Journal of the Siam Society* 58/2:30–44.

    1976   *The Traditional Music of Thailand.* Berkeley: University of California Press.

Musique Khmere
    1969   Phnom Penh.

Nginn, Pierre S.
    1959   "The New Year Festivities; Lent and the Water Festival," In *Kingdom of Laos: the Land of the Million Elephants and of the White Parasol,* ed. Rene de Berval, 283–287. Saigon: France-Asie.

Pranee Jearaditharporn
    1973   "The Relationship of Music and Society as Seen in the Thai Case." M.A. thesis, Cornell University

Randel, Don, ed.
    1986   *The New Harvard Dictionary of Music*. Cambridge and London: Harvard
            University Press.

Ratanavong, Kham Ouane
    1973   *Apprenez le Khene: Essai d'une Methode Moderne*. Vientiane: Bulletin des Amis
            du Royaume Lao.

Sahai, Sachchidanand
    1980   "The Phra Lak Phra Lam and the Laotian Cultural Tradition," *Southeast Asian
            Review* 5 (2):67–84.

Sam, Sam-Ang
    1988   "The Pin Peat Ensemble: Its History, Music and Context. " Ph.D. diss., Wesleyan
            University.

Souvanna-Phouma, Tiao
    1959   "Music," In *Kingdom of Laos: the Land of the Million Elephants and of the White
            Parasol*, ed. Rene de Berval, 87–88. Saigon: France-Asie.

Stieglitz, Perry
    1990   *In a Little Kingdom*. Armonk and London: M.E. Sharpe.

Stuart-Fox, Martin
    1986   *Laos: Politics, Economy and Society*. Boulder: Lynne Rienner.

PERSONAL INTERVIEWS

Thongtanh Souvannaphanh, Springfield, Virginia, February 1989
Bounthan Xayprasith, Riverside, California, April 1989
Sisouphan Kounlavong, Nashville Tennessee, April 1990
Chandeng Pongphimkham, Des Monies, Iowa, August 1988, June 1990
Thongmouane Vilavong, Des Moines, Iowa August 1988, June 1990
Seng Chitdalay, Santa Ana, California, May 1989
Sinouane Oudomhack, Pomona, California, May 1989
Chanthy Chanthasouk, Charlotte, North Carolina, December 1988
Somlith Prasasouk, Des Moines, Iowa, August 1988
Lamse Trechanh, Nashville, Tennessee, February 1990
Oulinh Manivong, Santa Ana, California, May 1989

TRADITIONAL VERBAL ARTS IN LAOS:
FUNCTIONS, FORMS, CONTINUITIES, AND CHANGES
IN TEXTS, CONTEXTS, AND PERFORMANCES

Carol J. Compton

OM.
Be patient,
Be very patient with me
And protective of me
As I come to offer you
My sung poetry today...

May my words come as quickly
as a speeding chariot...
My the Lord Buddha protect me...
My all of my teachers watch over me
As I come before you
To present you with these songs. (C. Compton 1986:93)

It is with such verses as these, paying obeisance to the Lord Buddha and respect to one's teachers, that many a performance of Lao verbal arts might traditionally begin. However, a wide variety of elements have affected these arts in modern times, bringing about changes and limiting or eliminating some of the aspects of their performance. Such changes can be found in both the forms themselves and in their functions, reflecting a number of influences, both internal and external. However, the process of change has been gradual, so that the continuity is evident between modern performances and earlier descriptions.

Two prominent areas of continuity in most of these forms are the use of poetic language and the influence of Buddhism in the texts of these materials. Changes in the presentation of Lao verbal arts in modern times can be seen in a number of performance aspects; these include objectives, themes, length, context, music and/or dance accompaniment, audience composition and interaction, and costumes, makeup, and choreography (see Table 1 for a chart inducating some of the changes and how they may affect a performance). In addition there have been chances in the selection and training of those who will perform.

Before we look at some of the continuities and changes as reflected in one particular form of Lao verbal art, we will present a brief survey and descriptiion of soome of the ways the Lao have used language in performance. Much of Lao literature—which is generally thought to have reached its heights in the period between the thirteenth and sixteenth centuries (C. Compton 1983:9)—has had a performance orientation. With the exception of the chronicles, much of it has been written in poetry designed to be read, recited, or sung for an audience. Thus, the physical presence of an audience was assumed to be part of any presentation. Most of the verse forms used are described by the Lao scholar Maha Sila Viravong in a number of his works (1962) and include some which reflect Sanskrit influence (i.e., *kaap*) and those which are felt to be truly indigenous forms (*lam, haay*) as wel as a form said to reflect Pali influence (*pranyaa*). Different verse forms are generally associated with particular contexts for verbal performance in Laos; for instances, "*haay* is generally used for *suut khouan* or *thet* because it is pleasant to listen to (ibid.:218, my translation). The *suut khouan* (*suut khuan*) he mentions is often referred to in the literature on Laos as a *baci* (*baasi*), the ceremony for calling of the spirits (see C. Compton 1979:202-203; Heinze 1982). The thet (*theet*) is the chanting form used by monks to present Buddhist teachings to the people (Maha Sila 1962:218).

Another verbal performance style involves the poetry form called *aan* or *aan nangsyy*, meaning literally "to read" or "to read books," and is the form used "to present long poems or epics when reading so that people can listen to and know those stories" (ibid.:204). "For the most part, these are the stories of the fifty lives [of the Buddha] of the Jatakas and include such stories as *Kalaket, Sin Xay*, and *Kay Keo*" (ibid.:205). The *kham phanyaa* have traditionally been "exchanges between young men and young women situated in one place and competing with sharp, pointed, or clever sayings, challenging the other to respond in like manner (ibid.:255). Finally, the Lao verbal art probably best known to outsides is the *lam*, the essentially extemporaneous, sung poetry of a skilled performer called *mohlam*. This form, which involves the synthesis of poetry, singing, instrumental music, and to a lesser extent dance and gestures, will be our focus as we look at the kinds of changes and continuities to be found in Lao verbal performng arts today.

CHANGES IN CHANNEL

One of the most obvious changes in the performance of lam has been in the ways this form has been presented to audiences. Where once the eyes and ears of the audience received the songs of the mohlam directly in a context in which both singer and audience might be sitting on the same mat on floor of someone's porch in a village, now the sounds and the scenes of a performance may be received in other ways. The modern mohlam now may send out his or her verses over the radio, through television, on cassette tapes, on records, or through films and videos. The poetry the mohlam composes may end up in print in books and magazines and small pamphlets; his or her performance may be heard over a loudspeaker attached to a microphone sitting on a stage that cannot even be seen by someone listening to the mohlam from another nearby house. In each of these instances the components of the performance may differ, for the channel indicates some of the ways in which the performance is going to be received by his or her now-often-absent audience. Since the singer may not be able to see how the audience is reacting, on-the-spot adjustments to content or style which might have been made to please a particular audience are now no longer possible. Therefore, other techniques for drawing the audience in and keeping their interest may be tried.

We can see how the channel may affect the performance byusing the examples of lam performed on radio stations. In the past, a performance of lam was just that, a live event in which the audience was usually in close proximity to the singer. Dance and gesture were integral components as the performers were both seen and heard. With the advent of radio, lam became very popular and many more people could hear a single performance of radio lam than could attend any one village performance. As a result, though, the visual element was lost; dance and gesture could no longer be included and the performer thus lost an element that had from time to time carried certain subtle or not so subtle messages.

At the same time, however, there were advantages to singing over the radio. A much wider audience could be reached much more quickly, and if a mohlam were indeed good, the radio audience could make him or her famous almost overnight. Higher prices for live performances could then be obtained, and some radio artists were thus invited to other regions of Laos and northeast Thailand for substantial fees. A number of them became rather well-off as a result of this new channel. Another effect of the radio was that new styles of lam or regional styles of lam from other areas of Laos or northeast Thailand would be heard sooner by larger audiences including other mohlam, who might then take ideas or styles into their own repertoire.

Some mohlam who were hired to sing over the radio stations in Laos during the 1960s and 1970s chose to remain anonymous because of the propagandistic nature of the topics about which they were asked to sing. Generally, when mohlam lam, somewhere within the text of the song they identify themselves by name. For instance, in the text of a song which was simply about courting between two young people, a performance having no explicitly political message, the singer's name would be mentioned somewhere in the verses, perhaps a number of times. If a pair of singers alternated verses, they might refer to each other by name. An example of such a "signature" is found in this verse from a performance of courting lam by a famous southern Lao mohlam. Note that she laments her new role as a political propaagandist:

> I, Duangphaeng, was born into this life
> With excessive torments.
> The life of a singer
> Is like that:
> I have found only sadness.
> I've wandered and traveled from place to place,
> Trying to create
> Gardens of pleasure, not fields of rice. (C. Compton 1979:77-78)

On the other hand, the full text of a radio performance of lam telling of the difficulties faced by the Lao people and their families due to the war contains no such signature by either the male or female singer (C. Compton 1975) and numerous other tapes on such topics to which I have listened omit the singer's name. Whether or not singers today are inserting their own names into the texts of their performances, given the absence of conflict, is an interesting question. However, a large number of radio performances would have to be analysed before a pattern could be noted.

TABLE I

MEDIUM	CONTROL OF THEME/TEXT	LENGTH OF PERFORMANCE	PLACE OF PERFORMANCE	INSTRU-MENTATION	USE OF DANCE a) PERFORMER	b) AUDIENCE
LIVE	Singer and or sponsor	Usually very long (9 pm until dawn, two nights in row, or longer)	Porch of home underneath home; on the ground	Typical for style and region of the country	Yes, seated or standing, depending on style of lam. Maybe if Sithandone	Yes if it is Saravane or Tang Vay; No for a number of form
LIVE WITH MICRO-PHONE	Singer and or sponsor	Long but usually ends by 1 or 2 am (i.e., many hours)	Usually raised stage outdoors; sometimes indoor stage	Traditional or mix of traditional and Western instruments	Yes, usually standing	Yes if it is Saravane or Tang Vay, otherwise no
RADIO	Government, producer, and singer	Usually short 15 minutes to half-hour; lam lang is longer	Radio studio or home studio	Traditional or mix of traditional and Western instr.	No	No
TV	Government, producer, and singer	Usually short 10 minutes per performer, but lam lyang is longer	TV studio	Traditional or mix of traditional and Western instr.	Generally yes	No
AUDIO CASS. OR RECORD	Producer, singer	As long as the original performance, or short, edited sections	Recording studio or anywhere	As in the original	No or N/A	No
VIDEO CASS.	Government, producer and singer	As long as the original or short clips of a performance	Usually TV studio or stage; can be anywhere	As in the original	Generally yes	No
FILM	Producer, and singer	To date, short	"On location"	As in the original	Sometimes	No
BOOK	Singer and publisher	Long if full traditional story or can be a set of short pieces	Created or imagines	N/A	No	No

TABLE I (continued)

COSTUME	MAKEUP	AUDIENCE COMMENT VERBAL INTERACTION	AUDIENCE POSITION
Lao skirt and blouse for woman, pants and shirt for man	Man, no woman, maybe	Yes, almost always	If seated oin mats, usually semi-circle toward singers; if singers on stage, audience may be seated on the ground or standing
Lao skirt and blouse plus jewelry or flowers man in pants and shirt but may add phakhoma (traditional textile wrapped around waist)	Man, maybe woman, often	Yes, usually if the stage is outside; perhaps when stage inside	If outside, seated on mats or grass; if inside stage, usually seated on chairs or mats
Daily wear of the singers (i.e., nothing special)	By individual taste	Almost never has audience	N/A
Yes, may be same as in live performance or more elaborate	Yes usually noth man and woman wear makeup	Almost never has audience	N/A
No	No	None, unless recording a live performance	Usually not applicable
Yes, may be same as in live performance or more elaborate	Yes, usually both wear makeup	None, unless taping a live performance	Usually not applicable
Yes, may be same as in live performance or more elaborate	Yes, usually both wear makeup	None, unless filming a live performance	Usually not applicable
No	No	No, except as reader	Usually not applicable

Another channel used for many years to record and present lam has been film. Films, videos, and live television present a different set of issues for the mohlam. With radio, these media share that distance from the audience that prevents some of the traditional verbal and visual interaction between mohlam and audience. Like radio, they have time constraints that require, for the most part, very short periods of time for what has generally taken place over many hours over one or more evenings. While village festival performances and performances at homes in rural Laos once might have lasted until dawn, those produced for radio, television, or film must be squeezed into short segments to meet the needs of the producers. Fifteen minutes to half an hour over the radio for any one mohlam is generally the time limit, while troupes of mohlam may be given somewhat longer time slots for a whole episode on radio or television. In any event, an outsider, not the mohlam, now decides when to start and stop and how long to continue. In addition, mohlam may be asked to put on costumes and makeup they might never have worn had they been performing live in a village setting. One advantage for the mohlam at a television station is that he or she can once again make use of dance and gesture as part of the presentation. However, such dance or gesture is now directed at an unseen audience, so that the subtle interaction possible between mohlam and audience in live performances is still missing. The same, of course, holds true for video and film performances.

In the 1960s and 1970s forty-five rpm records of lam were made (in Thailand) and sold throughout northeast Thailand and the Mekong River valley towns of Laos. Financially astute mohlam might receive a percentage of the sales as well as an initial payment for the performance itself. Since many of the mohlam worked on both sides of the Mekong, central Thai and Western influences reached into many Lao-speaking areas of Laos through the presentations made by these widely known singers.

Following quickly on the heels of the records was the production and copying of cassette tapes of mohlam performances. Though a professional singer would be well paid for a live performance, people began to bring their own tape recorders to the homes of friends and record their favorite mohlam. Others would copy these tapes and certainly some paid performance opportunities were lost as people began to play the cassettes of performances already held instead of setting up new ones and hiring the singers. In addition, they were now able to buy tapes of mohlam from northeastern Thailand.

Though most mohlam are performance-oriented, the older well-known mohlam—once they had passed performance age—might write up poetry from their repertoire and give it to a printer to print up and sell to bring in additional money. In addition, some people who were skilled at writing these poetry forms, but who had never or rarely performed themselves, began to write and get their materials printed. Sometimes poetry was written out too, before it was broadcast live on the radio, if the topic were particularly sensitive (C. Compton 1979:117).

Live performances of lam, then, have had to compete with and have been influenced by performances designed for and presented over the radio, on television, and in film and on records, tapes, and books. It is not surprising, then, that the ways in which singers are trained has also been changing. In addition, the structure and needs of the society in which they live have been changing, so that the circumstances under which they learn and the context under which they perform are no longer the same. The objectives of lam, which might once have been a matter between a professional mohlam and the individual or group hiring him or her, may now also be a concern of the larger society and even of the government.

CHANGES IN TRAINING AND PERFORMANCE OBJECTIVES

Twenty years ago in Laos, and probably before that, the choice of becoming a mohlam rested primarily with an individual and his or her family. Once the decision was made to study lam, the next step was to find the appropriate learning situation and the appropriate teacher. One might go to study with a teacher and work in the mohlam teacher's rice fields to pay for the opportunity. A whole group of young people could be found studying and working in such circumstances at the same time. If a family member knew the lam poetry and performance techniques well, a lucky individual might study at home with a father, grandfather, aunt, or other relative. Other individuals would go to a nearby temple to study poetry forms used in lam under the tutelage of a learned monk, or in some cases, a monk might leave the temple after many years and eventually become a mohlam (ibid.:111). In the course of such study, many of the stories and teachings of the Buddhist tradition would be studied and this literature would serve as a resource for the mohlam to draw on throughout his career. Often the themes of the suffering humans undergo because of their excessive desires would appear in the texts of singers trained in this tradition. For example, in an unpublished excerpt from a translation of such a performance, first the male mohlam (Sunee) and then the female mohlam (Duangphaeng) expresses the pain caused by such suffering.

> Sunee:
> My heart is uncertain and restained,
> But my desire is excessive.
> My soul is possessed, churning up
> Like water whipped into waves.
>
> Duangphaneg:
> I wait patiently until dawn for you,
> But you don't even think about taking me...
> My misery is excessive...
> Tears flow, washing my cheeks;
> Alas, I look for you, but you're not to be found. (C. Compton)

In addition to references to Buddha and Buddhist literature, the oral performances in the 1960s and early 1970s contained references to other religious figures, gods, and literatures with an Indic background. Thus we find Indic references scattered throughout both the introductory sections of a performance in which the singer pays respect to his or her teachers (*wái khúu* or *ñok khúu*) and the main sections of a performance. The following examples from a recording made in 1973 (C. Compton 1986:95, 97) include a number of such references.

> 30c   Along with the merit of the ancient gods
>   Of all the Four Guardians of the World,

31d   Of the Earth, of the Naga King,
       Of Mekhala, the Little Goddess of Lightning,

32c   And of Siva. The listeners will be overflowing;
       Indra himself will come to watch me.[1]

Once facility in the composition of poetry forms appropriate to lam has been learned, young singers would strike out on their own, searching for contexts in which to perform (and get paid) and working on their performance skills, thus building a reputation and a clientele. Such mohlam were professionals; this was how they earned their living. During festival seasons they would tour about from village to village where they had been hired in advance as one of the main attractions of the *boun* (*bun*), or village festival. They worked hard; at the height of her popularity, one singer reported to me she had performed thirty nights in a row in a wide variety of towns and villages. She was, of course, exhausted; she was also financially better off than many of her friends, however, living as she did in a nice house, having a stereo, jewelry, and other material goods.

Under the present government (the Lao People's Democratic Republic), there have been some changes in the way the performing arts and performers are viewed. When we look at the functions of the verbal and performing arts in a society, we need to look at their past history, their current situation, and also at what the future seems to hold for them. As we consider these arts in Laos, we need to look at the large picture of the role of culture and the arts in society. For socialist countries, the perforning arts have been an area of great interest, research, and utility. By this I mean that socialist countries have generally viewed the performing arts as having an important role in the development of the socailist state. For instance, General Kaysone Phomvihane, chairman of the Council of Ministers (1975–) and head of the government, has stated that one of the cultural aims of the government is "to select and use the precious heritage of the culture of our fatherland and its nationalities" (cited in Doré 1982:107).

Performing arts in the service of the state are able to achieve many things written literature cannot accomplish, particularly in a country such as Laos which has uneven literacy rates in the various ethnic groups and segments of society. Messages can be sent to the people visually and orally through performing arts which may touch them more deeply than the same messages presented in written forms. In addition, since a performance may often have a a rather larger audience than in the past, a group feeling or spirit may develope in the audience as the result of a successful performance. People may talk about or refer to the content (message) of such a performance at a later date. It becomes both a shared experience and a source of shared, common information. This use of folk media to reach large segments of rural populations with a particular message has also been used with some success in rural development efforts in other nonsocialist areas of the world (J. L. Compton 1984). In societies such as Laos which do not have high levels of literacy, the use of verbal and performing arts to present messages and themes to the public can be very effective. An example of such a message exhorting listeners from hill area ethnic groups to follow new agricultural practices was broadcast a few years ago on Lao radio. A song on the state radio admonishes:

Oh, hill-tribe girl, stop cutting and
destroying the forest; come live with me
in the lowlands and we will grow paddy
rice together in a cooperative.   (Ireson 1988:5)

Research on traditional texts and attempts to preserve them are an important part of the activities of the National Institute for Artistic, Literary, and Linguistic Research of the Ministry of Culture of the Lao People's Democratic Republic.

> This institute was organized in 1983 for research in the arts, literature, and culture and to distribute that research to the Lao people. There is a staff of 27 trained in the S[oviet] U[nion], India, and Vietnam. . . . The main task at present is to preserve artistic and literary traditions and to recapture those which have been lost. (McDonnell 1988:16)

One area of activity in the preserving of these forms has been the videotaping of festivals and celebrations at which the performance traditions of both lowland Lao and various ethnic groups are presented to the public. This videotaping helps preserve old elements of the culture, "and then a new ensemble is built up by the addition of new elements and selected ancient fragments" (Doré 1982:108). One short selection from a 1986 videotape which I have viewed gives an excellent illustration of such a synthesis. On the tape, a beautiful young woman in traditional Lao silk skirt and scarf (and a non-traditional blouse) sings in Lao about the nice aspects of love of country. In another tape we see an audience sitting in rows of chairs viewing a performance of short excerpts from a wide variety of musical and verbal arts from many different ethnic groups. A sample is presented of forms which sometimes would have had audience participation, but which are now presented, costumed, and choreographed for more formal presentation. It is important to note here that some of these changes, such as the presentation of shorter segments of larger works for the viewing of a (modern, Western-style) formal audience, are ones which have been taking place gradually in Laos, and similar though much smaller productions of a variety of choreographed ethnic dances and arranged ethnic music were given at the National School of Music and Dance (Natasin) in the early 1970s under the Royal Lao government.

There have also been changes in who may perform, or who choses who may perform, and these appear to be more significant than many of the other changes mentioned. Since the mohlam have traditionally been quite independent, an exchange of letters between readers and the editor of a column in the newspaper *Vientiane Mai* in 1983 is of particular interest. These letters discuss a policy of having "amateur cultural troupe controls" and various musicians and performers ask questions about how such controls will affect them and what they will be allowed to do. The regulation to which they are referring, regulation number three in the amateur troupe control plan, reads

> that a private person or family which has musical instruments or a private Lao folksinging troupe whether they are cardres, hold government office, or are merchants, anyone who used these instruments and skills to earn revenue for himself, are absolutely not allowed to get up and travel around to perform on their own for gain. (16, 17 February 1983)

However, the announcement does go on to say that they should fill out a "form requesting permission for the Vientiane Capital propaganda and cultural training section" (ibid.). Clearly this registration is a new situation for many performers, and one would think it might have some long-term effects in the growth and development or continuation of mohlam at the local and regional levels. It is not clear what the situation for these sohlam will be nor how they will be regarded in the future.

Another aspect of the traditional form of a verbal arts performance that has changed as the functions of the performances have changed is the *wai khuu* or *nyok khuu* section of a performance in which one pays respect to one's teachers. In a full, traditional performance many verses of poetry at the opening might have been devoted to paying respect to the Lord Buddha and one's teachers (C. Compton 1986). In the modern contexts on television, video, or cassette tapes, this segment may be shortened to only one or two verses—or even a phrase—and in some cases it seems that this segment may even be absent or at least extremely obscure. Certainly a significant change in this important tradition of acknowledging one's debt to those who have guided the artist has been taking place.

Clearly the Lao verbal arts traditions are still highly regarded, and videotapes of mohlam are being made by the government. An attempt to strengthen the growth of *lam lyang* has also been noted. Whether or not such growth and development in this area of the Lao verbal arts is going to be determined at the state level, there have certainly been a wide variety of new channels and new contexts for Lao verbal artists to use, and new challenges no doubt lie ahead for the modern mohlam and other performing artists of Laos.

The Lao verbal arts, and most particularly the lam, have had a long and rich tradition. Their ability to adapt to the variety of changes in society have kept them strong. As these verbal arts enter another period of change, we look forward to seeing what direction they will take next. For centuries, the mohlam of Laos have shared their songs and stories, their history and culture on open porches and stages and *salas* throughout the nation. Their flexibility, creativity, skill, and commitment to lam, have set them apart from others. We look forward to hearing again and again their sung poetry as they create and preserve the traditions of their people.

Olanoh.

NOTES

1.   The Lao transcription of each of these is: cătŭl âat thán sii (Four Guardians); thɔɔlaníi (Earth Goddess); nàak (Naga King); náan nɔɔy méekhăláa (Mekhala, the Little Goddess of Lightning); ſiisŭun (Siva); and phaſñáa ſiin(Indra); For Mekhala (Kerr (1972:936) gives three definitions: "angel of the clouds; goddess of lightning; goddess of the sea." However, the Lao with whom I discussed this translation preferred "Goddess of Lightning" for her.

REFERENCES CITED

Compton, Carol J.
  1975   "Lam Khon Savan: A Traditional Form and a Contemporary Theme." In *A Thai
              Festschrift for Acan Gedey*, ed. Thomas W. Gething, 55–82. Southeast Asian
              Studies Working Paper No. 8. Honolul: University of Hawaii.

  1979   *Courting Poetry in Laos: A Textual and Linguistic Analysis*. Center for Southeast
              Asian Studies Special Report No. 18. De Kalb, Illinois: Center for Southeast Asian
              Studies, Northern Illinois University.

  1983   "Lao Literature." *Encyclopedia of World Literature in the 20th Century*, III:9–10.
              New York, Praeger.

  1986   "A Wai Khru for Acan Gedney." In *Papers from a Conference on Thai Studies in
              Honor of William J. Gedney*, ed. Robert J. Bickner, Thomas John Hudak, and
              Patcharin Peyasintiwong, 91–106. Michigan Papers on South and Southeast Asian
              Studies No. 25. Ann Arbor: The Center for South and Southeast Asian Studies,
              University of Michigan.

Compton, J. Lin
  1981   "Folk Media and Development in South and Southeast Asia." In *Indegenous
              Knowledge Systems and Development*, ed. David Brokensha and Dennis M.
              Warren. Lanham, Maryland: University Press of America.

Doré, Amphay
  1982   "The Three Revolutions in Laos." In *Contemporary Laos*, ed. Martin Stuart-Fox,
              101–115. London: University of Queensland Press.

Heinze, Ruth I.
  1982

Ireson, Randall
  1988   "Laos: Building a Nation under Socialism." *Indochina Issues* 79:1–7.

Kerr, Allen D.
  1972   *Lao-English Dictionary*. Washington D.C.: Consortium Press (Catholic University
              of America Press).

McDonnell, Mary Byrne
  1988   "Report on a Trip to Indochina." New York: Indochina Studies Program, Social
              Science Research Council.

Sila Viravong, Maha
  1970   *Santhalaksana waynyaakoon laaw, phaak sii* (Manual of Versification, Lao
              Grammar, part 4). Vientiane: Ministry of Education of Laos.

A MELODY NOT SUNG: THE PERFORMANCE OF
LAO BUDDHIST TEXTS IN NORTHEAST THAILAND

Terry E. Miller

However you wish to define "ethnomusicology," its very being depends on the existence of "music." John Blacking has offered a universal definition of music: "humanly organized sound" (1973:10). John Cage has asserted that everything we do is music. Neither Blacking's oft-quoted phrase, which does not seem to eliminate speech, nor Cage's philosophical assertion, takes into account the reality of how individual societies define music. One of the most devastating questions that can be asked of a Western classical music major is "what is music?" They work with music every day, but who has thought about defining it? Indeed, neither that hoary Bible of Western musicology, the *New Harvard Dictionary of Music,* nor the *New Grove Dictionary of Music and Musicians* have definitions for "music."

Even within our own society there are radically different views on what music is and is not. Some years ago I wrote to an old Primitive Baptist elder in North Carolina. Wanting to know whether his congregation used notation, I asked the late Elder Walter Evans, "When you sing, do you use music?" His answer confused me: "We don't have any music in our church; all we do is sing." Through this experience I came to understand that for many people "music" means instruments. A Black student in a class related that when he was young he attended church with his grandmother. After one particularly moving part of the service, he asked her, "Grandma, why were you singing?" She corrected him: "I wasn't singin', I was prayin'." Examples can be drawn from throughout the world; by our definition, and by Blacking's, these phenomena, which are usually but not always vocal, are music, but according to the culture which produced them, they are not music. Therefore, how does the ethnomusicologist approach phenomena that have melody and rhythm but which the informants do not consider to be music? Are we ethnocentric in studying "non-musical" phenomena as music? Even more troubling, do we suspend research in societies that have no term for music? This is precisely the dilemma with Lao society, for strictly speaking there is no equivalent term for "music." The few terms that one finds in the dictionary (e.g., *dondee*) or in old literature (e.g., *nontri and duriya*) are of Pali origin and refer to instrumental music. *Mahori* also meant instrumental music originally but came to denote a particular ensemble of instruments. There is thus no equivalent term for "music" as used by Blacking, Cage, or most schooled Western musicians, since this includes both vocal and instrumental phenomena.

Nevertheless, in studying the "music" of the Lao people (meaning Lao speakers in both Laos and northeastern Thailand), one encounters a number of phenomena that easily satisfy universal and Western classical definitions of music but which are not considered music by the Lao. All are vocal and all are text based. Indeed, most derive their musical qualities from the tonal inflections of the words. All exhibit musical elements, including mode, contour, rhythm, and texture. The performance of none of them, however, is described with a verb meaning "to sing" (*hawng, kup,* or *lum*). Most importantly for the subject at hand, all derive aspects of their musical nature from the text, which may or may not begin in written form. They include 1) Buddhist chant (*suat*), 2) Buddhist sermons (*tet*), 3) special Buddhist sermons for telling the story of Prince Wetsundawn (*tet lae*), 4) a ceremony to call back the "spiritual essence" (*soo-kuan* or *ba-see*), 5) reading stories written on palm-leaf manuscripts (*an nungsü*), 6) responsorial singing during celebrations, especially the rocket festival (*süng bung-fai*).

To most listeners from outside the Lao culture, these genres sound like singing—some more than others—but none is considered singing by the Lao. What distinguishes them as a group from "singing" noted earlier is the fact that all are associated in some way with ritual or at least spiritual matters. "Singing" is reserved for entertainment situations. Therefore the distinction is based not on style but on function. Similar kinds of distinctions are made elsewhere in the world and for similar reasons. For example, in the context of Islam, the call to prayer (*adhan*), reading the Quran, and chanting the name of God (*dhikr*) all have musical characteristics—some require considerable "musical" ability—but none is considered singing.

BUDDHIST GENRES

The Theravada Buddhism of the Lao, whose ultimate sources were India and Sri Lanka, makes use of a sacred language, Pali, which is related to Sanskrit, the sacred language of Mahayana Buddhism. The temple was traditionally the center of literacy in the village and town, and Buddhist monks and novices learned to read and write palm leaf manuscripts called *nungsü bai lan* or *nungsü pook*.

The scripts used to write the Pali sounds varied by area: *dua müang*, derived from Shan, in northern Thailand; *dua tam*, similar to dua müang, in northeast Thailand and Laos; and *dua kawm*, which is essentially Khmer, in central Thailand (i.e., the old Kingdom of Siam). Originally these scripts were derived from early Indian alphabets used to write Pali and Sanskrit and adapted as a means to write Khmer, Siamese, Lao, Burmese, and variants of these. Previously these languages were unwritten. In addition to adapting the scripts, these languages also borrowed varying amounts of vocabulary. Only the more learned monks could actually read the sacred scripts; boys and men ordained for a limited time, sometimes no more than a week, obviously would learn little if any. Today few monks read the old scripts, and instead the texts are printed in books using Thai or Lao letters but in a spelling system peculiar to Buddhism. Sermons, however, are sometimes in Lao and therefore written in the Lao alphabet in Laos or Thai in Thailand.

Chant (*Suat*)

Strictly speaking, Buddhist monks are not permitted to sing or entertain. Although chant may resemble song, it is not song because the verb used for recitation of the sacred texts, *suat*. Suat, refers to "chanting" with or without a written text before the reciter; ultimately the words had been written but could be memorized. Resident monks and novices chant two required services each day, one in the early morning (*tum wut sao*) and one in the late afternoon (*tum wut yen* or *tum wut kum*). In addition special chants are required for funerals and various kinds of merit-making rituals (*tumboon*). Chant is normally done from memory, but since not all know the chants equally well, problems often occur. As a result the usual chanting may exhibit mispronunciation, stumbling, errors of memory, and apparent disagreement over melodic inflection. During a performance individual monks cease singing for short periods at will according to their memory, throat condition, and interest. During a recording session of the morning service at a northeastern Thai temple in 1973, the monks suddenly broke off and requested that I turn off the tape recorder. After leaving the *bot* (building housing the Buddha image), they returned with books in hand, to record the service accurately rather than the more usual way.

Since Pali is nontonal it is theoretically possible to chant on a monotone, but in practice this is rarely the case. Monks are not trained to chant in a systematic way; they imitate those who have greater experience. Without a central authority requiring uniform practice or notation to guide the monks, a variety of techniques emerge. This results in different scale forms having from two to four pitches, one of which is a reciting tone. Using pitch G as a notated reciting pitch, one group of scales exhibits a falling to F, and the other group to D. (N.B. The pitches of the chant have been given hypothetical letter names taken from Western theory to facilitate discussion. Their relationships only approximate the equal temperament implied.)

Group I	Group II
(1) F G	(1) D G
(2) F G A	(2) D G A
(3) F G B^b	(3) D G B
(4) F G A B^b	

While Pali chant cannot be transcribed into a fixed meter, the rhythm expresses the difference between long and short syllable lengths and phrasing. Two versions of what is perhaps the best-known chant to pay respect to the Buddha, "*namo dut sa, pakawadoh, ahrahadoh, sum-mah sum poot-tut sa*" [We worship the Blessed One, Arahat, Supreme Lord Buddha], are found in figure 1, the first using scale I (3), the second using scale II (2).

Palm leaf manuscript in *tai noi* (old Lao) script

Figure 1. Two *namo* chants recorded at Wut Mahachai in Mahasarakam, Thailand.

Since Pali does not require melodic inflection, is there a logic for divergence from the reciting pitch? The most logical reasons given are that inflection relieves the voice, better expresses the text, and beautifies the delivery. It is also true that the text is written phonetically in Thai or Lao letters which have built-in tonal implications. For example, the syllable *sum* is written with the letter *saw* (ส) which is pronounced with a rising tone. Consequently, the tonal inflections inherent in the Thai/Lao writing system have evidently affected the way non-tonal Pali is chanted.

Buddhist sermons (tet)

While Pali chant varies in its details from temple to temple, it is far more predictable than sermons, which vary from austere chant style to highly embellished melody—what we would call "singing." Some kinds of sermons resemble entertainment singing (lum) and have a close musical relationship, though without instrumental accompaniment. Certain kinds of sermon delivery require exceptional vocal control and musical ability, and while monks do not in theory "sing" or entertain, in practice they do. For special sermons delivered in tet lae style, specific monks are hired because of their vocal abilities and because the lay people enjoy listening to them (see following section on tet lae). But because the context is ritualistic and the purpose is didactic, the resulting event is not "singing" but "preaching"; the verb *tet* is derived from Pali *tet-sana*, "to teach."

Unlike Pali chant, whose meaning is obscure to most lay listeners and many monks as well, sermons are normally given in Lao, albeit with some phrases in Pali. Tambiah (1970:125–6) lists three categories of tet among the Lao.

1. Sermons appropriate for merit-making occasions, when the monks tell of the advantages of making offerings. Typical occasions include *boon katin* (ceremony of giving to monks), *kao pansah* (beginning of Buddhist Lent), *awk pansah* (end of Buddhist Lent), and for funerals and cremation services. These sermons were formerly written in a sacred script, now in Thai, and were delivered in a manner similar to Pali chant, using scales of two to four pitches.
2. Sermons for celebrations observing the opening of a new or repaired preaching hall (*sala*), building housing the Buddha image (bot or *wihan*), or monks' living quarters (*gootee*). Sermons of this type are similar in delivery to the previous type.

3. Sermons that tell stories (*tet nitan*), both sacred and quasi-sacred. Some are used throughout Thailand and are consequently in a mixture of Thai and Pali, but those that are of local origin or have been localized are in Lao with or without Pali words. Sermons in Lao, the language of the people, tend to be the most highly appreciated. Tet nitan can be grouped into three sub-classes.

   a. *Batom sompot* sermons tell both the life of the Buddha and of his previous 547 lives, called *jataka* stories—stories of exemplary princes and other high characters. The language is Thai mixed with Pali delivered in a plain style similar to chant.

   b. *Tet boon prawet* sermons concentrate entirely on the story of Prince Wetsundawn (Vessantara in Pali), the penultimate life of the Buddha just before enlightenment. The language is Lao mixed with Pali, in a verse form called *rai*, and chanted in a wide range of melodic styles, some among the most ornate heard among the Lao.

   c. *Tet nitan pün müang* sermons tell local stories and regional myths of noble princes and beautiful princesses, romance, wild animals, and the triumph of good over evil. Among the most famous are *Pa Daeng Nang Ai* [Mr. Daeng and Mrs. Ai], *Tao Sowat* [Prince Sowat], and *Sio Sawat* [name]. The language is Lao and the style is somewhat more interesting melodically than the other types, sometimes using five tones. These preached stories are also told in various kinds of lum singing, especially for theatre (*lum moo* and *lum plün*).

Of these, 3.b.—tet boon prawet—will be discussed here.

THE STORY OF PRINCE WETSUNDAWN: TEXTS, CONTEXTS, AND PERFORMANCES

Prince Wetsundawn, known for his generosity since childhood, is approached by Brahmins who seek the kingdom's white elephant whose magic will bring rain to end the drought. Angry citizens force the king to exile his son for this deed, and his family joins him. During their exit, Wetsundawn gives away the chariot, and they continue on foot. An old Brahmin, Choochok, tests the prince's generosity by asking him to give the children into servitude, which the prince does. The deity Sakka tests Wetsundawn by asking for his wife, which he agrees to. When the king hears of his son's misery, he pays Choochok a ransom, and Choochok dies a glutton. The royal parents go to the forest and bring Wetsundawn and his family back to the kingdom in triumph.

Because Prince Wetsundawn was the last human incarnation before buddhahood, his life was exceptionally meritorious and serves as an apt model for humans in lower levels of development. Although the jataka tales came to the Tai peoples in Pali, they were not only translated into Thai and Lao but localized as well, making Wetsundawn (in this case) a Lao prince observing Lao customs. The reading of the story constitutes a major Buddhist festival throughout Thailand and Laos.

In central Thailand it is called *tumboon mahachat* ("great birth") and takes place in late October or early November after the Buddhist lent is ended (awk pansah) and before the harvest. Each of the thirteen chapters, called *gun* or *bun* (from Pali *kanda*) is followed by instrumental music played by a classical Thai *beepat [piphat]* ensemble. Among the Lao the festival is called *boon prawet* and occurs after the harvest, in late February or early March, lasting from one to three days.

In a three-day festival the first day includes a ritual inviting a water spirit to come, so that the growing season about to begin will be a good and wet one. During the afternoon of the second day villagers assemble in the sala to hear the story of Pra Malai, called *malaiya soota*. Pra Malai was sent to hell (*narok*) to preach to its inhabitants and observe its tortures, then to preach in heaven (*sawan*), and finally went to earth where he described what he had seen. Numerous temples decorate a wall in their sala with large, gory engravings showing Pra Malai's travels and in explicit detail the horrors of hell. This tale, which is included with most modern printed "manuscripts" in Lao, falls into two sections, *malai mün* ("ten thousand flowers") and *malai saen* ("one hundred thousand flowers"). These are, however, not normally a part of tumboon mahachat in central or north Thailand. The chant style is similar to that of ordinary tet nitan, i.e., restricted to perhaps three pitches in speech rhythm.

The third day begins sometime after midnight when the villagers assemble to invite the *tewadah* (divine angels), then process around the sala three times and finally enter to begin the story. Because the northeastern Thai/Lao version has fourteen *gun* or *bun* (chapters) instead of thirteen, fourteen monks must be invited to read them, each of whom is sponsored by a family which makes offerings, usually of rice, to the temple. If done completely, recitation of the entire story takes up to fifteen hours. During the day villagers may process about the temple grounds and throughout town carrying artificial "money trees" (*don dawk ngun*) soliciting donations for the temple. Periodically a monk will leave the sala to receive and bless these "money trees." During the preceding evenings and after the reading itself is completed, many temples have a fair within the compound featuring, besides food and drink stands, such entertainments as movies, boxing, *rum wong* popular dancing, and traditional lum singing, both theatrical and nontheatrical.

The texts from which the story is read are now printed on palm-leaf using Thai rather than inscribed in the traditional manner and written in a sacred script such as dua tam. Although these are said to be published in Bangkok, the version used by Lao speakers is in the Lao language but written in the Thai alphabet. Each section has a title leaf followed by the text printed on five lines recto and verso divided into three columns. In central and north Thailand there are but thirteen chapters, but a Lao-language text used in northeast Thailand has eighteen, because it includes the story of Pra Malai.

1. *Gun piset* ("special chapter") entitled *malai mün* ("ten thousand flowers"), the first portion of Pra Malai's tripartite journey.
2. *Gun piset malai saen* ("special chapter, hundred thousand flowers"), which completes Pra Malai's story.
3. *Gun don* ("beginning chapter") which is also called *sung-gat* (Pali *sakaraj*, "time" or "year"), gives a brief review of the Buddha's life.
4-17. Fourteen main chapters describe the virtuous life of Prince Wetsundawn. The numbers in parentheses are the actual numbers of the *gun*. In central Thailand 8 and 9 are combined into a single chapter. The titles and their translations follow.

4 (1).   *Totsapawn,* the giving of ten blessings

5 (2).   *Himapan,* a word referring to a large, distant forest

6 (3).   *Tanagun,* the section in which a beggar receives gifts from Wetsundawn

7 (4).   *Wanabawet* or travelling into the forest, a humorous section

8 (5).   *Choo-chok,* the name of an elderly and well-known beggar

9 (6).   *Joolapon* or "small forest" describing the life of Wetsundawn and his wife, Muttee, in the forest

10 (7).   *Mahapon* or "large forest" continuing the account of their lives

11 (8).   *Gooman gun don,* the first portion describing the unfortunate fate of the children

12 (9).   *Gooman gun blai* which completes the story of the children

13 (10).   *Muttee* (*Mut-see* in Thai) concerning Wetsundawn's wife, generally considered the most emotional chapter

14 (11).   *Sukaban* (*Sukabap* in Thai) meaning "supreme god" and referring to the help rendered by Pra Intra

15 (12).   *Maharat* meaning "great emperor" or "king"

16 (13).   *Hokgasut* (*Chaw-gasut* in Thai) meaning "six kings"

17 (14).   *Nakawn gun,* the return to the city and a triumphant end to the story

18.   *Soot-Tai* meaning "last" or *cha-lawng* meaning the "celebration."

The story is recited by a monk seated in lotus position within a small raised pulpit with a roof called *tamat* placed in the center of the sala amidst decorations and flowers appropriate to the festival. Many temples also display a long strip of cloth tacked to the inside framework illustrating the life of Prince Wetsundawn. The monk reciting each gun reads with dignity from the text as villagers, more women than men, listen with hands held chin high in the *wai* or prayer position.

The vocal styles of tet boon prawet show great variety. Four informants, two currently monks, two formerly so, recorded *tet sung-gat* or *gundon,* the introduction to the Wetsundawn story. Three used the same scale pattern, F G A C D (G as the reciting tone). The fourth followed a pattern associated with Pali chant, i.e., F G B♭ C. It was also agreed by informants that the chanting style for sung-gat differs from that of other tet. Figure 2 illustrates the beginning of sung-gat as recorded by two monks from different temples. It will be seen that while tempos differed considerably, the overall contours of the melody did not. While both men conformed to the same scale pattern, each inflected the word tones in his own manner.

Figure 2. Two examples of *tet sung-gat.* I was read by Pra Boon-song og Wut Ban Bah-yang of Roi-et city and II was read by Pra Boon-ah-yoo of Wut Mahachai in Mahasarakaram.

Of the eleven informants who recorded excerpts from the main body of the story, all but one conformed to the same scale pattern, F G B♭ C D, which was extended by some to the higher F and G. One skilled practitioner stated that tet boon prawet recitation varies from province to province, while that of the sung-gat section, cited above, remains much the same throughout the region. The differences noted from monk to monk and from province to province, however, were more in terms of tempo and ambitus, not scale pattern. Factors other than geography, such as skill, may also have had an impact on this sampling. Further, monks assigned to a given temple in a given province may well have come from elsewhere. The following two examples, using the same text, were recorded by the abbot of a small temple in northeast Thailand to illustrate the styles of Kawn-gaen and Yasoton provinces, but it is unknown to what extent his versions would conform to other samples from those areas.

Figure 3. Two examples of *tet* from the story of Prince Wetsundawn read by the Abbot of Wut Glang-kosum in Kosum-pisai, Thailand. I. is in the style of Kawn–gaen province, and II. is in the style of Yasoton province.

I
II
jawn dung sawn (lawn liap) lawn sa prung liap fung num moot ja lin
si rü sa bah mai puk chee lae mai gawk mai kut mawk lae yom pah
sah too mee mai lin som hawm awn foong da lop awk hawng hui hui
continues similarly
tr
nik kun tee mai yang pai gwai ging kawm kao kah awm ah som sa ra nik kun
tee krüa jan jüa gio gin gwang da ling ban ngam

Gun (chapter) 10 entitled *"Muttee"* is traditionally the most emotional. Wetsundawn, in a test of his generosity, is asked by a stranger to give up his wife, though the stranger is really the god Pra Intra trying to protect Muttee. A monk from a village southwest of Roi-et city in northeast Thailand recorded a favorite passage in a style he called *siang yao* or literally "long tones," which is transcribed in figure 4. The term apparently relates to *lum tang yao* in lum entertainment singing, which is similarly melancholy and emotional. The scale form is that of ordinary tet boon prawet, but the ambitus is an eleventh (from F to b^b).

Figure 4. *Tet* from the story of Prince Wetsundawn, chapter 10, read by Pra Boonsong of Wut Ban Ba-yang southwest of Roi-et city, Thailand

Except for figure 4, all examples seen thus far have been fairly simple melodically. They can be seen as kinds of heightened speech influenced by the word inflections but also conforming to a regular scale pattern. The verb for preaching is simply *tet*. Interestingly, monks sometimes refer to the tum-nawng (melody) of the preaching, which suggests a recognition of the musical nature of the delivery. Nonetheless, it is still not singing (lum, kup, or hawng). Figure 4 pushes this assertion to the limit, but the excerpt in figure 5, taken from gun 14 and "preached" by a former monk, exceeds any expected bounds because of its elaborateness. Even so, a certain emphasis on the reciting tone G still harkens back to the relative simplicity of Pali chant.

Both figures 4 and 5 exhibit evident examples of text painting. Figure 4 includes melismas on the syllables *sah lah* (sala meaning "preaching hall"), *nakoh noh* (Pali of uncertain meaning) or perhaps *nakon* meaning "city," and on *yung* (alive or not yet dead). In Figure 5 nine melismas are indicated by number. They translate as follows: 1) *nüng* is "one"; 2) *perit* is possibly Pali *proet* meaning "excellent"; 3) *bua* is "lotus"; 4) *saeo* means "to swoop down"; 5) *mak* means "much" and modifies *liam lut* meaning "excellent" or "bright"; 6) "*ka*" means "expensive"; 7) "*lut*" means "to move easily"; 8) *yawng pong* refers to puffy cotton implying good quality; and 9) *yap* means "bright" or silver in color. Expressing certain of these words in melismas makes sense (e.g., 5, 7, and 8), but others do not seem to suggest it. It was reported that some singers tried to choose appropriate words for embellishments, but others simply showed off their voices as they pleased.

Figure 5. *Tet* from the story of Prince Wetsundawn, chapter 14, by Mr. Jundee Juntawan, age twenty-six, at Wut Glang-kosum in Kosum-pisai, Thailand.

rit- - - - - - - - - - - - - - - sen fai lüt dui yai- - - - - bua⁽³⁾- - - - - - - - - - - - - - - - -

chüng chai hua sen saeo⁽⁴⁾- - - - - - - - - liam lüt   laeo dui mak⁽⁵⁾- - - - - - - - - - - - - - - - - - - -

- - - - - - - - - nai   na   kawn gwang taw ben pün bang sa bah paeng pon kah⁽⁶⁾-

- kum   saen   dun da

wah waen   chup   sün   chang yai   yün yaw kao- - - - - - - - - hao taw ben

pün bang   bao   piu pawng gra tum dui (sen) fai lüt - - - - - - yawng yawng - - - - - -

-   pong - - - - - - - - - - - - - biu bui   yong - - - - - - -

yee   yap -

Special Buddhist sermons (tet lae).

Tet lae, unlike ordinary preaching, is not read but is delivered from memory. The written texts are in *gawn* form (in stanzas of four lines, each with a particular pattern of tone marks) and purchased from the teacher. Interestingly, these poems are quite similar to those used by entertainment singers called *mawlum*, i.e., a skilled singer of lum. It is worth noting that many monks have taken the robe for a temporary period; some were singers in lay life. Monks with good voices may wish to learn to do tet *lae* because they can earn some money if called to other temples for tumboon festivals. While monks are forbidden to sing and certainly do not entertain, in fact this is what they are doing but under the verb *tet*, "to preach." The term *lae* may derive from *nan lae* ("as it has been said") which concludes ordinary sermons, having a function akin to "amen" in the Christian tradition.

Lae style is especially prevalent in the boon prawet festival where both monks and lay people tend to prefer the gawn poetry to the more prosaic blank verse interspersed with Pali phrases, usually recited in a plain style. At first only gun 10, the evocative "Muttee" chapter, was given in tet lae, but now the entire story may be told in this manner. Because the poems can be short or long according to the writer, the story may be reduced to just a few hours if necessary rather than the usual fifteen hours. Temples compete to schedule the most talented monks of the area for their boon prawet to assure good attendance and generous offerings. Oddly, it is traditional to hold the palm-leaf text even when chanting tet lae. In one festival observed in northeastern Thailand in 1974 three talented monks seated themselves in a triangle, each taking the part of an individual in the story. Each attempted to outdo the others in displaying an impressive vocal technique. Lae is not restricted to boon prawet. The most usual form heard outside this festival is called *lae uipawn* which is sung at tumboon or other festivals to thank donors publicly for their gifts. If the temple has a talented monk, he will perform the lae, but if not, a lay outsider, even a mawlum singer, may perform it. Lae singers must know a certain number of lae uipawn poems with blanks which may be completed with the names and offerings of the donor, misleading some into thinking that the performer is improvising his text on the spot.

Lae also embraces poems teaching about the life, works, and philosophy of the Buddha, Buddhist theology in general, instructions to laymen concerning behavior at festivals, how to dress for temple activities, comments on current fads, and at one extreme entertaining poems which imitate animal noises, especially birds, and bring open laughter from the audience, this within the confines of the preaching hall. It may come as no surprise, then, that listeners, especially those who have had a bit of alcohol, are inclined on occasion to clank coins loudly into a basin for the performing monk yelling *motana*, a Pali word from *anoo motana* meaning "I am happy to give this." While most singers procure their poems from teachers, the less fortunate may purchase printed versions for a few *baht*.

Figure 6 was performed by a young monk from Galasin province, northeast Thailand, who had studied with a former monk. He is often called to entertain at tumboon because his voice is not only beautiful but his poetry is enjoyable, even comic. He enjoys showing off, performing extensive vocalizations with trills, repeated notes, and even bird calls. In one poem heard he spoke of his singing technique and illustrated several ways to sing, but in caricature. The following example, with a range of an eleventh, uses (in the transcription) D, F, G, A, C, D, and F, with most activity in the lower four notes. This scale, indeed, is identical to what can be called the *yao* scale in lum singing, but the listener would never confuse the two since lum is accompanied by the *kaen* free-reed mouth organ.

Figure 6. *Tet lae* performed by pra Tawng-sai, age twenty-six, of Wut Suang-ahrom at Choom-tang village, Galasin province, Thailand.

27. sün kün bai nung ban kun num prum tai wai

28. yaw mü wai brah sai tam kao

29. sao sa nit sen nee noi ban hak si mee

30. poot tüng mah ree nee wah wao ben pet awn

31. dawng ruk sah ge sawn

32. briap bra doot dawk mai hawm foong

33. wah glin glai dü ----------- (oo) -----------------

--- naw

Ceremony to the vital spirits (soo-kuan)

The soo-kuan ritual derives distantly from Hinduism, though some of it suggests an animistic origin. It is one of a number of rituals which co-exist peacefully among a people which is officially Buddhist but in fact accepts non-Buddhist practices easily. The ceremony is normally called soo-kwun or *tum kwun* in Thai, *soo-kuan* in Lao, and *ba see* or *bai see* when performed for Buddhist monks. Its purpose is to restore to a person his/her *kuan*, which has been translated variously as "psyche" or "morale" (Haas) or "spirit essence" (Tambiah). Some have compared it to the soul, but this is considered incorrect by Thai informants who understand the Christian concept. While a person has thirty-two individual *kuan* representing various parts of the body, it is the collective kuan which is involved in the ceremony. The kuan is said to be a timid spirit inclined to flee at times of stress, danger, important changes of status, and even during a long trip. The loss of the kuan may result in afflictions and misfortunes, and its flight must be checked **before** the crisis if at all possible. The rite is conducted in a variety of situations including marriage, ordination, promotion, pregnancy and child bearing, before a long trip, at the beginning of the Buddhist lent, before an important enterprise, for the sick and dying, to reintegrate people back into the community after, e.g., prison or military service, and after a bad omen such as a lightning strike.

The ceremony may take place in a home or in the *sala* of the temple but always around an altar called the *pa kuan*, a kind of symbolic tree placed on a tray together with the *kuang buujuh* (*puja* things), offerings consisting of a boiled egg, bananas, flowers, and a lump of cooked glutinous rice. The ritualist, called *pam* (after the Hindu *brahman*), *maw kuan*, or *maw pon*, seats himself before the *pa kuan* with the persons involved to his sides. Reading from a palm-leaf manuscript written in dua tam alphabet or reciting from memory, he intones a text appropriate to the occasion. Afterwards the witnesses tie pieces of string around the person's wrist symbolically binding the kuan to the body.

The *pam*, however, is far removed from the traditional brahman. He must be a lay male who is both a householder and a village elder and commands the respect of the people. Ironically the pam, although attaining office directly from a retiring pam, begins the study of the texts as a Buddhist monk in the temple. While currently robed monks do not officiate, they may be participants in the case of ordination, promotion, or other events which involve monks as well as laymen. Besides being of mature years, often more than fifty, the pam must be literate in the learned alphabets, particularly dua tam. He is free to exchange texts with other pam since the words are not secret, but is prohibited from improvising. Some texts have been published locally. The language is Lao, because the people must understand in order to benefit, but some phrases, particularly at the beginning, are in Pali.

The manner of reciting the text is again melodic, but not considered singing. The verb used is *soot*, a word which is derived from the Sanskrit *sutra* meaning "formula." Scale evidently varies widely, since there was little agreement among the four men recorded, three being pam at the time and one a robed Buddhist monk who agreed to record outside the context of the ritual.

Mr. Saman Soo-pompun of Mahasarakam province, northeast Thailand, age fifty-two (1973), had been a novice for three years and a monk for seven days and learned soo-kuan from another man of his town. Mr. Saman also functions as a *mawdoo* (fortune teller), a duality not at all unusual. Parts of the manuscripts from which he recited were written in dua tam on palm-leaves twenty-five centimeters long, while others were on cardboard written in Thai to replace original leaves that had deteriorated. Of the four examples recorded, three were for specific occasions (ordination, marriage, and for a sick person) and the fourth was a prayer in Pali to invite the tewadah angels to come and witness the ceremony. The latter was exceptional in that it was recited on only three tones, E^b, G, and B^b, with G as reciting pitch. The reading of the three specific texts all used a scale of six pitches—E, F, G, A, C, D, with G as reciting tone—but that for a sick person (*soo-kuan kon bui*) was preceded by an introduction, partly in Pali, using only D, G, and B, which is seen in figure 7.

Figure 7. *Soo-kuan kon bui* (for a sick person) recited by Mr. Saman Soo-prom-pun in Kosum-pisai, Thailand.

An elderly Lao *pam* now living in California also recited his text to a scale of only four pitches that closely resembled that of Pali chant, F, G, B♭, and C with G as reciting pitch.

The fourth pam recorded, Mr. Ken Wong-ha-gaeo, age sixty-nine, of Mahasarakam city, northeast Thailand, also used a similar scale of three tones (F, G, and B^b) but only for the Pali introduction. His reading of the main text was exceptional in a number of ways. Although Mr. Ken had impressive credentials and was literate in sacred scripts, having been a monk for five years (1924–1929), he no longer read his texts because the manuscripts were too badly deteriorated but instead delivered them from memory. One of them, *soo-kuan kon bui* for the sick, was in gawn form, the same kind of poetry used by mawlum singers. In most cases Ken recited to a five-note scale—G, A, B, D, E, with G as reciting tone—but sometimes ascended to the octave G as well. In at least one case, *soo-kuan nak* (for ordination), he used only three pitches—F, G, B^b—similar to the pattern used by other pam and in Pali chant. Figure 8 illustrates an excerpt of *soo-kuan daeng-ngan* or *pua mia* for marriage using a five-tone scale with octave G.

Figure 8. *Soo-kwum daeng-nganor pua mia* (for marriage) recited by Mr. Ken Wong-ha-gaeo in Mahasakaram city, Thailand.

To read a book (*An Nungsü*)

Ironically, the genre having the closest relationship with singing is considered the least musical, for *an nungsü* means literally "to read a book." The book, however, is not a modern printed volume but a traditional palm-leaf manuscript called nungsü pook ("book in a pile") or nungsü bai lan ("palm leaf book"). The art of copying such books is now nearly lost, for printed texts have tended to replace the traditional ones. According to older informants, such books were written using a stylus to scratch the letters. The leaves were then covered with lampblack which impregnated and highlighted the scratches. Although such manuscripts tend to deteriorate rapidly because of climate and insects, many temple libraries have nungsü pook dating as far back as one hundred years. While monks often preach from similar books written in a sacred script, those used in an nungsü use the *tai noi* (old Lao) alphabet with poetry in gawn form.

Immediately after a person dies, relatives and close friends come to the home each evening for three successive nights to participate in the *ngun hüan dee* or literally "good house party." Traditionally young and old alike spent the nights listening to older men read aloud from the nungsü pook the epic Lao stories drawn from both jataka and local sources in a form of heightened speech. Today the practice is extremely rare as interest in traditional literature diminishes and fewer and fewer men can read "books" in the old way. Today's youths prefer to play cards, talk, and listen to their cassette tapes.

Few skilled informants who could still "read" texts were found in northeast Thai villages in the early 1970s. The custom was likely more widespread in conservative Laos before 1975, but few Lao refugees are known to have the skill. Some of the older men could hardly read because of poor eyesight, a condition only aggravated by the fact that reading takes place at night with only a small oil light or at best a glaring kerosene lantern. Stumbling and other mistakes are therefore inherent to an nungsü.

The relationship between an nungsü and lum singing is found both in the poetry and in the scale. Both use gawn poetry, written in stanzas of four lines with requisite tone marks over certain syllables. But *gawn lum* (poetry for singing) differs somewhat from *gawn an* (poetry for reading) in that it adds opening and closing sections and makes use of more prefixes (*kum boopabot*) and suffixes (*kum soi*) appropriate to the courtship-dialogue of entertainment singing. Most importantly, gawn lum has rhyme between lines whereas gawn an does not. In terms of scale, an nungsü uses a five-tone scale which can be expressed as D, F, G, A, C, with D as the point of relaxation or tonic. This same pattern is found in several Lao genres (e.g., *lum dung-wai* or *tangvay* and *kup sum nua* or *Sam neüa*) as well as in northeast Thailand in the *lum tang nyao* portion of a *lum gawn* performance and in certain genres of theatre (e.g., lum moo). Because the singing of these entertainment genres as well as an nungsü is in speech rhythm, the most obvious difference is that singing is accompanied by the kaen mouth organ. But for reasons logical to the Lao, *an nungsü* is "reading" while *lum* is singing.

Figure 9 is an excerpt from the well-known story *Jumba-seedon* (Four Jumba Trees) read by Mr. Loon Saen-kot, age forty-two (1973) of Barabü district in Mahasarakam province, northeast Thailand. Mr. Loon read skillfully from an 80 year-old manuscript nearly one foot thick.

Figure 9. A *nungsü* from the story *Jumba-seedon* read by Mr. Loon Saen-kot in Nawng-weang village near Barabü, Thailand.

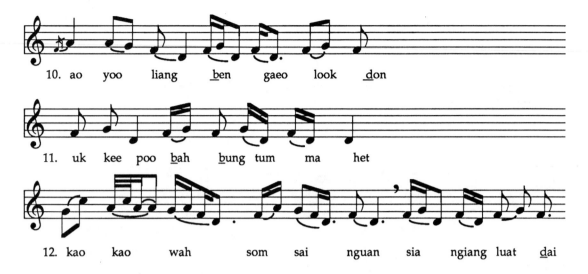

10. ao   yoo   liang   ben   gaeo   look   don

11. uk   kee   poo   bah   bung   tum   ma   het

12. kao   kao   wah   som   sai   nguan   sia   ngiang   luat   dai

Secular responsorial songs (*süng*)

A far more lively tradition, though having a more distant relationship to lum singing, is called süng. By definition süng is a kind of non-religious responsorial chanting with dancing that occurs during certain festivals. In northeast Thailand and parts of Laos süng is encountered most often at the *bungfai* rocket festival just before the rains return; near the Maekong river it is also associated with boat races. Ordinary villagers, usually male and more often than not inebriated on cheap rice wine, dance and sing from home to home begging for donations which will be used to maintain their blissful state of drunkenness. The poetic form used is *gap* whose lines normally consist of seven or eight syllables, the last of which rhymes with the third of the following line. Gap poetry is therefore not written in stanzas but in a continuous and interlocking form. The leader first sings the line, then the rest repeat the phrase in a responsorial manner. Though members often carry a few kaen, drums, or other instruments for marching, the süng itself is not normally accompanied.

The melody for süng, like the most of the genres described above, is generated by the word tones to a preconceived four-tone scale pattern, D, F, G, A, with D as the tonic. While correlation between word-tone and pitch/interval is very close, the melodies sung by leader and chorus may in fact differ slightly. Süng is therefore not a fixed melody but created from a restricted number of pitches according to the singers' whims tempered by habit.

Figure 10. *Süng bung-fai* recorded during the *bung-fai* rocket festival in Mahasakaram, Thailand.

♩=100   Leader   Chorus

1. Oh   hao   oh   ga   sut   tah   hao   oh   (same)

2. Om   poot   toh   ga   na   moh   ben   kao

3. pün   pah   dao   ga   ao   boon   bung   fai

4. heet baw lai ga kawng lung pün gao

5. dap dae tao tüng look lan len

6. kaw hai _ben ga dung kum pom _bat

7. baw bung at ga puak look puak lan

8. bah kao tan ga pawm gun müt moo

9. mah yün yoo ga pawm nah piang dah

10. oh hao oh ga sut tah ao oh

CONCLUSIONS

Thao Nhouy Abhay (in Berval 1959:348) has written, "Intended as it is to be read aloud or sung, Laotian poetry, or verse, is essentially musical and rhythmic." All of the genres surveyed are delivered in some kind of melodic fashion, plain and ornate. In all cases there is a close relationship between the word tones and the contour of the resulting melody, the latter being built on a restricted number of discrete pitches. Consistency of scale form for a given genre was limited, although for, e.g., Pali chant, there was a tendency to use F, G, B$^\flat$ and for an nungsü to always use D, F, G, A, C. None was accompanied by a musical instrument except süng. The verbs used varied by genre:

Pali chant—*suat*
Buddhist sermons—*tet* (to preach or teach)
Special Buddhist sermons (*tet lae*)—*tet*
Calling back the "spiritual essence"—*soot*
Reading palm-leaf manuscripts—*an*
Non-Religious responsorial singing—*süng*

Regardless of how entertaining we may find any these genres (there is no doubt that many Lao find certain of them quite entertaining) they are not functionally entertainment. Anything associated with Buddhism is obviously ritualistic, even the "preaching" of a fine tet lae master. Calling back the kuan is a serious matter and reading stories at funeral wakes is too, although the stories are well liked by the people. Even the seemingly raucous süng for the rocket festival is associated with a kind of fertility rite when symbolic phalluses in the form of rockets are sent to break the clouds to bring rain as well as inform *Payah taen*, the god of the sky, that the people need rain for life to continue. All this is different, at least to the Lao, from hiring one or more singers to perform for an audience, even if associated with a temple festival. That is the basis of the difference between "singing" and these performance practices which are melodic but not considered singing.

While the foregoing describes "how" the Lao classify these phenomena, it does not directly address the question "why." Answers to that are far more difficult and far less empirical. One can only speculate. On a more superficial level one notices a certain melodic flow in the contours of tonal languages such as Thai or Lao. The relationship of the level tones tends to create discrete pitches. The contour tones tend to produce ascending or descending intervals. One can therefore argue that the phenomena observed here are merely stylizations of the natural inflections of speech. But what of the fact that similar phenomena occur around the world among speakers of non-tonal languages? What about American auctioneering and old-fashioned chanted preaching? Why in so many religious rituals are the sacred texts intoned rather than merely spoken? Heightened speech similar to Pali chant is found within virtually all the world's religions, and few if any of these phenomena are considered singing. Although humorous, one of my teachers of many years ago had a valid point when he said, "You just don't talk to God the same way you talk to a Howard Johnson waitress!"

David Tame (1984:22), in *The Secret Power of Music*, asserts that the vibrations of sound are of primal importance.

> In ancient times sound itself, the very basis of all music, was thought to be intimately related in some way to non-physical and sacred dimensions or planes of existence. Why was this? Because audible sound was considered to be but an earthly reflection of a vibratory activity taking place beyond the physical world.

One of the purest manifestations of primal sound was the "*Om*" of Hinduism. But if sound vibrations are desired, would not ordinary speech work? It appears that speech is too random in its vibratory levels to achieve efficiently what is described by Tame. It needs organization. Said Yehudi Menuhin:

> Music creates order out of chaos; for rhythm imposes unanimity upon the divergent, melody imposes continuity upon the disjointed. . . . Thus a confusion surrenders to order and noise to music. (quoted in Tame 1984:14)

Rouget, in his book *Music and Trance*, (1985:120) notes that music is experienced physiologically, psychologically, affectively, and esthetically. He asserts that "music has a physical impact upon the listener and that it produces a sensorial modification in his awareness of being." He argues that while altered states of awareness can be self-induced without the aid of music, music (i.e., organized sound) makes the process more efficient and consistent. "In the dimension of time, music modifies our consciousness of being to an even greater extent. It is an architecture in time" (ibid.:121).

Apparently, then, it is more than mere sound that is important; it is the regularization and organization of vibration that are efficacious. And nowhere is that more important than in the context of ritual. Continues Tame:

> The role of music and the role of religious intonation and liturgy was to release into the earth a form of cosmic energy which could keep civilization in harmony with the heavens. . . . the voice of the priest within the realm of time and space becomes a vehicle for the energizing Voice of the Creator to manifest its forces through. (Tame, 1984:24)

If these ideas have any validity to the Lao, then one can understand why terms for music and singing, which are associated with genres reserved for entertainment functions, are differentiated from terms for the delivery of ritual texts. The former type—entertainment—is primarily for those on the earthly plane while the latter type—ritual—joins the earthly plane to the higher realms. Consequently these texts must be delivered musically so as to attune the ritualist and the listeners to the supernatural side of life which, to a religious person, is as essential as speech.

REFERENCES CITED

Berval, Rene de.
   1959   *Kingdom of Laos: The Land of the Million Elephants and of the White Parasol.* Translated by Mrs. Teissier du Cros, et al. Saigon: France-Asie.

Blacking, John
   1973   *How Musical is Man?* Seattle: University of Washington Press.

Haas, Mary R.
   1964   *Thai-English Student's Dictionary.* Kuala Lumpur: Oxford University Press.

Miller, Terry E.
   1985   *Traditional Music of the Lao: Kaen Playing and Mawlum Singing in Northeast Thailand.* Contributions in Intercultural and Comparative Studies, Number 13. Westport, CT: Greenwood Press.

Rouget, Gilbert.
    1985   *Music and Trance: A Theory of the Relations between Music and Possession*. Trans. and rev. Brunhilde Biebuyck and Gilbert Rouget. Chicago: University of Chicago Press.

Tambiah, S. J.
    1970   *Buddhism and the Spirit Cults in North-East Thailand*. Cambridge: Cambridge University Press.

Tame, David.
    1984   *The Secret Power of Music*. Rochester, VT: Destiny Books.

THE *LAM LÜANG*, A POPULAR LAO ENTERTAINMENT

Houmphanh Rattanavong

Translated from the French by Amy Catlin

Whatever the reason for visiting Laos, one will almost certainly spend an evening viewing the national entertainment called *lam lüang*. Performances may be staged in a temple courtyard of a village, in a public setting, or, best of all, in a district auditorium.

Lam lüang is a type of national play, a theater of song and dance consisting of many different forms, within which ancient mythology and modern epics are commonly presented. Whatever the subject, the lam lüang has always held first place in the Laotian notion of enjoyment. What is this art? How did it originate, evolve, and what role does it play in society?

Etymologically, lam lüang consists of two Lao words, *lam* and *lüang*. *Lam* means to sing, as well as song, or songs. It is, however, only one category of song, for in Laos there are many terms designating song. Lam are sung in Laos and northeast Thailand among the people of Lao origin. Among these songs are many specific and diverse types: for courtship, contests of love between young men and women, singing about the beauty of nature and the countryside, singing about happiness and sadness, telling myths and enacting dramas, singing about political life, praying, or for singing religious texts. In fact, one may sing about anything which touches on human life and society.

There are various genres of lam: *lam theung san, thang gnao* and *thang long, lam teuy, lam khu, lam kon, lam konsavan, lam som, lam sithandon, lam phra vet, lam phüne*, etc. Their character differs regionally, so that, for example, the lam of Vientiane, Sithandon, Leuy, Ubon, Khonkhen, and Korat are each distinctive.

The Evolution of Lam Lüang from Lam Phüne

The word *lüang* signifies myth, narrative, story, or legend. It is synonymous with the word *phüne* (as in lam phüne) but with a subtle distinction. Lam phüne signifies to sing a myth, story, or legend, while lam lüang means to sing a myth, story, legend, narrative, epic, or drama. Compared with lam phüne, the lam lüang presents a more modern character, more realistic and lifelike. It is a recent creation and is the fruit of the development of lam phüne.

During the 1950s and 1960s and going back to the 1930s, lam phüne was already being sung in the Mekong basin and the region of the Korat plateau in Thailand. At that time, the lam phüne was executed by a single singer accompanied by a *khene* player. The singer tried to enact all the roles of the story, gesturing while singing. These presentations were probably successful, not to say that everything was perfect and that there were no lacunae which the artist strove to remedy. Certainly, objective realities require that artists continually perfect their work in order to respond to the context.

From the 1940s a new name, *lam mou* (meaning lam with props) began to appear. Lam mou employed many singers who embodied the different roles and was certainly a step forward in the development and transformation lam phüne into theater. This name did not reflect the typical character and nature of this art which portrays myths or stories. Moreover, it could easily be confused with the other lam styles which at times also used multiple singers. For this reason, in the 1940s the name lam lüang replaced lam mou. Since that time, lam lüang has been well known in Lao society as a unique type of performance, distinct and original.

The Popularity of Lam Lüang

We noted that the lam lüang became a unique performance genre, a national form favored by the masses of Laos from north to south. In other words, it represented the fruit of a historical process born of the simple and common origins among the Lao population. In feudal Laos, however, not only did this art receive no encouragement, it was even considered to represent an inferior class of humanity.

During that time, there were two categories of art. One was called elite, or the Great Tradition, which served the needs and interests of the feudal class, the bourgeoisie. The other was the art or culture of the masses, the Little Tradition, serving the interests and needs of the inferior class, or the laboring masses. The elite arts of *Yike* and the famous dance of *Pha Lak Pha Lam* (*Ramayana*) were diametrically opposed to the lam lüang, which was continuously being perfected and renovated by the laboring masses who always considered it their own. Lam lüang never was performed in the palace for the king and his followers since the lam lüang was considered to be a lowly art form. The bourgeoisie, intellectuals, functionaries, as well as anyone considered to belong to the upper echelons of society, maintained contemptuous attitude toward this genre—but it was very well suited for the man in the street, for peasants and novice monks. *Pha Ek lam lüang* ("heroes of lam lüang") became a perjorative expression designed to ridicule the lam lüang actors (the same is true in Thailand). Nonetheless, lam lüang still developed into a vivid, unique, and irreplaceable art, loved and adored by the masses where it survives among the people it has always served.

Lam Lüang as a Syncretic Art Form

According to the rule, evolution is the only means of survival for anything which is otherwise condemned to death. Lam lüang also cannot remain beyond this law of nature. It has evolved and must evolve for its survival. In evolving in a specific social context among the most ordinary masses whose economy is rudimentary and whose intellectual environment is generally minimal, lam lüang has maintained two authentic characteristics until the present.

First is its pronounced popular character. No other art in Laos has captured the heart and respect of the people as lam lüang has. Public places are always completely filled whenever lam lüang is staged. The audience may spend an entire night there in order to see its favorite performance.

Second is that lam lüang is a syncretic art, with many forms and mixtures. Many foreign theater specialists and scene designers assisting in lam lüang presentations are struck by the mediocrity and bastardism of this art, which sometimes seems to evade all logic in its constructions, scenarios, musical accompaniment, and various borrowings. In it one can find practically every ancient and modern technique, national and international, so that everything seems completely jumbled. This unfamiliar character, which is difficult to define, instead of vexing the audiences seems to suit their taste, requirements, mentality, psychology, and aesthetic level. That is why, at every stage of history, lam lüang has always survived as a popular art among the most ordinary people and has evolved as a function of the technical and intellectual levels of the masses.

The Future of Lam Lüang

In 1969–1970, during the war, in the liberated zone of Viengsay, a tentative first step was taken to modernize lam lüang into a dance and song form which we call *lakhon lam*. A central troupe of this type of theater was established, led by Sommay Lommonty, head of the official lakhon lam troupe. During this time they performed not stories and legends, but revolutionary narratives such as *Sithong*, *I Plia*, "The return of the Voice of Justice," "Leave Sithandon," and others. These presentations were enormously successful in the liberated zone and then among the people in the occupied zone during the national reconciliation.

What is lakhon lam? The answer is simply that lakhon lam is a development or modernization of lam lüang. In lakhon lam there are more theatrical elements; modern songs are inserted as well as modern dances. Also, instead of having only a khene as the basic musical accompaniment, an entire orchestra plays modern as well as classical compositions.

In all of Laos today there are tens of lam lüang troupes. Only one lakhon troupe is known, however, that being the much-appreciated central troupe. It should be mentioned that in retaining the name lam lüang, this art has evolved, and continues to evolve. Because of the demands of the audience, with its growing aesthetic sense, lam lüang is becoming increasingly like lakhon lam.

Both lam lüang or lakhon lam are always strongly encouraged by the authorities of the People's Democratic Republic of Laos, which has ranked them among the national arts and which considers them as a precious artistic treasure of Laos. Our present concern is to constantly maintain the quality, perfectionism, and improvements which are consistently renewed for this sort of performance. Whatever the circumstances under which lam lüang and lakhon lam evolve, this Lao national genre will be responsive to each new day—to the demands of the moment—to the needs of art in Lao society for the Lao as well as for the foreigner.

MUSIC AND INSTRUMENTS IN LAOS:
HISTORICAL ANTECEDENTS AND THE DEMOCRATIC REVOLUTION [1]

Houmphanh Rattanavong

Translated from Lao by Kingsavanh Pathammavong and Katherine Bond

The sound of music can be more powerful than a warrior about to conquer a mighty enemy. Its power can hypnotize more deeply than that of a witch or a sorcerer. Music can make people laugh or cry, feel happy or sad, strong or weak. Sometimes, it is more sacred than holy water. It enables people to emphasize life, not death. At other times, it is filled with more lethal poison than an evil curse.

What is this music and what is the sound of music? Simply put, music is a type of art expressed through sound. This sound has been selected and organized by humans to express their spirit, their moods, and their soul within an art form. It is made by humans for other humans. It evokes feelings and thoughts, sets moods and stirs the imagination. The difference between this and other types of art is that it is based on sound waves that occur at different speeds and intervals. The waves then enter the ear to form an image or idea, evoke a feeling or mood. Other art forms are experienced through the eye which focuses on multiple objects interacting together such as in the circus, theater, or film.

Although it depends on only one sense, hearing, music demands that we examine it at several levels. Music induces an atmosphere or reaction according to the prior experience of the audience. Clearly different people, different listeners, will respond to the same music with different feelings and mental processes.

We must first learn about sound before we can understand how music is performed through sound. Sound is a natural phenomenon occuring when an object vibrates, thus influencing the atmosphere. These vibrations enter the ear, making us perceive the sound.

In general, there are two types of sounds: complex and basic sounds. Complex sounds are born from nature and cannot be manipulated; for example, thunder, wind, rain or the sound of a simple engine. Simpler sounds are created by humans through work, ideas, and research. Sounds of high or low pitch, short or long duration have different values in different systems of rhythm, such as in the sound of *mohlam, pi,* and *khaen.* Both complex sounds and simpler sounds are good and emerge from vibrating objects. The difference between them is explored in the compositional process: how we choose, control, and make the sounds into art to serve the needs of humanity.

These sounds have great benefits for individual experience as well as for the general advancement of society and humanity. They are a clear mode of communication that thoroughly expresses feelings and moods in the form of performance. We use sound to communicate, to teach, and to express love, hate, understanding, or disagreement. Once sound has been chosen and refined and ideas have been researched and developed, the production process follows. The process of producing art forms leads to the production of culture. Sound has many benefits: It can create moods, alertness to ideas, and good in humanity. It can also emphasize love and agreement, understanding, the creative process, and the spirit of fairness. It makes humans fresh and happy, calms and supports a sad and lonely heart, nourishes us with energy when we are busy, and helps us relax and rest when we are under pressure from work.

WHAT IS MUSIC AND WHAT IS AN INSTRUMENT?

Among the many works that refer to instruments, Alexander Buchner's[2] is worthy of reference. He indicated that instruments are the sources of sound created by humans to make music having value and tone and able, as a form of art, to create a reaction that pleases the mind. Those specific characteristics are the basis of each country's traditions and make up one specific part of history.

Sound, deriving from various sources such as instruments, can be produced with the following qualities:

1. Volume. The degree of softness or loudness depends on the sources that create high or low intensity vibrations. These elements help the instruments to fully express moods or feelings analogous to the sound of humans speaking. For example, when talking about love, the tone of voice will be soft and sweet, but when angry, the tone of the same speaker will be unpleasant.

2. Pitch. Pitch refers to the frequency of the sound, either high or low—treble or bass—in musical terms. In normal language we would refer to pitch as small or big sounds. Some instruments, however, can produce only one sound, such as *kong, khong, kasaik, gnapgneep,* and other percussion instruments.

3. Length of sound. Short or long sounds can be easily classified.

4. Timbre. This defines the personality or character of the sound. For example, if two people say the same word with different timbre and similar pitch, it does not sound the same. We are able to identify the speaker by hearing the sound even without seeing the speaker's face.

5. Rhythm. Rhythm is another component of sound, a combination of length and accent. These two elements determine the measurement and dynamics of the sound. In other words, the rhythm is the spirit of the music. Without rhythm there is no music, no art, and no mood. In contrast, with rhythm but no music we can somehow have fun. If melody is added the sound is surely completed. There are many kinds of rhythm, from *lamvong, lamteuy, lamlong, hot van,* tango and slow-dance to contemporary rhythms that leave disco outdated.

Types of Instruments

Laos is interesting in that it is a country with numerous ethnic groups: Australasian, Austronesian, Mon-Khmer, Lao-Thai, Sino-Tibetan and Sino-Burmese. Although the statistics are incomplete, there are more than forty ethnic groups present. Those that have been counted are characterized by regional differences. In the arts, for example, the styles of the Lowland Lao of Luang Prabang differ from those of the Lowland Lao of Vientiane or Savannakhet.

Lao sources classify musical instruments into four categories: plucked, bowed, beaten, and blown. Up to the present day, we still maintain the use of these categories in Lao music. However, the classification has several weak points that create confusion about percussion instruments. There are beaten instruments made of wood, metal, and skin. Following ancient Indian ideas, as in the work called *Natya Sastra*, instruments were classified until the fourteenth century (the period of King Fangoum of Laos) according to the raw material that created vibrations. Joramet Demurit and other nineteenth-century writers classified the instruments into three categories: string, wind, and percussion instruments. This classification has been used through the present. In 1878 Victor Mahillon, a Belgian, classified instruments into four categories, aerophone, chordophone, membranophone, and idiophone, used later by Erich von Hornbostel and Curt Sachs. They collected information from around the world, including that from ancient Indian texts, and classified instruments into more scientific categories based on the source of vibrations they produced. Although several musicologists have since tried to develop new types of classifications for instruments, the system of classification by Sachs and von Hornbostel is still popular.

Arranged as Lao types, the categories might include vibrating instruments, rhythmic membranophone instruments, string instruments, and wind instruments.

1. Vibrating instruments. A vibrating instrument can be clapped together or beaten to create vibrations from the whole object. This type of instrument can be described in the following shapes: pole, pyramid, pipe, box, plate, pocket, circle, triangle, corner, flat, zig-zag, and smooth.

   a. Wood: *lanat* (xylophone), *gnap gnap/ngop* (wood blocks), *kasaik, kalo* (vertical wooden xylophone), *kalophenkalo, deodeo, keung, bangthing, lantbang, kob, pong, kik, lakok.*

   b. Metal: *kongbang, kongchoum, kongnongneng, kongvong* (gong circle), *phanghat, pongno, lakangnongneng, lakangluang, lakanguang, seng, sing* (hand cymbals), *kading, kaleng, hevan, pong, kik, lanatlek* (bronze xylophone).

2. Rhythmic instruments [membranophones]. A rhythmic instrument is a type of percussion instrument that is beaten or struck, but it must have a leather cover, such as a drum. Examples are *kongluang, konglammana, kongtapon, kongkan, kongping, konghang, kongpeung.*

3. String instruments. These instruments use strings to create the sound: *so* (bowed lute), *kachappi* (lute), guitar, piano, *kim* (hammered zither), *takhae* (floor lute), and *phin* (plucked lute). They are played using the fingers to pluck or strum, wood

to beat, or bows. Other examples are *so ee, so oo, so kang, sobang, teunreek, sonamtao, kachappii, kachappii hauntao, tkimbang.*

4. Wind instruments. These instruments use wind that vibrates in tubes or air pockets to create a sound, such as *khaen,* accordion, *vot* (bundle aerophone), *pii* (free reed or double-reed aerophone), *khui* (fipple flute), trumpet, *kaneng,* seashell, *bangluang.* Other examples include Lowland Lao *khaen,* Lao Theung *khaen, pii tai, pii samouay, pii hu diaw, pii lue, banglouang, bangtov, baymai, sanai, sang,* whistle, cupped hands.

The four different types of instruments each consist of subcategories and each subcategory is composed of specific types according to region and ethnic group.

Sung Poetry

Because the Lao nation consists of many ethnic groups with many regional differences, there are countless varieties of lyrics and melodies. If we add forty other groups to the seven Lowland Lao regions, we would have our own United Nations that could account for hundreds or more. If we figure out that each group has five to six types of *khaplam* sung poetry, we would calculate between 200–250 types without counting those recognized by the nation.

The melodies of *lam* are very rich. Some kinds consist of *khaplam* that do not use instrumental accompaniment, some kinds use accompaniment, and some only use instruments. Two types of solo or ensemble *lam* do not need accompaniment. There are also four similar types of solo instrumental and ensemble *khaplam* that use instrumental accompaniment.

There are many lyrics and melodies to be played, but few instruments to accompany them, since the many ethnic groups use the same types of instruments. Also, some ethnic groups have their own type of instruments which cannot be used by others. Even if the instruments were used in ensembles, the stylistic techniques would reflect the particularity of the region, its particular culture and tradition, and would fit that region's particular image. The uses of the same instruments are seen not only in our country, but all over the world. It is noteworthy that all types of instruments are being used together without knowing who invented which first. Beside that, at present, all the countries around the world conform to similar types of modern musical ensembles.

The Uses of Different Types of Instruments in Laos

It is generally understood that humans have known how to use instruments since evolving from animals, since we began to have culture and exist as human beings. The proof of ancient man's love of art lies in the stone carvings in caves and other holes where he lived well over 10,000 years ago. Like the evolution of nature, the natural needs of humans led to the birth of music. At first it might have taken the forms of hands clapping, the beating of wood, or the sound of happy yelling after a successful hunt. From there music expanded to relate to events and to the spirituality of human beings. Since then the music of the world has expanded very quickly to include scientific types that can respond to the needs of psychologists and each individual in the society of the space and computer age.

Specifically in Laos, the use of lyrics, melodies, and the instruments mentioned above influences every aspect of society as traditions, customs, and resources that have been carried on from the time our culture began up to the present. The truth of Lao society shows us that there is no event, no activity, no emotion, and no atmosphere of any society that does not need music or musical instruments in warning us of danger; in a war cry; in gathering marching troops; in a commemoration or celebration; in the enjoyment of a group or individual; when angry, when in pain, if sad or lonely, if in love or heart-broken, if happy or proud. Those instruments developed from *kongluang* and blowing leaves or the smallest dry reeds.

Therefore, we can conclude that the instruments, or the sound of music, ingrained in the life and spirit, flesh, skin and soul of every ethnic group in Laos, are things that cannot be separated from subsistence, like rice, water, fish, or nutrition. Our Lao people use the sound of music, the sound of the *khaen*, to evoke a mood, and to comfort the heart at any time and under any circumstances. There will never be a shortage, except when one is asleep or working with deep concentration.

THE EVOLUTION AND EXPANSION OF LAO FOLK MUSIC AND MUSICAL ISNTRUMENTS

Developments in history show us that various groups, or various ethnic groups that have shared the land of Lan Xang in ancient times, have a mix of cultures. They exchanged and cooperated in culture to extract the best and synthesize it. We have still not been able to confirm which elements belong to which groups and can confirm only that we have seen an exchange and mixture of culture, an expansion beyond the nation, country, and region. A clear example is that we cannot say the *khaen* began among highland Lao rather than Lao Theung or Lowland Lao. Likewise, we cannot say that the architecture of a house or shop is typical of Lao Theung, Lowland Lao, Kampuchea or Indonesia.

The same is the case with instruments. We cannot say to which group the *pii, khoui* or *lanat* belong. What is important in this respect is the collection, selection, and combination of instruments that belong to everyone in the nation and to others in the same region.

We agree that the musical instrument has been through a natural stage of isolation, and to be complete it must have been combined in ensembles of many sizes. The development of the grouping of instruments into ensembles can be categorized into three stages.

The Period of Natural Dispersion

Following scientific terminology the period of dispersion was a period when ancient man did not yet have a strong, definite social order. The music of this period was diffused and began to group naturally in the forms of yelling, beating wood, clapping hands, blowing wood or reeds, etc. Following the expansion of society and the development of social hierarchies, the creation of classes (labor and owners of production) initiated the production of culture for the use of society. The musical instruments, or music created and developed, were formed into ensembles to entertain the upper class and administrators, to worship spirits of sky and sun and voodoo believers, and to entertain.

The evidence that the organization of ancient ensembles has been carried on, exhibited up to the present, is in the playing of *kongbang, kongnong neng, toy keung,* and *tang bang.* When the aristocratic regime expanded to higher levels, music played an important role in supporting class dignity, in inspiring spirituality, and in entertaining the aristocracy. It was during this period that the instruments were developed, created, researched, and organized into ensembles that initiated deference, respect, and acclamation for the administrative class. The significance of the music depended on the class, the group of people, the village, and the city. However, the most important points were to serve the aristocrats in supporting their daily functions or in special ceremonies (such as religious and official ceremonies) and to entertain villagers. In Laos we are able to observe that the instruments of various periods, as well as other aspects of culture such as literature, have characteristics similar to that of the Lao Huang period. Furthermore, based on experts' research of this period, it is agreed that there were students or Buddhist monks from neighboring countries who came to study in Laos, who probably contributed ideas on music from their homelands.

Instruments and Folk Music Under Colonization and Imperialism

Many well-known experts in the world have concluded, "War might be won in politics, but cannot be won in culture. To win completely is to win in culture." There is a history of lessons of life, such as the imperialist Mongol battle with China. In the end, China swallowed the whole of Mongolia only by cultural influence.

For our country, the most significant transition period was the loss of independence, when we, a heavy target of war, experienced both old and new types of colonization. It began at the time of the barbarian war of Siam in 1778. During that war, the capital city, Vientiane, was burned, Phrakeomorakot and Phrabang were taken to Bangkok, all Lao citizens were "cleaned up" to become slaves of all types, and all cultural property, gold and jewelry, was "cleaned up" to Bangkok. The artists, expert musicians and dancers were taken to serve in the palace in Bangkok. It was during this period that lyrics, melodies, dancing styles, and instruments fell into the supporting hands of Thai patrons. The implication of this is the decline of Lao art and culture for 200 years. During the downhill period when Laos fell under Thai colonization, the Thai aggressors took the Lao styles, both form and content, altering the original Lao art and losing a wealth of original Lao culture. In turn, that art was transformed to favor and praise the Siamese oppressor.

Following the "hunting period" of French colonization, the French, in cooperation with England and Siam, permanently divided Lao territory into two parts. The right side of the Mekong River to Dong Payafay belonged to Siam and anything beyond that region fell under French protection. The Lao nation lost power, unable to become self-sufficient. The Siamese had destroyed Lao culture on that side twenty to thirty years before, when they prohibited playing the *khaen,* learning the Lao alphabet, and identifying oneself as Lao. The revolutionary regime of the powerful Thai majority swallowed all that was of Lao origins through force, unlike the present period, when they allow one to sing in Lao as long as one acknowledges Thai nationality.

Regarding the French on the left bank of the Mekong River, they expanded and popularized Western culture there. They looked down on, subjugated, and took all measures to eradicate any resistance. They suffocated the art and culture of Laos. The sound of the *khaen, pii,* and *so* were substituted by guitar, accordion, violin, and trumpet.

During the period of new colonization the Lao nation fell as a target on two fronts. First, Vientiane became a target of expansion and the promotion of a culture of decadence, a dangerous society of individualism—scattered and dissolute, slovenly and drunken. The music sounded hot, besotten and without consciousness; it numbed the senses. The music covered the sound of *pii* and *khaen* to the point that the city people looked down on the nation's *khaen*—even the country girls knew how to "boogie" and sell their bodies. The second target was the liberation front, the disputed area where bombs were dropped, where the land was destroyed from the air. This territory was said "to have no house poles pointing to the sky." The damage was immeasurable. The surviving citizens lost the will to live. The wealth of art and culture suffered heavy losses. Only memory and what had been secretly hidden by the citizens was left.

Musical Instruments and Lao Folk Music Under the National Democratic Revolution

These weapons were important swords used to kill the enemy in battle. The sounds of singing and melody that came from the *khaplam* and *mohlam*, instruments, and various kinds of literature of that revolution, were a strong power, even more so than diamonds and sapphires, helping to win by killing the enemy. War destroyed and demolished the imperialist; it was able to destroy and stop everything except the spirit, ideas, mind, body, and soul of the nation's Lao citizens. The singing of songs and the sound of the *so* were destroyed, but the sound of music, of *khaplam*, were reincarnated. The *khaen, pii, so*, and other instruments became weapons alongside guns. The warrior could not do without it in the time of resistance. Tens of thousands of skilled warriors who slaughtered the enemy were also researchers of politics and artists—recruiters in the area of art and literature. They used folk instruments that they created on their own, modelled after the kinds they had seen before. Simple folk instruments adopted the lyrics and melody of the people, which got louder at every turn until the noise competed with napalm bombs, sounds of grenades and bullets, inspiring the hearts of warriors. Lao citizens, patient and strong, struggled and sacrificed together in the dog fight with the enemy. They beat the evil enemy who seemed a hundred or thousand times more powerful.

Other than that, elsewhere in the territory of the Central region, in Vientiane city and the provinces during the period of liberation, they organized musicians into ensembles. They grouped the folk music unit into troupes of *mohlam, lam lüang*, and others to inspire the warriors and the people of Laos to have confidence in the virtues of equality and fairness, and to exercise bravery in beating the enemy.

We are proud to show that the sound of *pii, khaen*, and *khaplam* from our folk could resonate and echo everywhere in the heart of Vientiane in 1975. The great resistance movement for the people of the capital, Vientiane, and throughout the country, could stand up and support the revolution and take control of the forces of the dictator.

Musical Instruments and Folk Music After the Democratic Revolution

It is accepted that our party and our government has always promoted and followed policies that protect and expand the most valuable heritage of the nation's culture, in agreement with the

Fourth Meeting of the party, "to preserve and expand the heritage and most valuable culture of the nation and of different ethnic groups." At the same time, the policy must exclude the out-dated culture, especially the debris from the ideology of the culture of the aristocracy and from the old and new colonial regimes. It would adopt the fruits of labor of world culture instead of selecting influences without discretion and combine the best of all from the old times, from the beauty of the country. It was an order to build a new culture, internally socialist, that displayed characteristics of the nation and of the people.

Musical instruments, voice, melody, and lyrics of various ethnic groups of the Lao nation lie within our nation's most valuable heritage that has been carried on from generation to generation. They are the fruits of labor, imagination, creativity, and ingenuity of people who excel throughout the nation. They are a gathering of lessons of life which evolved over hundreds of years. They became a heritage of culture that is difficult to find in the nation. Surely, to speak of the old things, some are complete, some incomplete, and some so primitive that they must be selected for development. The music, as well as the instruments themselves, are the same. The technique may be rudimentary but is still respected as the nation's heritage. It is that which has been carried on since ancient times. We are able to compose music, or play so it is characteristic of the nation. The characteristics of the nation are thus composed. The origin of the nation, the appearance of its spirit and the focus of its wish are mixed clearly, freshly, nicely, with the spirit of the West—socialism, and the progress of the period with respect to science and technology.

We have arrived at this point by following the agreements set forth by the major conference during various periods of the party; specifically, the agreement of the party's fourth meeting addressed the topic of culture. We have succeeded in many respects with regard to maintaining and expanding traditions in the field of music of Laos; for example, the first great festival celebrating folk and traditional art in 1986, and the first festival of the examination of *khaplam* across the country in 1987. Through these successes we can see very clearly something great of ours in this subject. Whatever the good, our explorations are still diffused and scattered efforts. We still do not have collections and research carried out with scientific methodology such as collections of museum objects, photographs, paintings of every type, explanations, classifications, and strengths and weakness in the scientific language, and the analyses of those strengths and weaknesses, and plans for expansion in the future. It is a way to help the scientist at the central and local levels to research, add, expand and apply the results. The subject, as mentioned, is very important. It is a types of methodology that will surely be successful, not only in the areas of instruments and folk music, but also in other areas.

CONCLUSION

The sounds of music, of *so*, of *pii*, of *khaen* that were created by our people, that entered their souls for thousands of years, used to be linked to labor, celebration, enjoyment, sorrow and joy, with beauty, with the senses, and with the kind of love we had in this nation. If we promote it, expand it, develop it, add color to it, support its goodness, it can be applied to the life and spirit of our nation. It will give us cheer, inspiration, motivation, and pride in the people. That will bloom a hundred thousand times. It is better than using the newest, hottest instruments or new inventions. It would take time for people to adjust to them and would develop in them a taste for more new things.

I hope in this first scientific meeting that participants and representatives will clarify, in depth and in general, the boundaries and ethnic groups in our domain. We have found, through exploration, the use of music in many special ceremonies. At the same time, we see that a variety of characteristics of lyrics and accents played a role in making our convention successful; in promoting the instruments and singing of the various groups in Laos; and in making the nation's character and each ethnic group look better, not only on the stage of the nation, but also on the stages of Western countries.

NOTES

1.   This paper was first presented to the Roundtable Meeting on Science and Lao Musical Instruments, March 16-18, 1988, Vientiane, Laos. H. Rattanavong, Presider

2.   *Folk Music Instruments of the World.*   Prague, 1972; English translation by Alžběta Nováková.

TEXT AND CONTEXT IN VIETNAMESE SUNG POETRY:
THE ART OF *HÁT Ả ĐÀO*

Stephen Addiss

HISTORICAL CONTEXT

The interaction of context, text, and musical performance over historical periods is clearly evident in sung Vietnamese poetry, *hát ả đào*. This art form extends back at least to the early eleventh century, when the female singer Đào-thị (literally "female of the Đào family") received awards for her singing from Emperor Lý Thái-tổ (1010–1018) (Khe 1967:147). It is generally accepted that hát ả đào (literally "singing girl Đào") comes from the name of this early songstress. Another name for this form is *ca trù*, the word *ca* meaning "song" and *trù* referring to a strip of bamboo once given as a prize for a fine performance.

During the centuries since Đào-thị was rewarded for her singing, hát ả đào has been transformed in accordance with changes in Vietnamese political and cultural history. From the Hồ dynasty (1400–1407), for example, comes a legend that gives another origin for the name of the music. This story significantly relates to the Vietnamese struggle against the Chinese who had invaded during the early years of the Ming dynasty.

According to this legend, in the village of Đào-xá lived a lovely maiden, Đào, who excelled in the arts of singing and dancing. When Chinese soldiers arrived, all the villagers fled or hid in the woods. The soldiers, fearing the sting of mosquitos, slept on the ground in reed pouches. One person who had won the confidence of the soldiers would tie the pouches with thongs at night and undo them in the morning. Hearing the songs of the Vietnamese girl, the soldiers invited her to sing and dance for them one evening. Her songs lulled them to sleep and with the help of the villagers she carried the soldiers to the river and threw them in. The strange disappearance of the soldiers was taken by the Chinese as an evil omen and they left the village alone thereafter. The village changed its name and built a small temple in Đào's honor. The village is still known as Đào-xá (Đề 1923:175).

From such early records we can infer that in its initial stages hát ả đào consisted primarily of singing and dancing by a young woman, probably with attendant musicians. During the fifteenth and sixteenth centuries, however, hát ả đào evolved into more elaborate forms, as is clear from the new names that were given to it: *hát cửa đình* ("singing at the meeting hall") and *hát cửa quyền* ("singing in aristocratic homes"). These two trends, the first towards performance in public and the second toward performance for the elite, sum up much of the subsequent transformation of hát ả đào.

At first the public aspects of hát ả đào seem to have predominated. During the fifteenth and sixteenth centuries it was performed to honor the patron saints of villages, to welcome the arrival of officials and the return of soldiers, and to celebrate planting and harvesting festivities. At this time a musical troupe under the direction of a trùm (chief) or quản giáp (leader) consisted of several female singers and male musicians. The orchestra included sao, bamboo transverse flute, địch-quản, double or transverse flute, trường cùng, split bamboo clappers, yêu cổ, double-faced, narrow-waisted drum with gelatinous rice to control its tone, and the three instruments still used in hát ả đào today: phách, wooden dowels struck by the singer against a wooden slab, đàn đáy, the long, three-string lute, and đan diện cổ, the single-face drum.

During this period of Vietnamese history, each province of the country (which consisted of former North Vietnam and two areas of central Vietnam) was divided into districts, each having two or three hát ả đào troupes. Among the most significant performances were contests between villages, usually in the fall after the harvest, at which troupes competed in dances such as the múa đèn ("dance with two lanterns"), múa trận hoa ("dance of wooing the tipsy girl"), and đi dây ("a dance on a tightrope"). Individual tests of skill included males balancing an umbrella on their upper lip or lifting a plow with their teeth, and females dancing with oil lanterns. The most important musical contests, however, were for women singers with men đàn đáy players. These had four sections possibly lasting ten to twelve days which took place before judges who played drums to indicate their commentary. First came preliminary songs called văn and selected passages for the đàn đáy to determine which performers could go on to the next level of the competition. Here twenty-eight selected songs called chầu thi were performed, followed by seventeen more songs called chầu cầm, three or four of which would be very difficult. Finally, contestants performed thi lại, the most complex songs, to establish the ultimate winners. The ten top finishers were then honored at a banquet at which prizes were awarded and special performances took place.

The importance of hát ả đào in Vietnamese society at this time was considerable. It was a major cultural event in the lives of farmers and villagers as well as entertainment for the upper levels of society, and also inculcated local pride in artistic attainment among the general populace. Singers took their art seriously, abstaining from sex and from eating meat for several days before the competitions, except for toad flesh which was supposed to be good for the voice. Village girls knew they might attract the attention of the emperor and move to court if they were beautiful and highly sklled performers. These singers became the feminine ideal of the age, much like operatic sopranos of nineteenth-century Europe or movie stars today.

None of the original music or dance survives from this "first golden age" of hát ả đào, which was gradually replaced in popularity by various forms of musical theater. In the seventeenth century Vietnam was divided into the Trịnh dynasty in the north and the Nguyễn dynasty in the south (now central Vietnam). Although the Trinh patronized hát ả đào, other kinds of musical performance usurped some of its traditional functions. For example, the folk theater hát chèo was growing in strength in the northern countryside. In the south, the Nguyễn Dynasty preferred classical musical theater hát bội (Addiss 1971). Theatrical forms had the advantage of telling a single, continuous story, whereas hát ả đào was made up of individual sections. As a result, by the eighteenth century, the ceremonial and public functions of hát ả đào largely had disappeared. In its new context, appealing to the scholarly elite, the art was now patronized by Mandarin intellectuals for whom the poetic elements of hát ả đào were extremely important. Private occasions required fewer performers, who were eventually reduced to the singer, who also played the phách, the đàn đáy player, and the listener, who drummed the diện cổ. Special houses were set up for hát ả đào, which also served as intellectual meeting places akin to a combination of salon and cafe. Despite the apparent decline in the popularity of hát ả đào, it remained an important cultural force. A literary renaissance in the nineteenth century brought a "second golden age" to the singing of poetry in this more refined form.

In its later manifestations, hát ả đào no longer included dance or acrobatics,[1] but was more closely tied to poetry than before. Folksongs were modified to fit the genre, adaptations of Chinese poems were made, and new poems were especially encouraged. A literatus, for example, might write a verse and dedicate it to a colleague. Instead of simply giving the poem to his friend, he could take it first to a singer. She would scan it for its form and note the tones of each word, and then accompany the poet to his friend's house with a đàn đáy player. The friend would strike the small drum in such a way that he could rhythmically comment on the poem. The drum part added to the musical totality making the friend both performer and critic.

In the last century hát ả đào has been maintained, but the vicissitudes that have afflicted Vietnam have been harmful to this complex and subtle traditional art form. Special houses where hát ả đào was performed often took on the qualities of a brothel or an opium den, giving the art a poor reputation. Furthermore, the influence of the French led many Vietnamese intellectuals towards Western culture and away from their own. In our own time, the long years of warfare discouraged young musicians from learning a form of music requiring years of study. After the partition of Vietnam, many performers came to the south, where they found that hát ả đào was neither understood nor appreciated. The form still survives, however, and is undergoing a revival in northern Vietnam, encouraged by the noted musicologist Trần Văn Khê. He has convinced authorities that hát ả đào represents a vital part of Vietnamese culture, that it is appreciated abroad, and that it has an important role to play in present and future Vietnamese musical performance. Historically, the context for hát ả đào changed significantly over the centuries. It will be of great interest to see how hát ả đào continues to change and evolve in the new Vietnam.

POETIC TEXTS

Hát ả đào utilizes a number of different poetry types, including verse inspired by such varied sources as folk songs, theater music, lullabies, drinking songs, historical declamations, love songs, the ballads of blind traveling minstrels, adaptations of Chinese poetry, incantations of shamans, and potpourris of all the above.

Centuries ago, a hát ả đào performance for the festival of a patron saint of a village began with presentation music for đàn đáy and drums, followed by the chanting for the presentation of incense, the lighting of incense, an instrumental interlude, a series of songs, and then dances. In contrast, performances during the nineteenth and twentieth centuries have begun with an instrumental opening, followed entirely by a series of sung poems,[2] the most important of which is *hát nói* (literally "singing-speaking"). This form begins with one or two introductory quatrains sung in free rhythm (*mưỡu*) and concludes with a poetic section of eleven lines. These are usually divided into five couplets with a single line at the end. The hát nói proper is expected to follow a strict poetic form with two introductory lines, two which "go to the heart" of the subject, two which follow Chinese style (in either 5–5 or 7–7 syllable form), two which recapitulate, two which widen the meaning, and a final concluding line of six syllables. Except for the fifth, sixth, and final lines, any number of syllables may be used, but the most common in paired lines is the typical Vietnamese poetic couplet of six and eight syllables.

Several combinations of elements in hát nói seem to have helped it achieve its great popularity in the hát ả đào genre. First, it includes a Chinese couplet for a sophisticated touch in an otherwise Vietnamese poetic style. Second, it combines strictness in its length and structure with freedom in the syllable count of all but three of its lines. Third, its introductory quatrains effectively set the mood and the tone of what follows. Finally, it encompasses a wide variety of topics within a fixed poetic framework. In 1932, the scholar Ôn-Như Nguyễn Văn Ngọc published a collection of more than two thousand hát nói poems, divided into the thematic categories of expectation, patience, pessimism, hedonism, descriptions of nature, love, didacticism, and humor (Ngọc 1932). Underlying them all, he felt a mood of searching for freedom from official restraints. His conception was perhaps exacerbated by the control of Vietnam by the French during this period; enjoyment of poetry and music was one form of release for the intellectuals of the time. A well-known hát nói from the nineteenth-century poet Dương Khuê (1836–1898) suggests this mood.[3]

Gặp Đào Hồng Đào Tuyết	On Meeting the Singers Hồng and Tuyết
Muởu	Introduction

Ngày xưa Tuyết muốn lấy ông	Once, Tuyết wished to marry me,
Ông chê Tuyết bé. Tuyết không biết gì.	I though her too young, she didn't know anything.
Bây giờ Tuyết đã đến thì,	Now Tuyết has come of age
Ông muốn lấy Tuyết, Tuyết chê ông già.	And I would marry—but she finds me too old.

| Nói | Poem |

Hồng Hồng, Tuyết, Tuyết,	Hồng Hồng, Tuyết, Tuyết
Mới ngày nào chưabiết cái chi chi.	It seems just recently you knew nothing.
Mười lăm năm thấm thoát có xa gì,	Fifteen years does not seem long at all.
Ngoảnh mặt lại đã tới kỳ tơ-liễu..	I turn my head and you are already grown up.
Ngã lãng du thì quân thượng thiếu,	When I was in my prime you were still a little girl.
Quân kim hứa gía ngã thành ông	Now you are ready to marry and I am an old man.
Cười cười nói nói thẹn thùng.	We smile and speak, but we are not at ease.
Mà bạch-phát vời hồng-nhan chừng ái ngại.	Between rosy cheeks and white hair, our talk is halting.
Riêng một thú Thanh-sơn đi lại,	My only joy now is to go to the hát ả đào house:
Khéo ngây ngây dại dại với tình.	I have become foolish, foolish with love.
Đàn ai một tiếng dương tranh.	Who is it now playing on the lute?

While the wistful emotion of this poem well expresses the resigned and escapist mood of many nineteenth-century literati, the verse itself displays a number of traditional Vietnamese poetic elements. These include the use of rhyme and partial rhyme, often moving contrapuntally over lines within two different couplets (lines 2—3, 4—5, 8—9), the preference for an even number of syllables per line when not imitating Chinese verse, and repetitions of words and sounds for their acoustic properties. In the Mưỡu or Introduction, for example, the name Tuyết occurs as the third word of the first line, the third and fifth of the second line, the third of the third line, and the fourth and fifth of the final line. Then in the main poem, the first line ends with a repetition, Tuyết, Tuyết. Later, the seventh line lightens the effect of the previous Chinese style couplet by the repetition cười cười nói nói, literally "smiling, smiling, talking, talking." We also find assonance, lăm năm thấm, in the third line. Finally, there are hidden rhymes and half-rhymes within the poetic lines, sometimes on the sixth syllable of an eight-syllable line to rhyme with the sixth (last) syllable of the line before it. All of these devices are proto-musical elements within the poem, which are then elaborated upon by the singer and lutenist.

In contrast with hát nói, a more ancient poetic form dates to the early days of hát ả đào when it was known as *thét nhạc*. Here the poetic rules are almost completely free, but the singer and musician are expected to pass through five different musical modes during the course of the piece. This is accomplished by making any note of the pentatonic scale the beginning of a new one; thus C-D-F-G-A can modulate to D-E-G-A-B, F-G-Bb-C-D, G-A-C-D-E, and A-B-D-E-F#. Pauses in the text are marked in the transcription by three dots. The emphasis upon musical rather than prosodic rules reflects the early ambiance of hát ả đào.

Thét Nhạc-Tiếng Dương-tranh

Tiếng Dương-tranh,
Đàn . . . ai đàn một tiếng Dương-tranh,
Chưng thỏ ngọc ô đàn nặo-nùng chiều ai-oán . . .
Nhạc Thiều . . . tâu,
Xa đưa tiếng nhạc Thiều .tâu,
Vẳng nghe chuông dóng lâu lâu lại . . . ngừng
Dường, hơi dường đầm . . . ấm . . .
Năm thức mây che,
Thức mây che rờ rỡ ngất . . . trời.
Nguyệt dãi thềm lan,
Thanh bóng trăng thanh dãi tỏ thềm lan . . .
Tiếc thay mặt ngọc thường ai,
Vậy là đêm là đêm đông . . . trường.
Rạng vẻ mây rồng,
Thiên, nam thiên rạng vẻ mây rồng,
Rực-rỡ nghìn thu,
Nghìn thu ngạt . . . ngào.
Lãng-uyển xa bay,
Luống thâu đêm, đêm nghe phảng-phất môi sầu tuôn,

Tuôn khôn nhịn ngân ngơ nỗi . . . buồn.

Thu, lá thu ngô đồng rụng . . .

Một lá thu bay, hơ sương lọt mày hơi

Sương lọt mày, ngồi nghe tiếng . . . đàn.

Sông, sông hồ nước biếc chín khúc cuốn quanh,

Đáy nước long-lanh, dạo ngồi chơi, ngồi chơi thủy . . . đình.

Nguyệt tà tà xế xế, ánh dãi chênh chênh,

Trên không hoa cỏ lặng canh dài,

Đỉnh Thân-sơn, đỉnh Thân-sơn mặt ngọc mày ngài,

Thấy khách hồn mai.

Dãi tường lâu,

Nguyệt dãi tường lâu đồng vọng bóng trăng thâu,

Nặng tiếng, tiếng đỉnh-đang,

Tiếng đỉnh-đang, xui lòng thiếu nữ . . .

Nhớ thương ai gửi bước đồng tường,

Bước đồng tường, chầy ai đã nện tường tư . . . sầu.

Vò-võ phòng hương,

Luống chực phòng hương,

Gửi cố-nhân tình thư một bức, gợi nỗi ái ân,

Tư, tương tư . . . sầu.

The Sound of the Tranh

The sound of the tranh . . .

Who is playing the tranh?

In the olden days, the instrument gave out lamentations . . .

Now the flute is striking up,

We hear the bell faintly at long intervals

Its sound is warm and melodious . . .

We recall its sonorous tones.

Five shades of clouds veil and dim the night sky,

The moonlight spreads on the verandah,

The moonbeams light up the orchid-lined verandah.

The face of the moon glows with affection.

This is the night, the long winter night . . .

The southern sky has a bright picture of clouds with dragons.

The pictures of clouds and dragons seem bright,

The sight, the sight will shine a thousand years,

A thousand years with sweet perfume.

The romantic tones of the flute fly far away,

All night long we hear the sorrowful sounds,

Never ceasing to convey sad thoughts and moods.

The autumn leaves fall from the trees.

One leaf flies away; a dewy mist comes into the eyes.
Sitting and listening to the music, the dew enters the eyes.
The waters and lakes and rivers wind into the nine streams,
Under the waters the streambeds gleam,
It is a pleasure to sit nearby.
The moon is slowly waning, its beams spread slantingly . . .
The grasses and flowers are silent all night long.
On the mountain, there is a face with curved brows,
A traveler kisses the cherry blossoms . . .
Along the wall of the house, the moon spreads its beams,
The house reflects the autum moonlight.
The bells sound deeply from afar,
The sounds thrill some maiden's heart.
She is missing someone who travels a long way,
A long road bears his footprints and a sorrowful heart.
Lonely in her bedroom, she waits by herself . . .
She sends a love letter to her friend, she sends her tenderness.
Ah, the sadness of love, the sadness of love and its sorrow.

The translation cannot give the full quality of the repeating patterns of words and images of the original, full of languorous delays and pauses. The lines, with four to eleven syllables each, are replete with alliterations, internal rhyme, and assonance, perhaps more than any other kinds of hát à đào poem. The lack of formal structure also distinguishes this *thét nhạc* style of poem.

Two more examples from poems in the hát à đào repertoire may suffice to point out some of the partially hidden "musical" elements of the verse forms. The first example is the opening six lines of a poetic form called *Nhịp Ba Cung Bắc* which is supposed to include the use of three different musical modes when sung.[4]

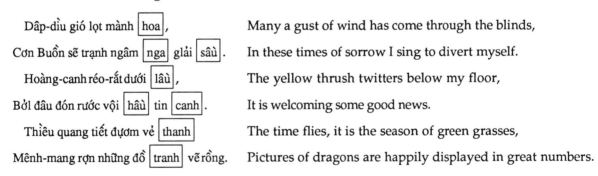

Dập-dìu gió lọt mành hoa,   Many a gust of wind has come through the blinds,

Cơn Buồn sẽ trạnh ngâm nga giải sâu. In these times of sorrow I sing to divert myself.

Hoàng-canh réo-rất dưới lâu,   The yellow thrush twitters below my floor,

Bởi đâu đón rước vội hâu tin canh. It is welcoming some good news.

Thiều quang tiết đượm vẻ thanh   The time flies, it is the season of green grasses,

Mênh-mang rợn những đồ tranh vẽ rồng. Pictures of dragons are happily displayed in great numbers.

This poem is in the *lục bát* (six-eight syllable) form, common in folksongs and often incorporated into formal Vietnamese verse. In this case the text has been marked to show the use of external-internal rhyme which occurs at the six-syllable mark, establishes a new sound at the end of the eight-syllable line, and then continues following the same principle.

The stresses in lục bát fall on the even syllables, in a form we might consider iambic. The tones of the words also play an important role in the structure. The Vietnamese consider the level tone a and the falling tone à to be "level," while the rising tone á , the mid-rising ã and ả join the low-rising ạ in being considered "sharp" tones. In lục bát, the fourth syllable in each line should be "sharp" while the second, sixth, and eighth must be "level." The pattern of the six lines in this case is:

```
SLLSLL
LLSSLLSL
LLSSSL
SLSSSLLL
LLSSSL
LLSSLLSL
```

Here the rules are strictly followed and we may note the additional tendency to repeat either "level" or "sharp" tones in patterns which are never completely symmetrical.

A final example of poetic acoustic devices is a couplet from an ancient form called *gui thu* (Sending Letters), entitled *But Hao Thao* (My Writing Brush).

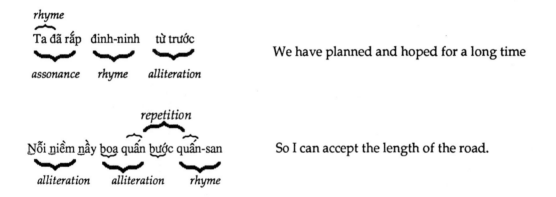

We have planned and hoped for a long time

So I can accept the length of the road.

Here we can see the use of rhyme, alliteration, assonance, and repetition to give a musical quality to the words, surely no coincidence in a poetic form meant to be sung.

MUSICAL ASPECTS OF PERFORMANCE

The non-Vietnamese listener, upon first hearing hát ả đào, is likely to be confused by the profusion of notes and complexity of vocal ornamentation that occur in performance. The vocal quality of the (female) singers is not the open-throated sound to which we are accustomed, and even coloratura singing in grand opera does not prepare us for the abundance of trills, vibratos of various kinds, grace notes, appoggiaturas, and other melismatic techniques of the Vietnamese songstress. Before we can fully appreciate the skill of the performers, we must come to some understanding of the structure of the music as well as the types of variations amd ornamentations practiced by the singers and musicians.

In his 1954 study of classical and romantic European music Heinrich Schenker demonstrated that underlying the most elaborate movements of symphonies, quartets, and sonatas, a simple structure can be detected that relies on the basic movement from either the fifth or third degree of the scale down to the tonic. Prolongations are accomplished in many different ways and in fact it is skill in these prolongations that distinguishes the finest composers from the mediocre; but the structures are always consistent within the tonal music of our tradition.

Basic melodic structures can also be found throughout Vietnamese music, although they are sometimes hidden by a great profusion of elaborations and prolongations. These are not conceptualized nor directly taught, but underlie all forms of traditional Vietnamese music through improvisation. In the complex art of hát ả đào, it is not until one compares various performers singing the same poem that one discovers what they all have in common (structure) amidst the variations of ornaments and elaborations (prolongation). In a previous article (1973) I described the structure of the Vietnamese version of Po Chu-i's Lute Song, called *Tỳ bà* in the hát ả đào repertoire. Here I will discuss the poem previous translated, *Gặp Đào Hồng Đào Tuyết* as an example of the hát nói form within hát ả đào.

First one must realize that because of the great number of poems used in hát nói, no single melody can be expected to fit them all, especially since a variety of tones in the words as well as varying syllable counts are possible in all lines but the fifth, six, and last. Nevertheless the poem chosen here is typical of how a hát nói might be sung.[5]

Gặp đào Hồng đào Tuyết

Surprisingly, this highly complex piece is based on only three notes, here given as A, C half-sharp, and E. Although in its sung version the passing tones G and D are also heard, the basic tritonic basis of the piece is quite clear and one might even consider that the structure is based only on the notes A and E. Another performance of the piece would have different elaborations: the time scheme might differ somewhat and the ornamentation would depend upon the singer and her particular expressive intent, but the fundamental structure would remain the same.

Why does such complex music have such a simple structure? I would like to suggest that this simplicity of structure allows the complexities to be perceived by the cultivated listener. Because there are only three main notes, all vibrato effects, sliding tones, grace notes, and subtle changes of vocal color can be kept in perspective and enjoyed in their full expressive potential. Were the structure more complex, the ornamentations could not be developed as thoroughly or the listener would be lost. In contrast, the twelve-tone music of Arnold Schönberg and his followers allows no extra elaboration, since the listener already has such a difficult time understanding the total structure of the music. Using a "home base" drone tone in the music of India, on the other hand, allows for the greatest melodic elaboration by master performers.

We may also note that the structural notes of the above hát nói outline what to a Western listener would represent the triad, an extremely stable relationship of three notes which here begins on the fifth scale degree and ends on the tonic. The interval of the fifth, which is easily produced by such natural means as overblowing a tube or dividing a string in quarters, gives a secure sonic structure to hát nói, while the "neutral third," between major and minor, imparts a sense of what most listeners would hear as a melancholy effect, perfectly suited to the poem.

To understand the structure of hát nói as the most important genre in hát ả đào, another hát nói poem may be presented to ascertain where it is musically similar and different from the one given previously. Let us examine a verse by the famous scholar-poet Nguyen Khuyen.[6] Although many of his poems express his personal integrity and disdain for those who collaborated with the French, in others there is a self-mocking humor such as in the following hát nói.

Hỏi Phỗng-Đán	Questions to a Stone Statue
Mưỡu	Introduction

Người đâu tên họ là gì,	Where did you come from and what's your name?
Hỏi ra trích trích tri tri nụ'c cười.	To questions you just smile, smile—
Vất tay ngoảnh mặt trông trời	Your arms are folded and you glance at the sky,
Cũng toan lo tính sự' đòi chi đây.	Perhaps you are brewing up something for the world?

Nói	Poem

Thấy lão-đá lạ lùng muốn hỏi	I see a strange statue of an old man and would like to ask:
Cớ sao mà len lỏi đến chi đây.	Why did you come here on this crooked path?
Hay mảng vui hoa cỏ nước non này,	Are you happy with the grass, streams, and hills?
Chừng cũng muốn dang tay văn hội lạc.	Probably you wanted to join the literary society!
Thanh sơn tự' tiếu đầu tương hạc.	The green hills laugh at my old head,

Thương hải đừng nghĩ chuyện đâu đâu,

Túi vũ-trụ mặc đàn sau gánh vác.

Duyên hội ngộ là duyên tuổi tác, chén chú

chén anh, chén tôi chén bác

Cuộc tỉnh say, say tỉnh một vài câu.

Nên chăng đá cũng gật đâù.

The blue seas don't know I am serene as a gull.

Stop thinking of far-off matters,

Let posterity settle the problems of the universe!

This meeting is good fortune, let's bring out the wine cups.

Here's to you, to you, to me, then to you again—

But to both good and bad ideas the statue keeps nodding.

It is clear that the structure is much like that of the previous hát nói. The basic melodic elements are the two tones A and E with the frequent use of the "neutral third" C (again half-way to C#), and finally the addition two more notes (G and D) as subsidiary tones.

Comparing the melodic structures, individual phrases have certain similar contours which serve as unifying elements that help to establish and define the musical genre of hát nói. However, since the words do not always have the same tones, the significant question is, how does the singer adjust the melody to the words? For example, to sing a word with a high-rising tone on a descending melody would change the meaning of the word, so this becomes a vital problem. The solution in musical practice is evident in the opening of the two mưđu:

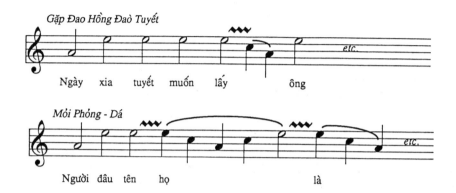

Here, although different word-tones lead to differing melodies, the basic melodic contour remains much the same. We can see the parameters: When a word has a high-rising tone, it must linger on a high note but may then descend. When a word has a low tone, it may begin on a high note only if it thereupon sinks rapidly. Accordingly the singer can maintain similar melodic contours in hát nói when singing different poems. For example, on the fifth word of each poem, the melody may change as follows:

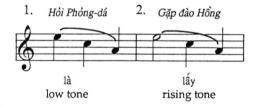

There are numerous conventions by which the singer must abide while bringing the poetry to life.[7] If this were not enough, the singer has an additional task in hát ả đào: she must use her phách to assist her performance. She produces tempo changes with the dowels on the wooden slab, and marks spacings between phrases. Before singing, she will often produce a steady tremolo called *phách rung*. Between phrases, she will use a dotted rhythm called *phách hoi*:

To speed up the tempo, she increases the speed of the dowel rhythm (*phách mau*), while slowing down is called *phách lá đầu*. Other uses of the phách include short spaces while the singer takes a breath (*phách khoan*) and the more rare use of the dowels while singing (*phách dọc*).

The most important instrument in hát ả đào is the đàn đáy. The typically male instrumentalist weaves around the singer in a heterophonic relationship; they are both playing the same basic melody, but in individual and complex variations. The instrumentalist also has solo passages before the singer begins and between her phrases. During these passages he will often use the form of transposition of the five-note scale described earlier; in fact he often seems to be straying as far as possible from the original scale, only returning deftly when the singer is about to begin her next phrase. The đàn đáy player must also maintain a subtle shifting sense of tempo in which there is never too exact a steady beat. He must bridge the gap between an obvious rhythm and total anarchy; his art is one of suggestion rather than statement.

The following opening of a performance of the poem Tý-bá (including the drum part) illustrates the relationship between the melodies of the singer and the instrumentalist. A full rather than structural notation is given to make this relationship clear

The đàn đáy player begins with a passage that leaves the scale unclear, but soon establishes the most important notes of C and G, along with D, F, and A, which establish the pentatonic scale. Before the singer enters, he reiterates the note G, leading to a C, which is the note that she reaches upon her entrance. The instrumentalist then plays the basic melody in a heterophonic relationship with the singer, outlining the structural notes just before or just after she reaches them. He tends to lag slightly behind the vocal part, as can be seen in the following structural notation:

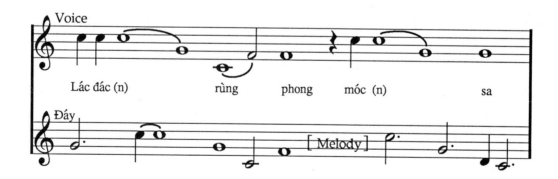

The question of whether the đàn đáy is leading or lagging behind the singer, however, depends on how one interprets the device of anticipation by the vocalist, who often reaches each structural note just before the new word is sung. If one considers when the singer first reaches the note, she leads the đàn đáy player:

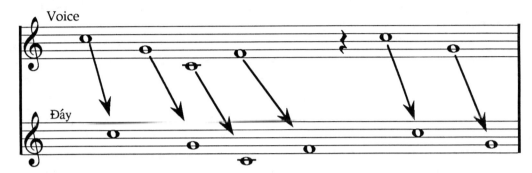

If, however, one considers the moment when the word is sung as the vocal structural point, then the đàn đáy player is sometimes ahead, sometimes even, and sometimes behind the singer.

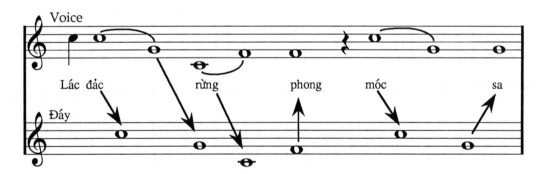

In performance, the shifting relationship of the voice and the đàn đáy is one of the subtleties appreciated by the educated listener. The structural notes may be reached in three different ways: when the singer anticipates them, when she begins new words on them, and when the đàn đáy player strikes them. Any two or three of these may be simultaneous, but they are more often slightly different, thus adding to the complexity of the rhythm that, like elaborations of the melody, give hát ả đào its sophisticated musicality in performance.

The art of the đàn đáy player is to strive for a subtle rather than an obvious musical relationship with the singer. His art is integrated into the totality, yet allows for a great deal of individuality by the performer. He generally eschews flashy runs or obvious feats of technical skill, instead working in a restrained and yet creative cooperation with the singer towards the total effect.

The small drum diện cổ completes the ensemble and is used for several purposes. As played by the guest or censor, it has both musical and extra-musical connotations. The guest may comment on the performance as it goes along as well as punctuating it rhythmically by the way he plays. In this way the original function of the judge in hat a dao contests is retained, although now without the aspect of direct competition.

Beats on the top skin part of the drum are called *tùng*, while hitting the wooden side of the drum is called *cắc*. These words are good descriptions of the actual sounds produced. Although the drum is small, it is rapped smartly so that tùng and cắc are quite piercing sounds. Different combinations of beats have specific meanings. Twelve cắc call the musicians, nine tùng tell them to prepare, and two tùng urge them to begin. Five, six, or seven cắc before a tùng indicate that the performance is inferior, while one cắc before several tùng signifies praise. This last combination in many variations is the basic pattern most often heard. In addition, two successive words that are extremely well sung can be applauded by tùng tùng cắc, and two words when divided by a vocal portamento can be honored by tùng cắc tùng.

The drum usually plays between phrases of the song. The drummer is not expected to set a beat, or even to play in whatever shifting sense of meter has been established by the singer and đàn đáy player. Instead, he punctuates the music freely with his tùng and cắc patterns, usually during pauses of the singer. He thus adds to the performance another layer of sound that has its own meaning and purpose. In a typical performance of a hát nói, one might hear the following drum patterns:

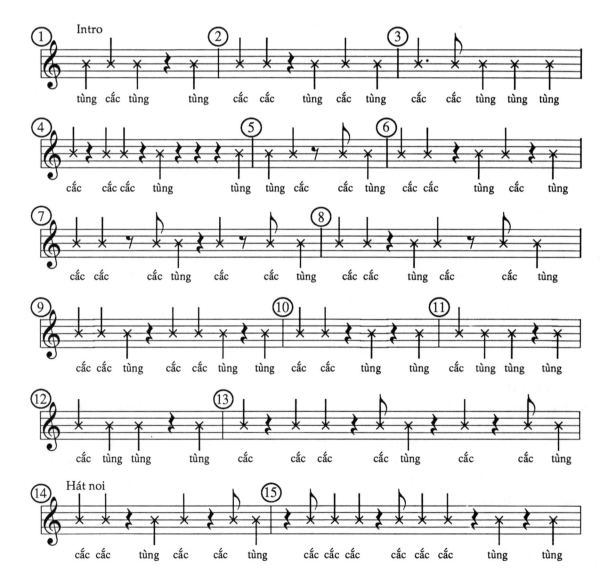

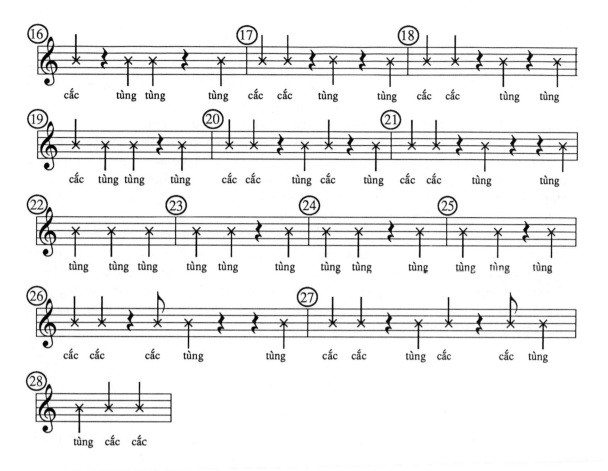

This example contains twenty-eight phrases, of which nineteen are different, displaying the variety of rhythmic effects one may hear in performance. In the following chart, the patterns are noted with a dot indicating a rest. Each letter indicates a single full beat, except for a half-beat cắc which is underlined (c̲):

1	t c t . t
2	c c . t c t
3	c̲ c t t t
4	c . c c . t . . . t
5	t c̲ c t
6, 20	c c . t c . t
7	c c . . c t . c̲ c t
8, 14, 27	c c . t c̲ c t
9	c c t . c c t . t
10, 17, 18	c c . t . t
11, 12, 19	c t t . t
13	c . c̲ c c t . c̲ c t
15	c c c̲ c c . t . t
16	c . t t . t
21	c c . t . . t
22	t t t
23, 24, 25	t t . t
26	c c̲ c t . . t
28	t c c

This chart shows us that the patterns are more simple at the beginning and end of the piece and more complex in the middle. One of the repetitions of phrases, three tùng, comes at the line of the poem about repeated drinking: "Here's to you, to you, to me, then to you again."

The other repetitions have no clear extra-musical meaning. In its most basic form the drum part is merely các tùng, but like the singer and the đàn đáy player, the drummer is expected to add variations to the simple structure of his part. He does this by means of repetitions (ccttt), rests within the phrases (c.cc.t...t), syncopations (c̲c̲ct...t), and combinations of these devices (c.c̲c̲ct.c̲ct). These may all be regarded as prolongations of the basic structural unit of các tùng.

The performance of the drummer involves a kind of improvisation with little direct musical relationship with the singing and đàn đáy except that he usually plays between the vocal phrases. His responsibility is to reinforce the phrases of the poem, comment on the performance, and add a free rhythmic element to the complex musical totality of hát ả đào. His role of commenting on the music while joining it is of some subtlety, and to be given the drum for a performance is an honor usually reserved for senior poets and intellectuals.

SUMMATION

As performed today, hát ả đào remains a complex combination of poetic texts set within musical structures, but the complexities are a result of elaborations on fundamentally simple parts. The singer follows a melodic structure that is often based upon only three different notes, to which she adds the ornamentations of trills, extra humming sounds, vibratos of varying kinds, melismas, grace notes, appoggiaturas, and other embellishments. She also performs rhythmically with her phách, often to help her clarify the different musical and poetic phrases. The đàn đáy player works within the same basic melodic structure, but utilizes complex heterophonic variations of the singer's melodies. He also has free solo passages between the vocal phrases, during which he may transpose the pentatonic scale. The drummer's improvisations consist primarily of variations on the basic pattern các tùng played most often between phrases of the poem. He also comments on the performance with signals of các and tùng that have specific meanings.

The combination of voice, phách, đàn đáy, and diện cổ can sound extremely complicated on first hearing, but when the elaborations are understood they become pleasing to the sophisticated listener. It is, in fact, these improvisational variations that give life to hát ả đào for the literati who have become its audience in the past two hundred years. In the context of Vietnam in the fifteenth and sixteenth centuries, the music must have been quite different, since its role at that time was more ceremonial. For dances, much hát ả đào was almost certainly quicker in tempo and more regular in beat than is now the case, and when it was sung in village festivals it could not have been as languorous in style as many performances are today.

It is clear that the changes that hát ả đào has undergone during its long history are closely related to the cultural history of Vietnam. At first performed both for entertainment at court and as an important part of the ritual life in the villages, it could not have survived without changing into an art of the intellectuals, with a nostalgic and escapist tone during the years of French domination. Today it is being revived and appreciated as a unique and significant heritage of

Vietnamese culture and remains a convincing example of how closely and directly musical performance can be related to both text and context in Southeast Asia.

NOTES

1. For a further discussion of dance, see "Hát Ả Đào" (Addiss 1973: 21).

2. For a description with examples of the poetry types, see *ibid.*:23–27.

3. The author would like to thank Phạm Duy and Nguyễn Ngọc Bích for their assistance in the translations of the poems.

4. The entire poem is given with a translation in "Hát Ả Đào" (Addiss 1973: 24).

5. The following notation has been greatly simplified, since the actual rhythm is always more complex and free and the singer typically uses sliding tones and a profusion of other special effects. Trills are marked with waving lines, but other vocal embellishments have not been noted. The note given as "C" is actually between a "C" and a "C#" (known as a "neutral third" between major and minor).

6. Nguyen gave up his bureaucratic position in 1885 pleading failing eyesight, distressed at the French rule of his country. This example is from a recorded performance available on *Music of North and South Vietnam* (Asch Mankind Series AHM 4219).

7. The art of the singer is to make the basic melodic contours come alive with original and subtle variations. She is expected to follow eight rules:

    *   Each word must be clear and therefore the tempo is slow.
    *   Each word must be rounded out using repressed tone.
    *   Each word must have an echo in sound, a hum, or an extra vocalization after the word, like a thread holding a necklace together.
    *   The singer must show strong breath control in long phrases.
    *   The feeling of the singer must be noble.
    *   The presentation must be dramatic and express the spirit of the poem being sung.
    *   The impression must be attractive.
    *   The singer must display vocal agility.

    More than fifty years ago, the connoisseur Nguyên Đôn Phúc (1923:288–286) gave his own description of a good songstress. "She must sing evenly and clearly throughout her range and must scan each word clearly. Every word must be followed by another sound in succession. Each word must be like a pearl and the extra sound like a string linking it to the others."

REFERENCES CITED

Addiss, Stephen
    1971   "Theater Music of Vietnam," *Southeast Asia* 1(1-2):128–152.

    1973   "Hát Ả Đào, the Sung Poetry of North Vietnam," *Journal of the American Oriental Society* 93(1):18–31.

Đề, Phương Vũ
    1923   "Hát Ả Đào," *Nam Phong* (March).

Khê, Trần Văn
    1967   *Vietnam*. Paris: Bouchet-Chastel.

Music of North and South Vietnam. LP. Asch Mankind Series. AHM 4219.

Nguyên, Đôn Phúc
    1923   "Khao luân vê cuôc hát Ả đào," *Nam Phong* (April):277–289.

Ôn-Như Nguyên, Văn Ngọc
    1932   *Đào Nương Ca*. Hanoi.

Schenker, Heinrich
    1954   *Harmony*. Chicago: University of Chicago Press.

TEXT, CONTEXT, AND PERFORMANCE IN VIETNAMESE BUDDHIST LITURGY

Phong T. Nguyen

Buddhism was first known in Giao Châu, present-day northern Vietnam, by the first century A.D. when a maritime trade route was established between Southeast and West Asia (the Middle East). Indian, Persian, and Central Asian merchants and monks brought this Indian religion into Giao Châu. According to an historical account of the thirteenth century, the *Thiền Uyển Tập Anh* (Selected Stories of the Well-known Monks in the Meditation Garden),[1] in the second century A.D. there existed in Giao Châu twenty temples, ten volumes of *sutra*[2] translated from Sanskrit into Chinese, and also 500 monks practicing their religion.

Buddhism is believed to have first blended with the local system of folk beliefs. With the import of early texts from the *Tripitaka* or Triple Collection (sutra, monastic rules, and Buddhist essays), translation, criticism, and recitation of texts became major activities of monks and lay scholars in Giao Châu from the second century A.D. The *Pháp Hoa Kinh* or *Saddharmapundarika* (Sutra of the Lotus of the Wonderful Law) is found among the first reciting texts known to scholars. This sutra was translated in 255–256 by Kalyanaruci (Chi Cương Luong) and Mahajivaka (Ma Ha Kỳ Vực) (Trần 1939:225). The chanting of this sutra was probably practiced in the propagation of Buddhism in both Vietnam and southern China during the ensuing centuries.

This long tradition of chant and its sociocultural context are my principal interest. In this paper I discuss the interrelationship of text, context, and performance in Vietnamese Buddhist liturgy.

LITURGICAL TEXTS USED IN VIETNAM

In general, existing liturgical texts came to Vietnam from a variety of sources. However, because of unsystematic scholarship due to wars among other reasons, many have been misplaced, altered, or destroyed. While it was a common phenomenon in Asia for Buddhism to be bound into the communal system, a national standardization of texts in Vietnam for liturgical services may not have been possible, particularly from the period of north-south division in the sixteenth century. Thus, in each region chant training may make use of texts in different versions or in a changed order while the ceremony may have the same title or purpose.

There are two categories of texts for a service or ceremony. One is the *kinh* (in Sanskrit, sutra), the main Buddhist texts comprising numerous long books that were translated from Sanskrit into classical Chinese and read in the Vietnamese way before they were translated into the vernacular language. The secondary texts called *kệ*, *bạch*, *sớ*, *điệp*, *sám*, and *tán* are mostly in poetical form, composed by monastic scholars.

Vietnamese and East Asian Buddhism commonly use the basic texts of the *Mahayana sutra* included in the *Tripitaka*. These texts, translated and/or transliterated from the original Sanskrit version into classical Chinese are called *kansan* and *bonsan* in Japanese and *âm* and *mật ngôn* in Vietnamese. The easily comprehensible texts of the second category, those composed by monks of each country, are in the vernacular language and are called *hwach'ong* in Korea, *wasan* in Japan, and *nghia* in Vietnam.

In Vietnam liturgical books include various texts of these two language systems arranged in proper order for each service. In the era of the Trần Dynasty (1225–1400) about ten liturgical books were officially used nationwide. Among these is found the *Khóa Hư Lục* (Teaching of the Emptiness), a famous literary and philosophical work composed by King Trần Thái Tông between the years 1258-1277 (Dao 1974:9). Chinese texts were imported in later periods, especially during the Ming Dynasty. About six such liturgical books were known in Vietnam (Nguyễn 1983:50), parts of which are included in today's services. During the Renovation movement (1920–1950) monks and scholars began to transliterate most Buddhist texts into romanized characters. The order of texts for services was revised, new ceremonies were created, and some new texts in the vernacular language were composed. At present texts in classical Chinese have almost disappeared from temples, particularly in cities; monks are now trained in the *chữ quốc ngữ* or romanized characters officially used today as the national written language.

Regardless of how the text is written, singing the texts is in Vietnamese and practiced by monks of all religious tendencies such as *Thiền Tông* (Meditation), *Mật Tông* (Secret), *or Tịnh Độ Tông* (Pure Land). In all instances the Buddhist chant is associated with various sociomusical elements of a particular country. As we can now see, there are regional distinctions of styles and arrangement of texts and services within Vietnam.

A Buddhist Ceremony.

Social Context of Buddhist Liturgy

Vietnamese Buddhism is not a separate and unique entity that can be easily identified like a Western religion. The Mahayanist tendency which occurred in India in the first century B.C., just before its introduction to east and southeast Asia (Nguyễn 1977:17), provided ample opportunity for change and adaptation.

Because of its doctrinal instruction, Buddhism comes to people as a religion of salvation. Religious men could use any available and appropriate means to help people understand its value. At this point, the question of "form" and "content" is raised. All means (forms) must serve the aim (content) in which compassion and salvation are realized. Therefore, the regionalization of Buddhism is understandable. Because a temple is usually a nongovernmental property of the village or district, Buddhist ceremonies carry a communal character. As a result, certain ceremonies and services in northern, central, or southern Vietnam aim primarily at responding to the needs of the local community. For instance, if a village temple is lacking monks, it may omit certain texts from the daily service or even some services of the day. Conversely, a large temple of twenty monks or nuns may have long services and recite extensive sutras. Ritual funerary ceremonies may vary according to the social position of the chief of the family, who would invite as many monks and musicians as he could.

There is also the communal custom of organizing annual ritual festivals. A wealthy community may be financially able to support one or more ritual festivals in the temple such as the *Thượng Nguyên* (First Quarter), *Trung Nguyên* (Middle Quarter), and *Hạ Nguyên* (Last Quarter), which last several days. A number of important texts may be used for these rituals. The specific date and circumstances of performance may require specific texts with a change of details such as name, location, and date. A text appropriate to a specific type of ceremony can be created quickly. It is interesting to note that in certain communities the Buddhist ritual is syncretized with those of possessionism or Taoism. Texts and ritual dances performed by possession ritualists and Taoists are sometimes included during one or several days of Buddhist ceremonies for the dead in private homes.

Correspondence between Text and Musical Context in Performance

The spoken Vietnamese language, a social aspect relating to music, weighs heavily on musical style. Pronunciation of words may differ from one region to another. Linguistic tones show a similar diversification. Vietnamese Buddhist liturgy therefore involves discrete regional musical traits. The musical performance of texts reflects two major aspects of the context: text for the service and music for the texts.

Text for the Service

Mahayana sutras, each of which is the main body of every service or ceremony, are used for all kinds of ritual performances.

However, there is a distinct reason to chant the following sutras, among others, for each circumstance because of the meaning of the story related in the text:

Kinh A Di Đà (Amitabha Sutra) for a funeral
Kinh Địa Tạng (Ksitigarbha Sutra) for the post-funeral
Kinh Phổ Môn (Universal Gate) for a wish of peace and wealth
Kinh Vu Lan (Ulambana Sutra) for the Salvation Festival
Kinh Lăng Nghiêm (Suramgama Sutra) for the monastic morning service
Kinh Hồng Danh (Sutra of Holy Names) for Repentance

An old text in classical Chinese : King Kim Cang (Diamond Sutra).

These texts are related to the type of service, time of the day, and sometimes even the number of people attending the service. There are secondary texts also included in these in ceremonies which are composed by monks in various poetical categories such as ke, bach, tan, and *xuong*, among others. Depending on the aesthetic and ritual contexts, the texts of a service are put in a predetermined order. Let us take the case of the *Công Phu Khuya*, or morning service (cf. Nguyễn 1982). The following texts are chanted one after another:

Title: *Công Phu Khuya* (Morning Service)

Preparatory part (in the belfry):
  1. *Kệ thức chúng* (Poem "Waking the Monks")
  2. *Kệ khai chuông* (Poem "Opening the Bell")

Service (in the reciting hall):
  3. *Niệm hương* (Poem "Offering Incense")
  4. *Kinh thủ lăng nghiêm* (Sutra Introducing "The *Suramgama*")
  5. *Chú lăng nghiêm* (Mantra "*Suramgama*")
  6. *Thập chú* ("Ten Mantras")
  7. *Bát nhã tâm kinh* (*Prajnaparamita Sutra*, "Heart of Understanding")
  8. *Tán thượng lai* (Praising Chant "Coming From the Heaven")

9. *Niệm Phật* ("Recitation of the Buddha's Names")
10. *Sám* ("Poem of Repentance")
11. *Tán lễ thích tôn* (Praising Chant "The World Honored One")
12. *Tứ sanh* ("Four Kinds of Beings")
13. *Tam tự quy* ("Triple Refuge")
14. *Hòa nam thánh chúng* ("Harmony in Monastic Life")

Concluding part (in the patriarch hall):
15. *Chú nẳng mô* (Mantra "*Namo*")
16. *Tán Thích Ca Văn Phật* (Praising Chant "*Sukya Muni Buddha*")
17. *Hồi Hướng* ("Honoring All Merits")

The *Công Phu Khuya* may be considered a typical example of religious liturgical aesthetics. From the aesthetic viewpoint the order of texts, each conveying certain ritual and educational meanings, comprises a kind of socioreligious ethos expressed in rhythm and sound. The rhythmic pulse is felt subtly in an arrangement going gradually from slow and nonmetrical to fast and metrical. After the *Kệ Thức Chúng* (Poem "Waking the Monks"), *Kệ Khai Chuông* (Poem "Opening the Big Bell") and the *Niệm Hương* ("Offering Incense") in free-rhythm chanting, the service becomes heightened with a tempo as fast as =400 in the *trì* cantillating style of *Chú Lăng Nghiêm*, the main text. For the latter the tempo is systematically accelerated at the beginning of each of the five sections, just in the middle of the service. However, this syllabic, regular *mantra* cantillation moves to the polyrhythmic *tán* singing style involving the *trống đạo* (Buddhist drum), *mõ* (wooden bell) and *chuông* (bowl bell). The morning service peacefully returns to a relaxing type of nonmetrical singing in the *Hòa Nam Thánh Chúng* ("Harmony in Monastic Life").

Conceptually, beautiful poetry is combined with aesthetically pleasing vocal expression regulated by physical control from low and soft to loud and dramatic exclamations, and from simple to complex melodies. The spiritual harmonization of the three religious sects mentioned earlier, called Thiền Tông (Meditation), Mật Tông (Secret) and Tịnh Độ Tông (Pure Land), is implied from the first to the last chant. Three musical styles called *tụng*, *trì* and *tán*, to be described further, illustrate this meaning.

Musical Performance of Texts

The Buddhist liturgy also results in the interaction of musical styles and texts. This may be understood in various ways, semantics playing a major role in each.

In a general way, the time and space in which the liturgical texts are chanted are seen as having musical significance. The *thiền* (meditation) is the predominant chanting mode for the monastic morning and afternoon services, these two services being reserved for monks or nuns. The thiền is a fertile musical concept expressing religious perseverance relative to the Meditation Sect (Thiền Tông) exposed through solemn melodies. On the contrary, the *nam* (south) mode, which is commonly known in secular music, may be used in public ceremonies provided with easy texts. Here the melody is soft and sad representing compassion, a social aspect of Buddhism. The meaning of the text emphasizes the salvation of souls in the Pure Land (Tịnh Độ) which is also the name of this sect.

One of the striking traits of Buddhist and traditional Vietnamese music is the ornamentation of notes regulated by the concept of *điệu* or *điệu thức* (mode) and *hơi* (breath or nuance). Two kinds of ornamental forms show characteristics of two contrasting điệus: the appoggiatura is for the thiền and the long vibrato is for the nam.

A main text (kinh) is chanted, and a composed text (kệ, tán) is sung. Chanting may be defined as a simple kind of cantillation with repeated melodic patterns. This style represented by the Vietnamese terms tụng or trì, is good for chanting long sutra texts. In contrast, short texts may be sung with more complex melodies and styles for which chanting skill is required. This latter type is called kệ, bạch, tán, xướng, and others mentioned previously.

Each text expressing a certain meaning and/or having a specific length should have an appropriate musical style for it. The correlation of text and music is thus significant. Among typical singing styles, the following may suggest how a text can correlate with a style:

(1) A text of Sanskrit transliteration representing the Mat Tong (Secret Sect) is restrictedly chanted in the trì ("perseverance") style that has three-tone repetitive melodic patterns and a narrow range. Conceived by this Secret Sect, which is close to Tibetan Tantrism or Vajrayana (Thunderbolt or Diamond Vehicle), the repetition of incomprehensible (nonsense) phrases of the mật ngôn or chơn ngôn (mantra = secret or true words) is intended to firmly keep the religious beliefs from loss.

(2) A text called kinh or sutra in classical Chinese or its translation into the vernacular language is chanted in the tụng (praise) style. Because of its length and storytelling character, the tụng, a rather easy four- or five-tone cantillation is found suitable.

(3) Beautiful poems glorifying the Buddhist doctrine should be sung in the tán (glorification) style. This constitutes the most complex ways of singing with instrumental accompaniment of the nhạc bát âm (in the north), đại nhạc (in the center) or nhạc lễ (in the south) ensemble. The feeling of honoring the Buddha's teaching are expressed in various substyles which involve particular polyrhythmic and heterophonic elements of the chant. While the thiền mode is utilized for a text containing happy meanings, the nam, a sad mode, is reserved for a text describing human suffering.

(4) The text Niệm Hương (Offering of Incense) is chanted in the niệm (thinking) style which is noted for its low register in a soft voice expressing the lightness and grace of incense fragrance and smoke.

(5) A text announcing the beginning of a chant or proclaiming the reason for a ceremony must be sung in the xướng (proclamation) style.

The above-mentioned Công Phu Khuya includes all and even more of these styles. In terms of tonal materials used in Buddhist chant, the kinds of text truly correlate with chanting styles: Mantra in prose is three-tone, trì and sutra in prose are four- or five-tone tụng, and poems are in the four-tone niệm, xướng, and the five- to seven-tone tán .

In addition, instrumental music, which is unfortunately a neglected aspect of most world liturgies, plays an important role in the Buddhist music of Vietnam. There are two distinct groups, the liturgical and the secular. The liturgical instruments are played by monks, the secular instruments by lay musicians. Interestingly, one can find the inclusion, not the exclusion, of "secular" music[3] in the religious context. Secular ensembles to accompany Buddhist chant may include the southern nhạc lễ, đại nhạc of the central region and nhạc bát âm of the north. But the liturgical instruments played by monks also function as a rhythmic foundation for every service. Their function and sound qualities have a tremendous meaning in daily monastic life. They seem to hold a central spot in all activities such as calling the monks for service and work and announcing the beginning and the end of or keeping the tempo for a given chant. Instruments made of wood, bronze, skin, and shell are used with the following rituals and functions:

1. Metal plays a conducting role for all services. For example, the bronze bowl bell called chuông gives signals for the beginning and the end and punctuates paragraphs of a sutra.

2. Wood is secondary, like the mộc bảng (wooden plate) to wake up or to call monks for ceremonies and the mõ (wooden "fish" drum) to keep regular beats in sutra chanting.

3. Skin and shell together are for a category celebrating the rituals. These instruments are trống bát nhã (big drum of Prajna, "Heart of Understanding"), trống đạo (small "Buddhist" drum), and pháp loa (conch).

Although these instruments are rich in rhythm and their use is mainly to support melodic chant, no stringed instruments are allowed to be played by monks. This exclusion might be connected to the idea that melodic instruments could become the means to self-entertainment that lies outside the duties associated with chanting.

The Buddhist liturgy of Vietnam depends, in essence, on texts provided by Buddhism. There is no way to conceive of Buddhism deprived of text chanting, which is possibly the most effective means of religious propagation, or of a liturgical music without Buddhist texts. In the union of religion and music as seen in Vietnam there is a lively context for performance of texts which will require further substantial research.

NOTES

1.   Meditation Garden here means Buddhism or Buddhist temples.

2.   *Sutra* is a Sanskrit term for recited Buddhist texts.

3.   A secular music ensemble includes musicians who are laymen.

REFERENCES CITED

Anonymous (13th century)
>   *Thiền Uyển Tập Anh* (Selected Stories of the Well-known Monks in the Meditation Garden).

Đào Duy Anh
>   1974   *Khóa Hư Lục* (Introduction). Hà nội: Khoa Học Xã Hội.

Nguyễn Lang
>   1977   *Việt Nam Phật Giáo Sử Luận* , vol. 2. Paris: Lá Bối.

Nguyễn Thuyết Phong
>   1983   "La liturgie bouddhique du Vietnam." *The Vietnam Forum* 2:44–55.

>   1982   "La musique bouddhique au Vietnam." Phd diss., Sorbonne University.

Trần Văn Giáp
>   1939   "Note sur la baniere de l'ame - A propos d'une ceremonie bouddhique a la memoire des victimes du 'Phoenix'." *Bulletin de l'Ecole Francaise d'Extreme Orient* 39: 224-272.

CONTRIBUTORS TO THE VOLUME

Steven Addiss, Chair of the Art History Department at the University of Kansas, is a composer, painter, and poet who has been studying Asian arts for three decades. His recents books include *The Art of Zen, A Haiku Menagerie, Tall Mountains and Flowing Waters: The Music, Poetry, Calligraphy, and Painting of Uragami Gyukudo, Art History in Education,* and *Narrow Journey to the Interior,* which he also illustrated.

Katherine Bond* received her Bachelor's degree in sociology and anthropology from Swarthmore College and has worked in the field of social services and health education with the refugee community. She is currently pursuing a doctoral degree in public health at the Johns Hopkins University School of Hygiene and Public Health. She is also a violinist and has conducted research in ethnomusicology in Chiang Mai, Thailand.

Amy Catlin**, President of the Applied Anthropology Network of Southern California and Managing Editor of Apsara Media for Intercultural Education, conducts applied research with refugees from Southeast Asia concerning their cultural traditions. She also frequently conducts fieldwork in India. Her doctorate in Music is from Brown University with a concentration in anthropology and its approaches to performance. Currently a research ethnomusicologist at UCLA, she has taught courses in Asian music and fieldwork there and at the California Institute of Technology. Among her ongoing research interests is the relationship of South to Southeast Asia. Recent publications include *From Angkor to America: The Cambodian Dance and Music Project of Van Nuys California* a thirty-seven-minute, narrated video tape, and *Khmer Classical Dance Songbook.*

Carol Compton has a Ph.D. in linguistics from the University of Michigan. She did fieldwork in Laos (1972–73) under a Fulbright-Hays Dissertation Research Grant and in northeast Thailand (1984–85) under a Fulbright ASEAN Senior Research Grant. She has published a monograph and numerous articles on the oral literature of the Lao people. Currently she is at the University of Wisconsin-Madison Center for Education Research.

Paul Cravath undertook doctoral research in Phnom Penh in 1975 for his study of Cambodian court dance. In 1985 he received his Ph.D. in Asian theater form the University of Hawai'i at Manoa based on his dissertation, "Earth in Flower: An Historical and Descriptive Study of the Classical Dance Drama of Cambodia." He currently teaches acting and creates original plays based on Hawai'ian myth, dance, history, and contemporary problems at the University of Hawai'i Leeward Community College.

John Hartmann is a professor in the Department of Foreign Languages and Literatures at Northern Illinois University, De Kalb. His teaching duties include Thai, Lao, and Southeast Asian literatures in translation, and his research and publications are in the area of comparative historical Tai and oral liteature and drama. He is currently doing a study of a Black Tai narrative of the hero Prince Therng and in January 1993 will be on sabbatical at Prince of Sangkla University in southern Thailand researching the shadow puppet theater of that region.

Terry Miller, professor of ethnomusicology at Kent State Univertsity, earned his B.A. in organ at the College of Wooster and two graduate degrees in musicology at Indiana University. His interest in Southeast Asian music dates to his service in the U.S. army in Vietnam and his first visit to Thailand in 1970. A specialist in the music of northeast Thailand and Laos, Dr. Miller did extended fieldwork there from 1972–1974, 1988–1989, and 1991. He organized and has directed the Kent State University Thai Ensemble for thirteen years, a group that plays both central and northeastern musics.

Phong Nguyen* comes from a family of professional musicians in south Vietnam who performed a wide range of music, from Buddhist chant to theater. By age ten, he was performing *Nhac Le* professionally. Dr. Nguyen studied and taught literature and Western music in Saigon before moving to Paris to study ethnomusicology at the Sorbonne in 1974. Through the mid-1980s he served at the CNRS and has since then taught on the faculties of the University of Washington, Kent State University, and UCLA.

Kingsavanh Pathammavong* is a researcher and Lao culture consultant for the Smithsonian Institution in Washington D.C. With an academic background in art, he has served as a co-presenter/translator for CBS News, the National Endowment for the Arts, and the Kennedy Center for the Performing Arts. He also produced and narrated the Laos AIDS Prevention Video, sponsored by the Indochinese Community Center of Washington D.C. Since 1988, he has been a research fellow for the SSRC ISP-funded project "Traditional Contexts of Lowland Lao Classical Music."

Frank Proschan* is a folklorist specializing in Kmhmu culture. He earned his undergraduate and graduate degrees in anthropology (folklore) at the Univesity of Texas at Austin. Between 1986 and 1989 he worked at the Smithsonian Office of Folklife Programs in Washington D.C. Presently he is conducting research among the Kmhmu in Laos. Since 1982 his life has been inextricably intertwined with the Kmhmu people—during research in California, other states, and Laos.

Herbert Purnell* is professor and Chair of the Department of TESOL and Applied Linguistics at Biola University. His major field research has been on the Mien language in Thailand and China. He is currently working on two Mien dictionary projects, a translation of a Mien wedding song book, and a collection of Mien folktales as told by refugees from Laos.

Houmphanh Rattanavong is Director of the National Research Institute for Art, Literature, and Linguistics of the Lao Committee for Social Sciences in Vientiane, Lao People's Republic. After his education in France in political science and economics, journalism and cultural anthropology, he served as an army officer and then worked for the Lao National Radio for sixteen years, becoming its vice-director in 1979. In 1985 he was appointed a member of the Lao National Committee for UNESCO. His institute's research has been supported by UNESCO, the Asia Foundation, the Jim Thompson Foundation, the Ford Foundation, the Toyota Foundation, the Santi Pracha Dhamma Institute and Chongsathit Company of Thailand, and the governments of France and Japan.

Chan Moly Sam* is a Cambodian dancer and choreographer who has represented Cambodia in world festivals and conferences throughout Southeast Asia. Since 1977 she has been teaching, performing, choreographing, and participating in conferences throughout the United States. Her publications on Cambodian dance include *Khmer Folk Dance, Khmer Court Dance: A Comprehensive Study of Movements, Gestures, and Postures as Applied Techniques*, and *Khmer Court Dance: A Performance Manual*.

Sam-Ang Sam* is a Cambodian performer and ethnomusicologist who has been studying traditional Cambodian music since the early 1960s. After completing his undergraduate education in Phnom Penh, he continued his studies in the Philippines and eventually in the U.S., where he earned his doctorate in ethnomusicology at Wesleyan University. Currently at the University of Washington, Sam-Ang Sam has published three books on Cambodian music and has performed widely in the United States, Asia, and Europe.

*   These scholars have received funding from the Social Science Research Council, Indochina Studies Program, whose support helped make possible the conference where the articles in this volume were originally presented.

**   These scholars are past recipients of funding from the Social Science Research Council for research on Southeast Asia.